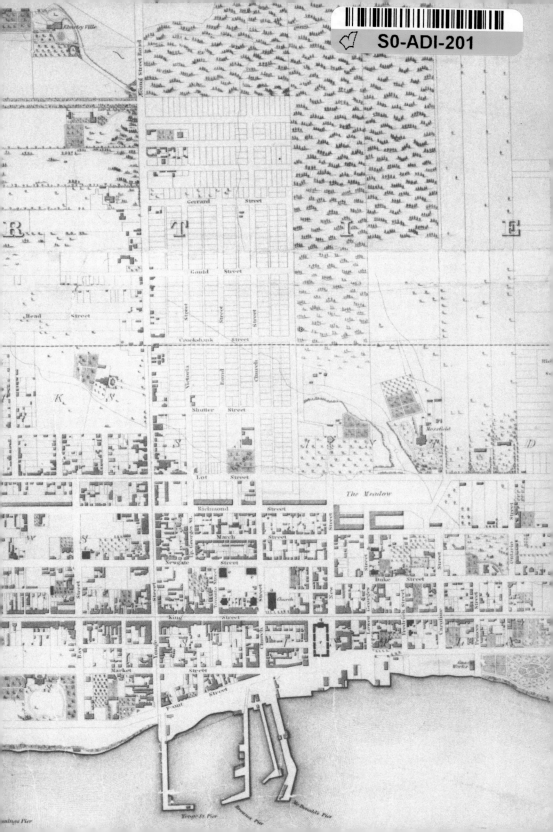

A

CITY

IN THE

MAKING

Progress, People & Perils in Victorian Toronto

by
Frederick H. Armstrong

Toronto & Oxford

Dundurn Press

1988

Design and Production:Andy Tong
Printing and Binding:Gagné Printing Ltd., Louiseville, Quebec, Canada

The writing of this manuscript and the publication of this book were made possible by support from several sources. The publisher wishes to acknowledge the generous assistance and ongoing support of **The Canada Council** , **The Book Publishing Industry Development Programme** of the **Department of Communications** and **The Ontario Arts Council**.

The author and publisher are particularly grateful to the **Ontario Heritage Foundation,** an agency of the **Ontario Ministry of Culture and Communications** for a research grant and a grant in aid of publication.

Care has been taken to trace the ownership of copyright material used in the text (including the illustrations). The author and publisher welcome any information enabling them to rectify any reference or credit in subsequent editions.

J. Kirk Howard, Publisher

Cataloguing in Publication

Armstrong, F. H. (Frederick Henry), 1926-
A city in the making

Bibliography: p.
Includes index.
ISBN 1-55002-026-9

1. Toronto (Ont.) - History. 2. Toronto (Ont.) - Biography. I. Title.

FC3097.4.A74 1988   971.3'541   C87-094975-6
F1059.5.T6857A74 1988

Dundurn Press Limited
2181 Queen Street East, Suite 301
Toronto, Canada
M4E 1E5

Dundurn Distribution Limited
Athol Brose, School Hill,
Wargrave, Reading
England
RG10 8DY

To
Maurice & Betty Careless
with many thanks

CONTENTS

Preface

Most of the essays in this collection first appeared in journals which are now long out of print; others were originally written as papers which were never published. For this book, all the essays have been updated and extensively revised with many sections added, rewritten or deleted. For some of the nineteenth-century documents which are quoted it has been necessary to add punctuation and to divide sentences to make the texts more readable. As a guide to further reading, a short bibliography gives a selection of the major sources on nineteenth century Toronto.

Thanks must be extended to those journals which gave me permission to republish materials on which I did not have copyright. These are the *Canadian Geographer*, the Canadian Historical Association's *Historical Papers*, the *Canadian Historical Review*, *Inland Seas*, the *Journal of Canadian Studies* and *Ontario History*. Acknowledgement of the original place of publication is made in the first footnote of each chapter. The Ontario Heritage Foundation has provided grants-in-aid for both the preparation and publication of this volume; Carl Thorpe, Lorne Ste. Croix, and Elizabeth Price, of the Foundation have helped me greatly with their advice. Some of the research for the original articles was prepared with the assistance of the Canada Council and the Social Science and Humanities Research Council. A great number of individuals have assisted in my research. Many are again thanked in individual chapters, but special reference must be made to those who have advised on several chapters, or have helped with the present revisions.

The idea of publishing these essays was originally suggested by J. Keith Johnson of Carleton University and was strongly supported by William Ormsby, the late archivist of Ontario, and my colleague at the University of Western Ontario, Gerry Killan of King's College. In the Department of History at Western, two other colleagues, Peter F. Neary and Jack Hyatt, have made invaluable suggestions, and the chairman, Robert A. Hohner, has been particularly helpful with word-processing problems. The manuscript has been typed by Chris Speed, Sharon Sjalund, Joanne Burns, Dorothy Vandendries and above all Julie Wray; they have shown exemplary patience both with word-processor difficulties and with this author.

The staff of the Regional Room and Special Collections of the D.B. Weldon Library at the University of Western Ontario, especially Edward C.H. Phelps, John H. Lutman and Guy St-Denis, have been called upon to supply innumerable details. Robert G. Hill of Toronto has, as always, been ready to advise on problems connected with architectural research. Henri Pilon and Charles Dougall of the *Dictionary of Canadian Biography* have also given much useful advice. At the Metropolitan Toronto Library's Baldwin Room, Sandra Alston, John Crosthwait, Robert Capido, Edith G. Firth, Christine Mosser, Bill Parker, Alan Walker, Winnie Woo and others have willingly provided information, as has Michael Pearson, the former history librarian. The staff of the Archives of Ontario have been equally helpful, beginning long ago with Sandra Guillaume and the late Miss J.M.L. Jackson, both of whom advised on many questions. The same is true of the staff of the City of Toronto Archives, particularly the former head archivist, A.R.N. Woadden. Curtis Fahey has been a most patient editor.

But, most particularly, I would like to thank my thesis supervisor, Professor Maurice Careless, who first led me through the intricacies of urban history in the early 1960s and gave sound advice on how to write articles, and his wife, Betty. It is to them that this book is dedicated.

Frederick H. Armstrong
London, Ontario
August 1988

Introduction

In a book comprised of essays written over a period of twenty-five years and devoted to subjects as diverse as the process of urbanization and the impact of major conflagrations, it may be appropriate to begin by explaining how I became interested in Toronto's nineteenth-century history and why I have written on such a broad range of topics over the course of my career. My historical research and writing, which has centred on the history of Toronto and more broadly on the history of Upper Canada/Ontario generally, arose from an interest in history and archaeology kindled by my mother's father, Frederick John Goode. A native of Birmingham, England, he trained as a landscape gardener and worked for the 3rd Marquis of Bute when the latter was turning Cardiff Castle into one of the most remarkable mock-medieval fantasies in Europe. As a boy at our Lake Simcoe cottage north of Toronto I listened to my grandfather's tales of excavating a Blackfriar's monastery under the lawns of the Marquis' estate and discovering the entombed enemies of some former Lord of Cardiff encased in the walls. There were other accounts, too, of the rebuilding, such as the tale of the kindly, but eccentric, Marquis mixing gold and silver dust with the plaster in order to make the walls of some rooms glitter appropriately. Grandfather's stories left me with a feeling for the magic of history that has remained with me ever since.

Wales is far from Toronto, but an interest in my own native city followed easily. In 1849 the Armstrongs migrated from the Minas Basin in Nova Scotia to York County, and by 1894 they had moved on to the city of Toronto itself. My father, Silas Henry Armstrong, was superintendent of playgrounds from 1913 to 1947 and during the Depression his blow-by-blow account of how the city politicians were cutting the parks and playgrounds budget was standard fare at home. Their theory seemed to be simple — trees and kids don't vote, so cut there. But on one occasion, when the budget for boys' basketball was pared, Father managed to strike back by cutting some women's evening classes in Cabbagetown instead. When a deputation arrived at his Shuter Street office demanding reinstatement of the classes, he explained that it was either classes or baseball. If the latter went, their sons would be home underfoot or out on the streets up to goodness knows what. Pressed on how the money for the classes could be reinstated, he told the women that they would have to go to the City Council. They went — and virtually invaded a Council meeting. An alderman was hit on the head with an umbrella and, miraculously, the funds for the classes were restored, Depression or not!

With the influence of my grandfather behind me, I studied history at the University of Toronto, though my research and writing in history did not begin until my return there for doctoral work in 1960 after many years in the insurance business — an experience that lies behind my studies of fires. It was while taking the Old Ontario graduate course given by Professor Maurice Careless — which was the training ground for a considerable number of Canada's historians — that I came across the Toronto City Council Papers for the years just after civic incorporation in 1834. They had been sent to the provincial archives in 1929 by a city employee who was ordered to clean out a vault and (thankfully) decided that they were too important to destroy (they have now been reclaimed by The City of Toronto Archives). These records of the first councils became the basis of my doctoral thesis, written under Careless' enthusiastic supervision. It investigated Toronto's rise from village to city in the late 1820s and 1830s.

When I did this study in the early 1960s urban history in Canada was a largely neglected field. Toronto's growth in the late nineteenth century had been examined in part by D.C. Masters' *The Rise of Toronto, 1850-1890*, one of the first scholarly studies of the evolution of a Canadian city, while Edith G. Firth had compiled two bulky collections of documents for the Champlain Society on Toronto's history from 1793 to 1834. But this left the years from 1834 to 1850 open to enquiry, and some of the most important documents relating to this period were available at the Ontario Archives. Two of the chapters in the present book — on the city's geographical base and on its first mayor, William Lyon Mackenzie — originated from my research into this valuable mass of material.

During my years as a graduate student, I was also influenced by the work of Canon Henry Scadding, the city's first historian, who wrote *Toronto of Old* in 1873 — a volume I subsequently edited for a modern edition. Scadding cast his net widely, examining virtually all phases of the city's growth: the shipping in the harbour, the expansion of Yonge Street into the north, the early educational system and even the migrations of the red light districts. Following his example, I have tried over the years to look into all aspects of Toronto's evolution, and studies such as that of the city's Black community arose from this approach. In my research I have also been much affected by the warning of one of my Classics professors at the University of Toronto, Gilbert Bagnani, that one should never accept a story at face value, however often it may be repeated, without checking it back to the original sources. Noting that any good story tended to be copied by one writer after another, Bagnani remarked that in one case he had traced an inaccurate legend back through three centuries of writers to a mis-translation in the sixteenth century. It was through thus checking the stories of the William Lyon Mackenzie family — stories that had been unquestioningly copied by later historians — that I began to see a very different historical figure emerge from that of the man of the legend.

Other essays in the collection at hand arose from articles I prepared for the *Dictionary of Canadian Biography*. Preparing entries for the DCB leads writers to family connections, business enterprises, recreational pursuits, and, indeed, every variety of human endeavour. Consequently, when researching such pieces, historians can gain a new perspective on the communities in which their subjects lived, as well as a new understanding of the forces that shaped the development of these centres. My *Dictionary* biographies hence mark the starting-points of several of the essays that follow in this collection. They also led me on to the study of the élites who ran the city: how they arose; how they retained power; and how they directed economic and political development

Such is the rather lengthy tale of how these essays came to be written. While the collection in no way attempts to provide an overview of the history of Toronto, its contents will, it is hoped, give some idea of the nineteenth-century richness and diversity of life in what was traditionally long regarded as the dullest and the most colourless of Canadian cities.

The use of the term Victorian to describe the period covered in this book may seem somewhat limited, for the story told in some of the essays reaches back into the late eighteenth century. But, as the focus of discussion extends from the York riots of

March 1832 to the Second Great Fire in April 1904, Victorian seemed an appropriate designation. Furthermore, most of the book deals with events that took place in the middle years of the century.

Some of the essays are built around an incident, some concentrate on an individual, and some do both. They are divided into four groups by theme: Toronto's geographic base and economic ambitions; Mackenzie, one of its most colourful citizens and controversial politicians; some of the types of Torontonians who gave the city its remarkable variety; and two of Toronto's greatest disasters. Each section has its own short introduction.

Though so much was different in the nineteenth century, Toronto's topographical underlay — its escarpment and river valleys, its harbour and grid-pattern streets — was in essence much the same as it is today. Thus, the urban picture of that time is understandable without too much explanation. Some things, however, have changed considerably. An example is the many revisions in street names that have taken place. Occasionally the same street has had more than one name change; sometimes several streets have been linked together and given one name: Bay Street and particularly Dundas Street are cases in point. To avoid confusion, the modern names are used throughout; but where there have been changes, the contemporary name is shown after the modern name in square brackets on the first reference in each chapter.

Another point in need of clarification is the monetary system of Upper Canada, which was a particular nightmare before the decimal system was adopted in 1857. As part of the British Empire, Upper Canada used the imperial system of pounds, shilling and pence: the pound consisting of 20 shillings and the shilling being divided into 12 pennies (240 pennies equalled one pound). Figures were written as £/s/d — pounds/shillings/pence. To complicate matters further, there were two types of pounds used in Upper Canada: the British pound or pound Sterling (abbreviated St.), and the local pound or pound Currency (Cy.). The latter, which was originally only a bookkeeping currency since there were no local coins or paper notes, was less valuable: five shillings Currency equalled four shillings Sterling. When the local banks began to issue their own paper money and tokens in the 1830s they used pounds Currency.

With no government-issued paper money or coins, and English money hard to import, and at any rate slightly different in value, almost any coins that drifted into the colony were accepted. American money was the most frequently met with, $5.00 American being roughly equal to a pound Sterling; but French, Spanish and other coins were to be found, as well as a variety of privately struck tokens. Even leaving aside currency fluctuations and interest charges, the simplest transactions could become nightmares and a good deal of business was carried on by barter. Not surprisingly, it was customary for people to keep running accounts at stores rather than pay for each individual purchase.

Trying to compare nineteenth-century figures and costs with those of today is thus very difficult, even without considering the various waves of inflation and deflation — which in the end left the 1914 American dollar very close in value to what it had been worth in 1815. The incredible technological advances of the era sometimes also resulted in drastic reductions in prices. In some cases examples of contemporary costs and wages have been added for comparison.

From the series Whitefield's Original Views of North American Cities, *No. 30, Toronto, Canada West, "from the top of the jail", 1851.*

Part 1: The Urban Background

The first section of this book deals with the physical land-scape of Toronto as it grew from a village in the 1790s to a town of more than 10,000 people in the 1830s. As well, it looks at the ambitions of early Torontonians, the limits of their economic power and their desire to expand their communication network and commercial hinterland. The first chapter provides a to-pographical and architectural description of the city as it had evolved by 1834. The second examines the extent of its hinter-land, the state of its commercial and communications network, and the nature of the services it provided for its population. Finally, the story of the first attempt at railway building inves-tigates some of the problems — organizational, logistical and financial — that afflicted the city's early ventures in economic development. It also tells, through their own statements, the hopes, ambitions and frequent frustrations of Toronto's busi-ness leaders.

In all these aspects Toronto provides a local microcosm of an international phenomenon. What was taking place in the city reflected the commitment to progress that was remaking the face of every town, village and hamlet across both Europe and North America. Some of the schemes that were attempted were ludicrous, but others — such as the railways — represent a crucial stage in the evolution of most of the largest cities of today. Their effects on Toronto show how a remote, backwoods, colo-nial city formed part of an international economic pattern, and demonstrate the almost instantaneous, world-wide transmis-sion of new technological developments in the nineteenth cen-tury.

Chapter 1

The New City in 1834: The Physical Layout[1]

When in 1834 the legislature of Upper Canada incorporated the Town of York as the colony's first city it simultaneously changed its name back to Toronto, a designation that had been discarded in 1793 by the first lieutenant-governor, John Graves Simcoe. The reason for incorporation was York's mushroom growth caused by the influx of English immigrants to British North America that began in the mid-1820s. Then, as now, York/Toronto was a major destination for arriving immigrants, both those newcomers who stayed in the town itself and those who went on to settle in the counties of York and Simcoe to the north. In 1826 the population of the town had been 1,710, in 1830, 2,860, and by 1834, 9,254. After incorporation this increase continued, usually at a slower speed, and by 1850 the city had a population of over 30,000. The effect of this sudden wave of migration was the virtual creation of a new entity. The village of 1825 was scarcely recognizable a decade later; but even the new city itself was soon changed drastically as the population expanded further, and new buildings and streets which still survive today made their appearance. Thus in 1834 Toronto was undergoing a physical as well as a political transition. At the same time, however, it was still semi-rural in many aspects. A survey of the city at that date demonstrates that many of the characteristics of modern downtown Toronto had developed, while many features of the former village lingered into the early metropolitan period.

The Form and Extent of the City

By 1834 the Town of York had attained what was, for Upper Canada, the advanced age of forty-one years. As originally laid out in 1793 by Lieutenant-Governor Simcoe, the town plot was merely a twelve-block rectangle bounded by Front (Palace), George, Adelaide (Duke) and Berkeley streets, but this area had long ceased to be the centre of the city. In fact, an observer looking at a map would have had trouble believing that this initial nucleus had ever been more than the eastern suburbs of the town. In 1834, within the eastern part of this original rectangle, Ontario Street was only partially built up, and east of it, towards Parliament Street, there were only scattered houses. Beyond the plot there was virtually nothing built north of Richmond (Duchess) Street. East of Parliament, stretching towards the Don River, lay only the undeveloped eastern Military Reserve. The provincial legislative buildings had originally been located in this area, but they had been torched in the War of 1812, again burnt in 1824 and were moved to the west end of the town in 1828.

The westward spread of York, which had left the original town so undeveloped, had come about because of several factors. Most obvious were the unhealthy swampy areas on the town's eastern margins around the outlets of the Don River, which was already known as Ashbridge's Bay. But there were also positive reasons for the spread of the town to the west. Old Fort York (then usually called the Garrison), situated on the western Military Reserve which extended west from Peter Street, exerted a pull which became stronger when the provincial legislative buildings were moved to the west end. Yonge Street, opened by Simcoe's Queen's Rangers in 1796, provided another reason for the shift westward. It became the main route north to Toronto's rich agricultural hinterland, stretching up to Lake Simcoe and potentially beyond to Penetanguishene on Georgian Bay. Yet another factor in the town's westward expansion was the pleasant lakeshore running from the mouth of the Don River towards the Garrison. Paralleling this strand, Front Street, then edging the harbour, rapidly became the preferred residential location of many of the most prominent citizens. Finally, as road conditions began to improve in the years immediately before incorporation, Queen (Lot) Street, which was then the road leading to Dundas Street and the west, began to exert a north-westerly pull away from the original town plot. Consequently, by 1834 the growth of the city had resulted in a fairly solidly built-up area stretching along the east-west axis of King Street, from Simcoe's town to York Street. West of York Street, a series of semi-built-up areas continued on to Peter Street and the Garrison.

Rooftop view of King Street, Yonge to Church Streets, 1841.

Reflecting this westwards expansion, in 1797 the area west to Peter Street had been annexed to the town by provincial legislation. At the same time, several plots of land near Jarvis (New) and Church streets were set aside for future public buildings; on this land would eventually arise St James's Cathedral, the St Lawrence Market, and, immediately west of the cathedral, the long-vanished courthouse and jail square. In the Reserve itself, which initially stretched north from the lake to Queen Street between Peter and Dufferin streets, were the fort and various other structures connected with the military. By the early 1830s its eastern portions were already subject to development schemes. These included not only streets and squares, but also an abortive plan for a new governor's house on what is now Clarence Square. The actual sale of lots in the western Garrison Reserve had begun by 1833.[2]

To the north the growth of the city was just as uneven. Simcoe and his surveyor, Alexander Aitken, had planned a series of 100-acre park lots, really farm properties, extending from Queen Street northwards. Queen Street thus stood as the baseline for the park lots (hence its old name "Lot Street"); it was also the first concession line of York Township. These lots, along with town lots south of Queen Street, were granted to the principal citizens as compensation for their giving up their homes in the original capital at Newark (Niagara-on-the-lake) and resettling in York

East of Yonge Street, northward expansion had been cut off by the Taddle Creek ravine. This creek, long an impediment to the development of the town, flowed southeast from what are now the university grounds and Queen's Park to cross Yonge Street between Shuter and Queen streets. After blocking Queen Street (which, as a result, had never been extended farther east than Church Street), the creek turned south to flow into the harbour near Ontario Street. East of Taddle Creek, across the future line of Queen Street, stretched the park lot estates of Samuel Peters Jarvis, the victor in one of Toronto's most famous duels, and William Allan, already very rich and eventually to become probably the wealthiest man in Upper Canada. The route from York to Kingston first ran via King Street, and then curved north to join what is today Queen Street East, just as King Street still curves north. Beyond the town to the east the Don River forked a short distance before it flowed into the bay. A bridge, called Angell's Bridge after the engineer who built it, had been constructed across the "Great Don" to provide access to what is now Toronto Island, then still a peninsula; but it had been rendered useless by the mid-1830s because the bridge across the "Little Don" had been destroyed.[3]

The town had also begun to spread northwest of Queen and Yonge streets. By 1834 the western park lots had usually undergone several changes of ownership, subdivision was taking place and lines of buildings were stretching both north up Yonge Street and west along Queen Street. Immediately to the west of Yonge Street, occupying the area covered by the city halls and Eaton's as far north as Albert Street, was Toronto's first suburb, "Macaulaytown," named after the original holder of the park lot on which it was located, Dr James Macaulay, who had come out as a surgeon with the Queen's Rangers. Basically this was a shanty town, far from such services as the market and largely occupied by poor immigrants. Up Yonge, scattered buildings reached towards the Toll Gate at Bloor Street, then called the 2nd Concession Line. Westward along Queen Street past Macaulaytown was the newly built east wing of Osgoode Hall and then a stretch of mostly frame dwellings running towards Spadina Avenue. Here, in what was still a remote corner, were situated the two most impressive streets of the village and, quite possibly, the Toronto of today: the broad stretch of Spadina Avenue running up to Spadina, the Baldwins' country residence on the hill to the north (the predecessor of the Spadina which still stands east Casa Loma); and University (College) Avenue, then composed of two parallel thoroughfares, the western one planned as the main entranceway to the projected King's College, now the University of Toronto. A 150-acre site for the college had been purchased in 1825, and the avenue had been planted with trees and shrubs since 1830. This whole area was sufficiently built up by 1834 to be constituted a separate ward named in honour of St Patrick.

The Approaches to the City

Surrounding York were the virgin forests, composed for the most part of pine, oak and other hardwoods, and interspersed increasingly with clearings. A unknown British soldier visiting the city in May 1840 wrote:

There is a good deal of cleared land in the vicinity
of Toronto but the forest still predominates very
considerably in the landscape and in many cases
forms the boundary of the town. The clearings
are made in three principle lines viz: in Dundas
Street, King Street, and Yonge Street, the two
former of which follow the shores of the lake and
the last is directed to Lake Simcoe. The first 10 or
12 miles in these three roads are very well constructed and kept up by turnpikes.[4]

In 1834 the surfacing or macadamization of main routes
from York — that is, covering them with a thick layer of pounded
gravel — largely lay in the future. The roads, however, had been
"opened" for many years: Yonge Street by Simcoe; Dundas
Street, the route to the west reached via Queen Street, by his
successor Administrator Peter Russell in 1796; and Kingston
and Danforth roads (after contractor Asa Danforth) by Russell in
1799. To the west, moreover, Lakeshore Road had been constructed through Etobicoke in 1804, but was almost impassable
for years. Conditions on all these roads are well described by a
traveller who said that when he approached York by a stagecoach about 1834, "the passengers [walked] up and down hills
in crossing several creeks to ease the horses."[5]

To the traveller approaching York by boat — the most
frequented and comfortable method — the first view of the city
was the long peninsula which would become the island when a
series of storms in 1858 created the eastern gap. Once the
traveller's steamer had rounded the peninsula through the
western gap and passed the still surviving Gibraltar Point
lighthouse, already an old landmark in 1834, the Garrison and
the Town of York came into view. The most famous account of
its appearance at that time, though far from the most favourable,
is that of the English author Anna Jameson:

A little ill-built town on low land at the bottom of
a frozen bay, with one very ugly church, without
tower or steeple; some government offices, built
of staring red brick in the most tasteless vulgar
style imaginable: three feet of snow all around;
and the gray, sullen, wintry lake, and the dark
gloom of the pine forest bounding the prospect.[6]

Though unflattering, the description would seem to be a fair one. Arriving unexpectedly on Dec. 30, 1836, Mrs Jameson not only found no one there to meet her, but also was immediately introduced to one of the worst hazards of travelling in the city at the time: "As I stepped out of the boat I sank ankle deep into mud and ice."[7] With such a first impression of the city it is surprising that her description is not even more scathing! Still, the winter harbour could have its pleasant aspects. William Henry Pearson, an early inhabitant who became manager of the Consumers' Gas Company, presents an appealing picture of boyish winter sports; the harbour, once frozen, provided an ideal recreation area for both skating and ice boating, stretching over some five or six miles from the western gap to the end of Ashbridge's Bay. Normally it was frozen from the end of the shipping season in December until late March, the only break in the ice being a fissure caused by the Don current, which crossed from the mouth of the river to the King's (later Queen's) Wharf at the fort.[8]

In summer the harbour could also be pleasant, the peninsula providing an escape from the heat of the city. It was forested in part, and on some portions wild strawberries grew in profusion. As well, it was a great resort for game with flocks of wild ducks, snipe, plover and other birds, and in the 1830s it was the site of various commercial fishing grounds. Although John Ross Robertson, proprietor of the *Telegram* and publisher of the six-volume *Landmarks of Toronto* (1894-1914), states that there were only three buildings as late as 1843, the original woods were already being cut down for timber, and the appearance of the peninsula — or as it was sometimes already called, the island — was consequently being drastically changed.[9]

Along the town side of the harbour there was as yet little landfill beyond the natural shoreline; the city was fronted with an embankment and a gravel beach, much as Niagara-on-the-Lake is today. As Pearson described it, "there was no Esplanade until about 1855. A bank from fifteen to twenty feet high extended the whole length of the waterfront, from the foot of Berkeley Street to the Queen's Wharf, with a pebbly beach at the margin of the bay." There were various plans for making the shoreline a promenade but they came to nothing, and in the end the railways were given the right-of-way. In the early 1830s the shoreline was still crown land, and was inhabited in part by squatters who had built huts and shanties there without the permission of the authorities. Other than these hovels there were few buildings along the south side of Front Street, nor were there as yet many wharves, though several were to be built in the next decade. The King's (later Queen's) Wharf beside the Fort (at the foot of Bathurst Street today) served the commissariat and was used for general government purposes. Commercially, at the time of York's incorporation, there was only Feehan's Wharf at the foot of Church Street, but a second commercial pier was under construction. Other harbour facilities were almost completely lacking, despite the fact that York had been a port of entry with its own customs officer since 1801. There was the Gibraltar Point lighthouse, begun in 1806 and later remodelled, but the entrance to the harbour, which could be dangerous, did not even have a proper system of warning buoys. However, by the 1830s, for all its limitations, the harbour was a scene of constant activity.[10]

The Appearance of the City

Stepping off the boat at Feehan's Wharf in 1834, the traveller immediately found himself in one of the main business sections of the town, Front Street between Church and George streets, although the main commercial centre was King Street to the north. Even on these busy streets the city would hardly be considered built up by modern standards — except for King Street, which presented a fairly solid line of buildings from York to Sherbourne (Caroline) streets, and lower Yonge Street, which was fairly well built up. Many of these buildings were of a rather inferior type of construction. As the soldier's diary of 1840 stated:

> King street is the great thoroughfare of the Town. The houses are principally built of brick and have their lower stories for the most part laid out in shops. This handsome street is, however, as is the case in all American cities, disfigured by an intermixture of mean wooden buildings with the more substantial edifices erected on the surrounding lots.[11]

Court House Square at north-west corner of Church Street and King Street, showing proposed new building, c. 1835.

By the 1830s these more substantial edifices— still built of red brick though white would soon be more stylish — were becoming the norm for new construction in the central area. Land values were increasing, and small frame structures were no longer practicable and presented a fire hazard. Row buildings were beginning to appear, an outstanding example being Chewett's Block at the southeast corner of King and York streets on the site of the present-day Toronto Dominion Centre. These were built in 1833-35 by a new arrival in the city, John Howard, soon to become one of its leading architects and surveyors, and eventually one of its great benefactors by his virtual gift of High Park to the citizens of Toronto. The corner structure in Chewett's Buildings was occupied by a famous hostel, the British Coffee House, one of the main social centres of the city. East of it a line of elegant stores and dwellings spread along King Street.[12]

But Chewett's Buildings were only one of several rows. In the mid-1830s the City Council began to demand that lessees' buildings on the city-owned "Market Block," covering the area immediately west of the market (today's St Lawrence Market) and bounded now by Front, Church, King and West Market streets, be rebuilt as substantial three-storey brick structures according to an overall design. Although the council's scheme ran into difficulties, largely because of the depression of 1837, by the early 1840s the King Street row had been completed and became known as the City Buildings. These survived the First Great Fire in 1849 with little damage, and some still stand across from St James's Cathedral today. Another early example of commercial row buildings were Bishop's Buildings on the north side of Adelaide (Newgate) Street between York and Simcoe (Graves) streets. Completed early enough to be listed in the 1833 Directory, these consisted of four houses which were obviously substantial residences since their tenants included Attorney-General Robert S. Jameson, Anna's husband. By the late 1830s other rows were making their appearance, especially in the choice business area along King Street East.

In the central business district many substantial hotels, such as the four-storey North American with its roof walk, were intermixed with the commercial buildings, as were various factories. Some of the latter presented a fire hazard which worried many of the citizens, but, because of good luck and dedicated volunteer fire-fighters, there was no major blaze up to

1849. Many of the factories were small, for example, the tailoring establishments along King Street; but others, such as Sheldon, Dutcher and Company's foundry on Yonge Street north of King Street, and Jesse Ketchum's tannery, were large enterprises for the period. Peter Freeland's soap plant, then rising at the foot of Yonge Street, was to become one of the most prominent structures on the skyline. In addition to these "downtown" factories there were others scattered throughout the city — such as that of Worts and Gooderham at the eastern end of town with its prominent windmill — and there were mills on the nearby streams, particularly the Don River.

Although the commercial heart of the city thus spread along several King Street blocks, the city's life might be said to have revolved around two foci: the offices of the local administration and market activity in the east, and the centre of provincial government in the west. That in the east was the older, and its traces can be seen today in St James's Cathedral, the St Lawrence Market, and many surrounding buildings, all of which were rebuilt after the Great Fire of 1849. This eastern focus could trace its origin to 1797, when Peter Russell first extended the town westwards and at the same time reserved space for the necessary public buildings. A decade later, the first St James's was built on much the same position as the present cathedral, though with an east-west instead of a north-south axis. Its grounds spread east of Church Street between King and Adelaide streets, covering much the same area as today. In 1832 a new church was built on the site, the earlier structure having become inadequate. John Ritchey, its contractor, was one of the leading builder-architects in the city at that date. In front of the church stood a row of popular trees, which added a rural touch to the business centre until they were cut down in 1845.[13]

South and southeast of St James's was the market, five-and-a-half acres originally set aside for that purpose by Lieutenant-Governor Peter Hunter in 1803. By 1834 the land fell into two sections. The western covered the already noted area between Church, King, Market and Front streets and was known as the Market Block; the land here was let by the town for various stores and other buildings on long-term leases. On the eastern half of the area, stretching from Market Street to Jarvis Street between King and Front streets, stood the market proper. This was a new red-brick structure which had been recently built to replace the original 1814 frame market. For a decade after 1834 it doubled as the City Hall. Immediately to the south of the market, on the site of the present south section of the St Lawrence Market, was one of the few structures on the lake side of Front Street, the Farmers' Storehouse Company. This was a co-operative, set up by the farmers of the region in 1824 both as a depot for goods going to Montreal and as a centre for sales in Toronto.[14]

The third area involved in this focus was the block immediately west of St James's surrounded by King, Adelaide, and Church Streets and the newly laid-out Toronto Street. The south part of this block was an open square faced on the north by two identical moderate-sized brick buildings with ornamental stone trim; these had been built in 1824, possibly to the design of Dr William Warren Baldwin. The one on the west was a combination gaol, debtors' prison and lunatic asylum, and by the early 1830s was already inadequate for its functions. Scene of the hanging of Samuel Lount and Peter Matthews after the Rebellion of 1837, this structure survived until recent times. The building on the east was the Court House, where the magistrates of the Court of Quarter Sessions — the governing body of the Home District (which included Toronto) — held their meetings. Immediately to the north of the Court House on Church Street stood a small building which was the first fire hall of the town, and beyond it on the southeast corner of Adelaide and Church streets was the second most important church in York, St Andrew's Presbyterian. Begun in 1830, and not quite finished when the city was incorporated, St Andrew's represented official Kirk of Scotland Presbyterianism. One other structure connected with this grouping was the small brick county registry office on the north side of Adelaide Street opposite St James's; it was built in 1829 by the registrar, Samuel Ridout, at his own expense.[15]

As for the western focus of the city - except for the much later St Andrew's Church, which was built on its eastern side in 1875 — all traces of it have disappeared. By 1834 three adjacent blocks were spreading north from the lake to Adelaide Street and occupied respectively by the House of Assembly on the south (the planned site for the CBC headquarters), then the lieutenant-governor's residence (site of Roy Thomson Hall), and finally Upper Canada College on the north. The Parliament buildings, begun in 1829, and its grounds occupied the entire six-acre block surrounded by Simcoe, Front, John and Wellington (Market)

King Street, Bay to Simcoe Streets, c. 1835.

streets. Facing the lake, they consisted of three two-storey plain red-brick Georgian buildings much deplored by Anna Jameson. The three were joined together in 1849, and in 1903 — a decade after the legislature moved to Queen's Park — were demolished. Immediately to the east across Simcoe Street were the impressive grounds around Anglican Archdeacon (later Bishop) John Strachan's residence.[16]

North of the legislature, occupying the area between Wellington and King streets west of Simcoe Street, lay the grounds of the governor's house or, as it was still often called, Elmsley House. The structure was a frame, roughcast building, the nucleus of which had been built by Chief Justice John Elmsley in 1799. About 1814 it was purchased by the government, and the next year it became the lieutenant-governor's residence. Its external appearance underwent various changes aside from those occasioned by extensions. Originally it was painted a pale green colour, but Sir Francis Bond Head redecorated it in a loyal British orange for the election of 1836. By 1850 it had settled down to a less conspicuous yellow. Toronto ceased to be the capital in 1841, when Upper Canada and Lower Canada (Quebec) were united as one province, but the government house continued to serve various official purposes: government offices, normal school and the residence of the Prince of Wales when he visited Toronto in 1860. Finally, just before it burned down in 1863, it became a barracks. When Upper Canada, renamed Ontario, again became a separate province at Confederation, a new government house was erected on the same site and continued in use until 1912, when the estate became railway yards. Surrounding the residence were landscaped grounds with groves, beautifully shaded serpentine walks, and a small stream running through a ravine.[17]

To the north again, the third component of this western nucleus, Upper Canada College, founded by Lieutenant-Governor Sir John Colborne in 1829, occupied the block between King and Adelaide streets to the west of Simcoe Street. It consisted of a range of plain, attached brick buildings facing south over gardens stretching towards the government house. Opened in 1831, the college buildings continued in use until 1891. West of the college some open ground stretched to John Street. Past John Street, also to the north of King Street, was the town hospital, built in 1820, ancestor of the present Toronto General Hospital.

Beyond all these structures, there were only a few homes of government officials and, across the Garrison Common or Reserve, the fort, now Old Fort York, which was already considered obsolete in the 1830s and after 1840 was largely replaced by the New Fort or Stanley Barracks, of which the Marine Museum is a survivor. Even though the Old Fort possessed a few more buildings in 1834 than it does today, it still was not an impressive structure.

There were few other public buildings in the town worthy of note. The first portion of Osgoode Hall, now the east wing, without its portico, had been built in 1829-32 on property purchased from Chief Justice John Beverley Robinson. Again John Ritchey was the builder. The old Court House also deserves mention, for it was still a regular meeting place for municipal functions in 1834, and was later to become the first House of Industry. A two-storey frame structure at the southeast corner of Queen and Yonge streets, it had originally been built as a dwelling by Alexander Montgomery but became the court house after the legislative buildings were burned in 1813. It continued to serve in that capacity until the King Street building was built in 1824.

Aside from the already mentioned St James's and St Andrew's, the only churches with any architectural pretensions were St Paul's Roman Catholic, which had been erected in 1822 on the east side of Power Street (where its successor still stands), and Adelaide Street Methodist, a brick structure seating a thousand persons which was opened in 1832. The other churches were little more than simple frame meeting houses, although they already represented a wide variety of denominations: various Presbyterian and Methodist sects, Congregationalists, Baptists and Unitarians. Three had been established up by Black congregations.

More conspicuous by their very number, and sometimes by their size, were the innumerable taverns, licensed and otherwise, that were to be found in all parts of the town. At the official granting of licenses on January 6, 1834, the magistrates of the Quarter Sessions of the Home District, who supervised the government of the area, received requests from only twenty-nine innkeepers in the town and one in Macaulaytown; but these hardly represented the total number of inns, for the licensing regulations were more often ignored than complied with. In addition to the taverns, general stores sold liquor in measures not less than quart. The licensed outlets themselves varied from quite substantial establishments, such as the British Coffee House and the North American Hotel, to "holes-in-the-wall" with none of the facilities of an inn except a bar.[18]

As the business centre for the western part of the province and seat of the provincial government and law courts, the town naturally possessed its share of wealthy men whose mansions frequently stood on extensive grounds. Pearson states that the most outstanding residences in the late 1830s were Justice D'Arcy Boulton's Grange, Archdeacon Strachan's Palace, William Allan's Moss Park, Chief Justice John Beverley Robinson's Beverley House, and Attorney-General Henry John Boulton's Holland House. He also noted that the principal residential streets by the end of that decade were, first, Front Street, and, then, Adelaide Street and part of Peter Street. The soldier's diary agrees, remarking that the principal homes were situated on Front Street or in the suburbs. The Front Street homes often occupied a full block. Usually they overlooked the lake, there being almost no structures on the south side to obstruct the view. Front Street had naturally been one of the earliest locations favoured by the rich and, although commerce was encroaching, it remained, as the contemporary descriptions show, the "Rosedale" of its day.[19]

The city also contained many substantial, but less costly, homes — often the residences of wealthy citizens who could have afforded more elegant accommodation. Jesse Ketchum, the philanthropist-tanner whose many properties were subject to the largest single assessment in the city's early years, lived quite simply in a frame house on Yonge Street near his tannery, as did many of the leading merchants, some of whose homes were above their stores on King Street. Many of the homes were frame, although brick houses were becoming much more common. There were even a few examples of construction with mud bricks.

There were also the poor districts, and, not too surprising in a boom town, the slums were rather extensive for a small place. Generally, the new suburbs spreading out to the north and west along Queen Street and Macaulaytown were not rich districts, nor was much of the eastern part of the town between Yonge Street and the original survey east of Jarvis Street. Lombard

(March) Street, one of the more crowded sections, was becoming infamous as the red light district, and the areas to the rear of both sides of Church Street were noted for their poverty. The worst alley of all was Henrietta Street, a lane running south from King Street to the east of the present site of the King Edward Hotel. All these areas presented a spectacle of congested frame shacks which constituted a major problem for the fire department. The crowded lanes also presented a health problem. When the first cholera epidemic broke out in 1832 Henrietta Street and the houses in Church Street were, predictably enough, centres of infection. An even lower level of existence was reached by the squatters along the banks of the Don River and along the lakefront.[20]

The Atmosphere of the City

Although it is easy to pinpoint the areas of commerce, wealth and poverty, it is much more difficult to recreate the atmosphere of the town. Basic facilities and services that we take so much for granted today were simply non-existent. There were no sewers and there was practically no municipal water supply. Two wells had been dug in 1824, one in the market and the other at the northwest corner of King and Princess streets, but no further additions to a public water supply were made during the ensuing decade of mushroom growth. Most people had their own garden wells; rain water was collected in underground tanks and barrels for washing. If further supplies were needed, water could be obtained from the carters who were a familiar sight around the city, supplying water for both domestic and fire-fighting purposes from their puncheons or large barrels mounted on wheels.[21]

In the Toronto of 1834, not only was there a lack of public services, but many conditions existed —and were more or less shrugged off as "nuisances"— which would today lead to public outcry. The report of the Board of Health in the spring of 1833 noted, for example, that "in Teraulay Street [Bay Street north of Queen Street] there are large stagnant pools of water, covered with decomposed vegetable matter, which already send forth the most noxious and poisonous exhalations," and many other parts of the town exhibited the same problem. While it was easy to report and pass motions, action was another thing, particularly considering the state of civic finances. Such pools and offal were often virtually permanent decorations on the landscape.[22]

The expansion of the business area along King Street, and the dispersal of the homes of the wealthy, were as typical of the spread of the population as were the growth of the foci around which Toronto radiated. One traveller said that it was difficult to pick out the main four corners of the town, which seemed to be really composed of a series of suburbs. Thus there was a certain sameness in many of the streets, a feature that was accentuated by the lack of thoroughfares of any notable width (except for Spadina and College avenues in the northwest suburbs) and by the fact that large and small, substantial and flimsy, structures were almost everywhere intermixed.[23]

Such was the topographical picture York presented in 1834. With its basic grid-pattern of streets and homes set back among gardens it must have resembled the Niagara-on-the-Lake of today in many ways, but the bustling activity and constant expansion of the town were far different from the peaceful atmosphere of that centre — the tourist season excepted. York in 1834 was not only a town that had just undergone a rapid burst of expansion; it was also a city whose leading merchants were already sure that it was destined to grow into a metropolis that would command the province, if not the nation.

Chapter 2

A Rising Metropolis: Expanding Toronto's Frontiers, 1825-1841 [1]

For several decades Canadian historical writing has concentrated upon the influence of the metropolis rather than that of the frontier, studying the spread of civilization and commerce from the centres along the St Lawrence and the Great Lakes, and developing what has generally come to be called the Laurentian school of historiography.[2] Thanks to the work of the Laurentian school, there is now general agreement among historians that cities have played a dominant role in our development, organizing the frontier instead of being organized by it. Yet, in spite of this interest in metropolitanism, much work remains to be done on the growth of the major metropolitan centres themselves. Take the case of Toronto. Throughout its rise to the status of metropolis of the nation, Toronto has played a key role in Canadian history. However, despite all the research that has been done on its evolution, there is still disagreement over such basic questions as which events and eras represented turning points in the city's development.

An extended, comprehensive history of Toronto is still well in the future; what is needed first are detailed studies of many important segments of the city's past. Through such studies the crucial changes will be more clearly pinpointed and the major trends arranged in connected sequence. For the earliest periods of Toronto's history a great deal of work has already been done, beginning with Canon Henry Scadding's *Toronto of Old* in 1873. The city's origins in the French regime were examined by Percy J. Robinson in 1933, and events in the Town of York from the 1790s to early 1820s have also attracted many writers. It is to the next major period in the history of the city that this chapter is directed — the few years after 1825 which saw the village of York turn into the thriving city of Toronto.

This transformation arose from the great population influx from the British Isles that began in the mid-1820s: within a

Sports in Toronto harbour, 1835.

decade the population of York leaped from 1,685 (1824) to 9,252 (1834), and its surrounding Home District (basically York, Simcoe, Peel, and the former Ontario counties) grew from 14,924 to 46,288. The town's mushroom growth, which was paralleled by the emergence of new centres such as Hamilton and London, allowed it to pull ahead economically of its rival Kingston — long the largest centre in the province. As it surged ahead, its character underwent dramatic changes that were most strikingly symbolized by its incorporation as a city in 1834, with the concurrent return to the original name of Toronto. But it is the economic transformation that concerns us here. Toronto in 1825 was a market village; ten years later the basis was laid for it to become an important metropolis.

This metamorphosis has been much discussed by historians.[3] D.C. Masters in his 1947 *The Rise of Toronto: 1850-1890*, an innovative foray into the then almost untouched field of Canadian urban history, began his study with the railway boom, regarding that pivotal development as the take-off point. Toronto did not attain a large population or an extensive industrial base until the second half of the 19th century; but the city was assuming the appearance of a fledgling metropolis by the time of the Rebellion of 1837. Thus the date for the emergence of Toronto as an important political and economic centre should be placed in the early- to mid-1830s since all the crucial factors necessary for its rise to metropolitan status were in place by that period. Establishing when it was clearly settled that Toronto would become the provincial metropolis is more important than trying to formulate the arguable criteria of when it attained that dignity. The great economic boom that unquestionably followed the opening of the railways in 1853-56 should be regarded as the city's second great economic upswing - when changes were more of degree than of kind— rather than the beginning of Toronto's metropolitan economy

The economic changes that took place in what might be called Mackenzie's Toronto — though many leading citizens of the era would shiver in their graves at the use of that designation, — have been overshadowed by the political ones. Mackenzie and the events of the Rebellion are colourful topics for discussion, routine details of commerce are not. Because of these political events, however, Toronto is usually seen as a provincial capital rather than an economic hub and thus an important aspect of its growth has been obscured. Certainly the fact that, almost from the start, Toronto was the provincial capital was the first significant factor in its success, but the effect of its political status after the late 1820s can easily be exaggerated. Of course, being the capital had advantages: the legislature, officials, nascent civil service and institutions such as the provincial courts and the land companies naturally located themselves in the seat of power. Yet these factors became progressively less important as Toronto grew in size and its hinterland expanded. In the end, losing the seat of government to Kingston in 1841 — a dozen years before the railways — had little adverse effect on the city.

In examinations of Toronto's early economic unfolding a framework that has frequently been used is Norman Gras's metropolitan thesis. His theory, based on the growth of London, England, appeared in 1922 and has been a favourite of Canadian historical writers. It divides metropolitan evolution into four phases: first there is a concentration on market or commercial facilities, then the development of manufacturing, which in turn is followed by the evolution of transportation and finally by the achievement of financial maturity. The strict application of this thesis to North American metropolitan centres, as Gras himself notes, should be undertaken with a certain amount of caution since there are marked differences between London and the newer North American cities. Still, these differences do not affect the first phase too greatly, because it is really based on the extension of existing village facilities rather than on new technological developments.[4]

The real divergence between Europe and North America concerns the manufacturing and transportation stages as they evolved in Britain and on this continent, for in many cases it could be argued that they began here before the marketing phase was complete. For instance, in Britain, where the market phase was complete and manufacturing improvements preceded communication systems, the stages to a large extent followed each other; metropolitan communications could not be improved until William Symington had invented his steamboat or John McAdam his road-surfacing methods. In North America, this was simply not the case. Since many advances in technology preceded the opening up of the interior of North

America, they were naturally applied immediately in newly opened areas, thereby telescoping the stages of metropolitan evolution. Further, new ideas and processes were constantly being adopted while the cities grew. Gras notes an example of the resulting duality of development in the evolution of Minneapolis-St Paul — the centre that he examined in the most detail — where manufacturing and transportation developments appeared together in the years 1870-1900. He concluded: "While in older districts, for instance, in England and the Atlantic states of America, the Industrial Revolution preceded the revolution in transportation, in the American Northwest these two movements were synchronous."[5] This meant that there was a different course of evolution in the metropolitan areas of North America, a difference that became progressively more apparent as civilization moved west

The rise of York/Toronto, therefore, did not follow the same basic pattern as that of the great European metropolitan cities such as London. In Toronto, Gras's market stage was still under way in the 1830s; however, at that time the manufacturing and transportation stages were reaching a fair level of advancement, although they were not to come into full bloom until after the railways were completed in the mid-1850s. Nevertheless, while Gras's model has its limitations, it does provide a convenient basis for an examination of the economic growth of the city. For that reason, it is used to set the structure of the following discussion.

The first stage of metropolitan economy, characterized by the appearance of all the market institutions necessary to service a large agglomeration of people — wholesalers, specialist merchants, warehousing, extended civic facilities — was well advanced in York by the early 1830s. The growing commercial importance of the town was particularly characterized by the emergence of several new wholesale firms, some established by local residents, others being branches of mercantile houses in Montreal or Kingston. Although the appearance of branches of Montreal firms in the city might be taken as evidence of the continuing domination of that centre, it can also be seen as an indication that York's trade could no longer be obtained by merely waiting for the city's merchants to place orders in Montreal. Also, York's selection as a branch-office site by Montreal firms confirmed its growing place in the western Upper Canadian economy.

That the citizens of York, perhaps rather paradoxically, regarded these new wholesalers as evidence of emancipation from Montreal is shown by an editorial which appeared in the *Courier of Upper Canada* on Oct. 20, 1832. The journal announced that there were now four Montreal wholesalers in the city, as well as five local wholesale firms, and added: "with all these numerous and extensive concerns, it will be obvious that Country merchants need no longer think of going to Montreal, since every article of Merchandise can be obtained at York, in equal abundance and variety, and upon Montreal terms." Further evidence of the fact that York was attempting to break away from Montreal control are the advertisements of such merchants as George Monro and Isaac Buchanan, who boasted that they had established direct connections with the Old Country. As well, a large volume of trade was being carried on with the United States.[6]

Paralleling the growth of the wholesalers was an equally rapid expansion of specialist firms. In the earlier years of the town, some merchants had claimed to be specialist dealers, but by 1830 large, sound businesses were making their appearance, such as Watkins & Harris hardware and the printing and publishing firm operated by Henry Rowsell. There were also a great variety of minor concerns: silversmiths, book stores, druggist's, hatters, even a cigar store and a used-clothing shop. Many of these businesses, of course, were ephemeral, but others were to grow and play a leading role in the city for decades.

Whether the new stores were wholesale or retail, Montreal-controlled or Toronto-owned, importers from England or from the United States, or both, they all had one thing in common: the desire to develop business both in the city itself and in its hinterland. Their newspaper advertisements frequently contained specific instructions for local papers in other parts of the province to copy them. By studying these instructions we can gain a good idea of the extent of Toronto's commercial influence during the period. Most of the places in which Toronto merchants actively solicited business were located in the western part of the province, or in the Niagara Peninsula: centres such as Hamilton, London, St Thomas, Niagara (Niagara-on-the-Lake) and St Catharines. In addition, the names of villages along the shore of central Lake Ontario, such as Cobourg, were to be found on occasion. That there were also Toronto trade connections to Lake Simcoe in the north is shown by the fact that as early as 1832 the firm of Murray, Newbigging & Company were operating a wagon route to that area, and had at least three co-partnerships there, located at Holland Landing, Newmarket and the Narrows of the Lake (Orillia).[7]

The converse of this expansion of in-bound trade, the growth of Toronto as the port of export for its hinterland, is more difficult to trace in the records. The only major merchant's correspondence that survives from the 1830s, the letters from John Spread Baldwin of York to his partner Jules Quesnel in Montreal, is quite fragmentary, though extensive; still, it shows that shipments of wheat and potash played a major role in business. This evidence is corroborated by the fact that the farmers of the Home District founded their own cooperative store on the Ontario lakefront as early as 1824. Planned as a centre for exports and imports and local trade, it operated successfully for some years.

Another aspect of Toronto's commercial and communications development was the flourishing newspaper business which had grown up in the city, and which, as is evidenced again by the commercial advertisements, was particularly important in spreading the capital's influence throughout the hinterland. York had had a newspaper since the official *Upper Canada Gazette* had moved from Newark (Niagara-on-the-Lake) in 1798, but the *Gazette* remained the only paper in the town until 1820. After that date new sheets appeared rapidly, and, though many of them failed, by the early 1830s there were usually six papers being published simultaneously in the town. Beginning with the *Courier of Upper Canada* in 1829, these tended to become semi-weekly. *The Royal Standard*, which flourished briefly in 1836-37, was the first daily in the province.

Newspapers were important to the growth of the city's influence because most papers of province-wide interest — or hopeful of attaining province-wide interest — tended to locate in Toronto. The *Gazette*, as noted, had followed the capital from

Newark; William Lyon Mackenzie's *Colonial Advocate* came from Queenston in 1824; Thomas Dalton's *Patriot* moved from Kingston in 1832; and George Gurnett had relocated his *Courier* from Ancaster in 1829. Of the two denominational papers, in Upper Canada the Methodist *Christian Guardian* moved to Toronto and the Anglican *Church* was sometimes published there.

The actual circulation of these papers is difficult to establish. Mackenzie, whose paper must have been one of the most influential in the province, once published a list of fifty-two agents scattered over a wide area, but the fact that he had appointed an agent for a particular village does not necessarily mean that he had subscribers living there.[8] The paper with the largest circulation was probably the *Christian Guardian,* for every travelling circuit rider was automatically an agent. On a more limited basis, the *Courier* had subscribers in the Gore, London and Western districts — what is today Southwestern Ontario and the Niagara Peninsula. This was almost the exact area where the commercial houses of the provincial capital circulated their advertisements and may well represent the limit of influence of most Toronto journals.

In addition to the development of commercial enterprises, there is another aspect of Gras's first stage of development — the organization of public services to handle the needs of the growing population. This type of change can also be seen in the Toronto of the 1830s. The very reason for incorporation was the inability of the appointed magistrates who governed the Home District — of which Toronto was also the district town or capital — to deal with the problems posed by the continuing waves of immigration. The preamble to the Act of Incorporation of 1834 stated the problem clearly: "whereas from the rapid increase of the Population, Commerce and Wealth, of the Town of York, a more efficient system of Police and Municipal Government has become obviously necessary." [9] In the years before incorporation the local magistrates had made valiant, but unsuccessful, efforts to expand municipal services to meet the growing demands of the population. Two wells for the town water supply were dug in 1823, a volunteer fire service was organized in 1826 and a new court house and jail opened in 1827. The inadequacy of these last buildings within a few years demonstrates the problem facing the government authorities. When the court house and jail were first planned in 1820 the population of the Home District was about 13,000; when they were finished seven years later it was 21,398, and by 1835 there were 58,308 inhabitants, 9,765 of them in Toronto. By the mid-1830s new buildings were under consideration and a new jail was opened in the city in 1841.[10]

In spite of the financial burden imposed by the court house and jail, and a taxation system that was far from adequate, the district magistrates were next forced to build a new market for the city to replace the old one which had become hopelessly overcrowded. This was done in 1830-32, but the cost involved (over £9,000) was the final difficulty that brought on incorporation for Toronto — some new system of governing and financing simply had to be found. The provincial government, too, occasionally attempted to aid its fast-growing capital, and Lieutenant-Governor Sir John Colborne was largely responsible for the opening of the first hospital in 1829.

William Lyon Mackenzie, as first mayor in 1834, proved to be singularly ineffective in alleviating the problems facing the new city, partly because the Tories and Reformers on the city council were more interested in doing battle with each other than in undertaking constructive measures, but mainly because of his own failings as an organizer, administrator and leader. After Mackenzie and his Reformers were decisively defeated in the election of 1835, civic government took a decided turn for the better. Robert Baldwin Sullivan, the Tory second mayor, began an organized municipal financial system, appointed an inspector of nuisances to clean up the streets, and, most important, started the construction of a sewer system. The Reformers returned to power the next year under a new leader, Dr Thomas D. Morrison, and began the macadamization of the city streets. At the end of his term, in January 1837, Morrison also played a part in the establishment of the first house of industry (poor house) in the city.[11]

In the years that followed the city's sewers and paved roads were gradually extended. Gas and water systems were also built in the early 1840s, though neither worked effectively for some years. Clearly, in terms of the basic civic services it offered its people, the city was well advanced in the first stage of metropolitan development.

Though Toronto was not to become an important manufacturing city for some years yet, sufficient progress had been made by the time of incorporation that the city had already entered the second phase of metropolitan development. Firms had been established which were to play a major role in the city's history and the larger industries had expanded beyond local-service requirements and were aiming at dominating the immediate hinterland. Some of these factories were located in the centre of Toronto's downtown area but others, including many varieties of mills, spread along the Don and Humber rivers. One of the most important of the mill complexes was developed at Todmorden on the Don River by the Helliwell, Eastwood and Skinner families.[12]

The central area of the city contained a wide variety of enterprises by the 1830s: Jesse Ketchum's tannery; Peter Freeland's soap factory, which was one of the main landmarks on the shoreline for many years; the famous furniture factory of Jacques & Hay; and various brickmakers, breweries and distilleries. These two latter lines of business provided some of the most stable firms in the city, including Copland's brewery, founded in 1830 and sold to Labatt's of London in 1946, and Gooderham & Worts, which was established in 1832. Heavier industry was also making its appearance; the largest manufacturing operation in Toronto was probably the foundry of Sheldon, Dutcher & Company, which was employing eighty men by 1833. Armstrong's axe factory was nearly as large by the rebellion period.[13] Thus, the manufacturing stage, though still in its infancy, was plainly in evidence in Toronto before the "market" stage was completed.

With regard to Gras's third phase, the development of transportation, Toronto had made definite steps forward by the 1830s. We have seen how the roads were being improved within the city; by 1833 similar macadamization projects were being undertaken in the surrounding townships, and stretches of macadamized highway were gradually being extended along Yonge and Dundas streets and Kingston Road. Horse-drawn carts for the transportation of both goods and people were also appearing and the first cab was built in 1837. For travel beyond the city, scheduled stagecoach itineraries had been established as early as 1816, and by 1833 there were regular runs of coaches from Toronto to all the main neighbouring centres. In the winter almost daily connections were available west to Hamilton, via both the Lakeshore Road and Dundas Street, east to the Bay of Quinte and Montreal, and north to Holland Landing on Lake Simcoe.[14]

Whenever the seasons permitted, the preferred method of travel outside the city was by boat. Water connections had developed rather earlier than land transportation. The steam-boat appeared on Lake Ontario with the *Frontenac* in 1817, and by 1826 one newspaper reported that there were no less than five steamboats on the lake and "the routes of each are so arranged that almost every day of the week the traveller may find opportunities of being conveyed from one extremity of the Lake to the other in a few hours." [15] In 1834 there were seven boats running from Toronto, five making a full circuit of the lake — which usually took a week — and two others providing more localized connections: one with Niagara, the other with Rochester, New York. Between them these boats connected Toronto with the stage routes leading to Montreal, the major American cities and the Upper Great Lakes.

At the same time that steamships were appearing on the Great Lakes the foundations of the canal system were being laid. The construction of the Erie Canal connecting New York City to Buffalo in 1825, and the extension of the canal to Oswego on Lake Ontario in 1828, simplified and improved Toronto's connections with the Atlantic Ocean from February to December. Soon construction was underway on the Rideau and St Lawrence canals in eastern Ontario and on the Welland Canal in the Niagara Peninsula. With their completion, or rebuilding, in the 1840s, Toronto's water connections with the Great Lakes and the world were in place.

The focal position of Toronto in water transportation in the years that followed incorporation is well illustrated by the number of piers built in its harbour. The 1833 *Directory* showed only the government dock, two small piers and a third commercial wharf which was still under construction. By 1842, when James Cane engraved the Sir Charles Bagot Plan of the city, there were no less than four new private wharfs. Nearly all of these, including the three main commercial piers, were in use by the time of the Rebellion. In addition, although Toronto was never the scene of much shipbuilding, its merchants were shareholders in many of the ships built around the lake, and Torontonians such as Hugh Richardson and the MacIntosh brothers commanded many of the most notable vessels.

Not satisfied with these steamer and stage connections, in the years 1834-38 the merchants of the city made their first attempt to improve communications with the city's hinterland to the north and northwest by planning a railway. The surveys originally called for a line to Lake Simcoe, but later they were altered so that the line would run to Lake Huron and thus to the American west beyond. The idea failed to materialize because of the depression of 1837; but it was to be revived when times improved in the early 1840s and would eventually become the Northern Railway (now part of Canadian National). Indirectly, Toronto's communications with its hinterland were improved with the 1839 opening of the Erie & Ontario Railway, which bypassed Niagara Falls.

In general, then, it could be said that Toronto had established quite adequate connections with a considerable hinterland region — considering the level of technology of the period — about the time of its incorporation. Moreover, the merchants of the city were already looking ahead to any new schemes, such as railways or additional canals, to spread their sphere of influence farther. In fact, Toronto's development in communications was, if anything, ahead of its advance in manufacturing. In sum, even though it had not quite completed the market phase of its metropolitan development, Toronto was entering phases two and three simultaneously by becoming both a centre of manufacturing and a hub of communications.

In the years we are discussing, the city was still far from the financial stage of metropolitan development, but, as Gras noted, financial evolution of a rudimentary sort takes place during the earlier phases. Such an evolution can be seen in the Toronto of the 1830s. The merchants of the city had always been alive to investment possibilities and, though there was as yet no stock market, a considerable trade in stocks had developed by the early 1830s. This was carried on partly by opening books for subscriptions to new enterprises, partly by banks handling stock transactions, and partly by various dealers in a variety of businesses also selling stock. Again, the city was a centre for the sale of land both within its limits and throughout its hinterland. As the seat of government it was the location of the Crown Lands Office. It was also the centre of operations of the powerful Canada Land Company, and of various independent land agents, one of whom, Joseph Talbot, in 1834-35 even published a weekly newspaper devoted almost exclusively to land sales.[16]

Banking in Toronto underwent a major boom in the years preceding the panic of 1837. For a decade after 1822, the government-allied Bank of Upper Canada — the first bank in the colony — was the only bank in the city. Its first real rival was the Commercial Bank of the Midland District, founded at Kingston in 1832 and partly controlled by Toronto interests, which soon opened an office in the capital. Because, like the Bank of Upper Canada, it was a Tory organization, its appearance in the city did not quell Reform demands for an independent bank. The Reformers soon quarreled among themselves, however, and ended up founding two new banks in Toronto, not one: the Farmers' Joint Stock & Banking Company, established in May 1835, and the Bank of the People, established in November of the same year by the more radical Reform faction.

Meanwhile, two English entrepreneurs had chosen Toronto as the site for a banking operation, opening the Agricultural Bank in the spring of 1834. This institution was far more enterprising in its policies than even the banks dominated by the Reformers — it was the only one willing to underwrite the first loan to the city, and the first to pay interest (three per cent) — on deposits. It was also the only Toronto bank to go under in the panic of 1837. Before the depression put a stop to banking expansion, another bank — the English-chartered Bank of British North America — chose Toronto as the site of its first office in June 1837.[17] On the surface, the collapse of the Agricultural Bank in 1837 might seem to indicate that the city's banking structure rested on shaky foundations. In fact, however, this bank's failure was the result not of its operations in Toronto but of crooked dealings and overexpansion in New York state. The success of the other Toronto banks in weathering the troubles of the later 1830s demonstrated that the financial expansion of the city was not premature. From this time on Toronto was unquestionably the financial centre of the province, and was recognized as such even beyond the provincial boundaries.

Another facet of Toronto's contemporary financial growth was the appearance of local insurance companies. Prior to this time the insurance business in the city had been handled by agents of English and American firms, but in 1832-34 a group of prominent citizens founded the British America Fire & Life Assurance Company, which continues in business today as Royal Insurance Canada. Although some Reformers were involved in the establishment of this company, other Reform figures decided to establish a second company, the Home District Mutual Fire Insurance Company, in 1837.

A final aspect of Toronto's metropolitan growth, perhaps, was the beginning of labour troubles — though these were of a very minor nature. The printers established a union in 1832, and in October 1836 staged an unsuccessful strike, calling down upon themselves the wrath of Mackenzie, who uttered statements worthy of the most authoritarian tycoon, when faced with a strike himself. The printers' strike was followed almost immediately by an equally unsuccessful tailors' strike. Although organized labour made little progress during the period, the apprentices in the stores had some success in limiting their hours, when, except for Saturdays, the merchants agreed to an 8 p.m. closing in August 1836, and a 7 p.m. closing in November 1840. Those merchants who declined to comply were quickly faced with replacing broken windows.[18]

By the 1830s Toronto, in spite of its small population and its lack of great financial resources, was well along the road to becoming much more than a market centre. If we accept Gras's terminology, the city had gone beyond the first stage and entered phases two and three of metropolitan economic growth, even though the great boom in both these stages would not come until the railways were completed in the mid-1850s. The city was also the centre of a growing hinterland which extended throughout most of the settled areas of the province to the north and west, and financially, to an extent, as far as Kingston in the east.

Leaving Gras's terminology aside, we may say that by 1834 Toronto was already much more to Upper Canada than simply the political capital; it was also clearly the prime focus of its business. Some of this business activity was admittedly concentrating there because Toronto was the seat of government; but by this very concentration the city was both developing into something more than an administrative centre, and at the same time, losing its dependence on its political status. In sum, though full metropolitan development might come later, the foundations were in place and the course clear by the 1830s. By the time of the Rebellion it was obvious that Toronto, not Kingston or Hamilton, would be the provincial economic centre. Indeed, so secure was the city's economic position that by the Union of Upper and Lower Canada in 1841 Toronto was on its long march to usurp the hegemony of Montreal.

Chapter 3

Developing Communications: the First Railway Venture[1]

Toronto's commercial importance during the French regime lay in its location near the beginning of the portage route to Georgian Bay and the fur-trading grounds of the west, a route which both by-passed the Niagara Falls portage and avoided the trip along Lakes Erie and Huron. In 1795-96 the value of this northern connection was greatly enhanced when Lieutenant-Governor Simcoe's Queen's Rangers first opened up Yonge Street and settlement began to develop in the rich agricultural hinterland spreading to Lake Simcoe. By 1830 the Town of York was rapidly becoming a city and the forests around it were giving way to cultivated fields. Its leading merchants were seriously considering ways in which they could both consolidate their hold over the counties of York and Simcoe to the north and, at the same time, exploit the advantages of the old French trade route to the upper Great Lakes and the rapidly developing American west.

The ultimate result was the City of Toronto and Lake Huron Railway, or, as it was known after 1858, the Northern Railway. Interest in the project can be traced back to the early 1830s; however, the panic of 1837 stopped construction in that decade. Revived in 1844 with the return of prosperity, the line was completed to Collingwood on Georgian Bay in 1855. From then until it was absorbed in the Grand Truck system in 1888, the Northern was one of the most successful Canadian railways, especially under the able management of architect Frederic William Cumberland from 1860 to 1881 when it became one of the main factors in the rapid commercial and industrial expansion of the city. Since 1921 it has formed a major link in the Canadian National Railway system.

Though unsuccessful, the first attempt, which began in 1834 and was virtually abandoned in 1838, is still well worth examining, for it shows the difficulties pioneer Toronto faced in both raising funds and for a railway and in determining its route. This attempt at railway building is also important for the light it casts on the politics of the period. More specifically, it underlines the fact that when it came to major economic projects, most Upper Canadians — regardless of their political faith — were ready to cooperate for the good of the city and their individual profit. Supporters of the railways included men of all political affiliations and a wide range of newspapers too — the radical *Correspondent and Advocat* backed the project just as strongly as the *Albion,* the *Courier of Upper Canada* and the *Patriot.*

By the early 1830s Toronto had quite an adequate system of communications in light of the technology of the period. The lake steamers, by far the most pleasant method of travel, regularly linked the city with all the major ports of Lake Ontario and the world beyond; but such boats at best could operate only from early April until November. For the rest of the year, both traveller and shipper were forced to rely on the stagecoaches and the roads. A fairly extensive system of roads radiated out from the city: Yonge Street to the north, Kingston Road to the east, and Dundas Street and the Lakeshore Road to the west. For passengers in winter, the snow made travel easy; in spring and fall, however, stagecoaches were often mired in mud, and in the summer, dust made land travel thoroughly unpleasant. The shipment of bulk goods to and from the growing villages north of the city, where there were no navigable rivers, was very difficult because of the bad roads. The enterprising Toronto firm of Murray, Newbigging and Company had already attempted to set up a wagon service to Newmarket and Holland Landing. Some more satisfactory system of transportation was obviously needed, however, and the citizens were quite ready to consider suggestions of a canal or a railway.

Developing communications to the north was complicated by the question of what route should be used. The most logical line for a railway — which was eventually taken by the Northern in the 1850s — lay from Toronto to Lake Simcoe and then on to Georgian Bay and Lake Huron. Such a route would benefit the city in two ways. First, it would link Toronto with the agricultural hinterland stretching north to Lake Simcoe. Here lay the chance of immediate profit, and, conversely, the danger that if Toronto did not act, one of the towns to the east, such as Port

Hope or Cobourg, might build a railroad and steal the capital's trade. The second advantage of this route was that it would again open up the old fur traders' portage route to the Upper Great Lakes and the American West — this time, it was hoped, on a much more profitable basis. If Toronto could build an easy line of communications across the portage, it could exploit its geographical position and become the great trade centre for the west.

Immigrants and goods could travel from New York, via the Erie Canal and the Oswego Feeder to Lake Ontario, then cross to Toronto and so on to the west. Conversely, trade would flow the other way as the west developed. Dr Thomas Rolph expressed this theory clearly in his *Statistical Account of Upper Canada*, published at Dundas in 1836, when he stated that:

> the country on both sides of Michigan Lake is rapidly increasing in population &c., and the country on the south side of Lake Superior, will in a few years be settled, so that by this line of communication, the principal part of the trade, &c., of that vast country will flow down this way to Montreal, and New York. [2]

Originally, the merchants of Toronto planned to build a railway to Lake Simcoe only, possibly with the idea that another group in that area would carry the line on to Lake Huron. This course was soon abandoned, and in its place some of the more adventurous entrepreneurs substituted a second route that ran directly to Georgian Bay, bypassing Lake Simcoe completely. Thus, the railway would not only fail to connect the city with its direct hinterland up Yonge Street, and thus possibly leave that area open to exploitation by rival centres; but also it would run through virtually unsettled territory with no local traffic to bear the operational costs. Although the whole idea was unsound, in the boom period of the mid-1830s almost any scheme looked rosy. Possibly, it was fortunate for Toronto that the depression of 1837 came when it did, before the city had had an opportunity to pour much money into what would almost certainly have been an unprofitable project.

The railway builders' efforts may be divided into three phases. In the first, which lasted from June 1834 until about early

1836, they were engaged in supervising the survey of the route from Toronto to Lake Simcoe by a local engineer, Thomas Roy. By late 1835, however, the more ambitious plan was under discussion and the dream of untold riches quickly overcame the more practical ideas of Roy and some of the original sponsors. American engineers were brought in from Utica — at much greater cost — to prepare a new survey, and an act was obtained from the legislature authorizing a direct line to Lake Huron. This second phase of planning lasted through 1836 and into 1837 while the new survey was being completed. Finally, in the summer of 1837, came the last phase of the operation, the actual attempt to organize a company. By that time, depression was settling in and raising the necessary funds quickly became a hopeless task. By 1838 the idea of building a railway had to be abandoned.

To return to the beginning, as early as 1832 meetings were held and a subscription collected to defray the expenses of a survey for a railway line to Lake Simcoe. The *Courier* asserted that, if practicable, such a railway would be of great advantage to persons near its route "who are at present subjected for at least half the year to the terrible annoyance and inconvenience of being dragged over that chain of mudholes called Yonge Street."[3] Nothing further developed at that time; but two years later the idea was revived, with the impetus coming from the Lake Simcoe area rather than the city itself. On June 23, 1834 many of the leading inhabitants of Simcoe County held a meeting at the village of Newton, on the Narrows of Lake Simcoe, to discuss how they could improve communications along the line of the old trade route from Toronto to Lake Huron. Among those present were Samuel Lount, later to be hanged for his part in the Rebellion of 1837, William Beverley Robinson, the representative for Simcoe County in the House of Assembly and a member of one of the most prominent Tory families, and Charles Thompson of Sunnidale Township, a justice of the peace, who later played an important role in Toronto business. The chairman of the meeting was the Reverend Charles Crosbie Brough, the Church of England incumbent at Newmarket

Discussion focused on a canal rather than a railway, and the meeting favoured a course northward to Georgian Bay rather than southwards to the capital. Presumably, those present felt that Toronto would itself undertake the construction of some type of communications from Lake Simcoe to Lake Ontario. The route that the Simcoe meeting selected was naturally the Toronto-Lake Simcoe-Georgian Bay connection, not the direct Toronto-Georgian Bay project attempted during the second phase of the project. After approving the construction of a canal the meeting resolved:

> That such a canal would promote a direct chain of water commencing from Lake Ontario to the Shores of Lake Superior, through the centre of this vast Province, encourage Emigration, facilitate the settling of Back Townships, as well as those on the shores of Lake Huron, and open to enterprising individuals the Fisheries of the Great Lakes.[4]

A committee was then set up to promote the enterprise.

This activity evidently inspired a revival of interest in Toronto, for on July 26 a public meeting was held at the Court House, located across Church Street from St James's Cathedral. The meeting was attended by many who had been present at the Simcoe gathering, as well as many leading members of the Toronto business community. William Botsford Jarvis, the sheriff of the Home District, was elected chairman, and James Newbigging was appointed secretary. Newbigging was to be one of the most active promoters of the railway, acting as both secretary and treasurer until his sudden death on Feb. 9, 1838, at the age of thirty-two. His interest is hardly surprising since his firm, Murray, Newbigging & Company, as already noted, was active in the trade of the Lake Simcoe region.

The July meeting debated the idea of building either a canal or a railway to Lake Simcoe, to connect with the Lake Huron canal that the Simcoe meeting had already approved. To facilitate action, subscriptions of £1.5.0 (to be credited against future stock purchases) were received from nineteen individuals. A separate Toronto committee was appointed which included various representatives from both the Lake Simcoe area and the townships between the lake and the city. W.B. Robinson, Charles Thompson and Benjamin Thorne of Thornhill were members, along with many representatives from the city such as Peter Robinson, commissioner of crown lands and a brother of

W.B. Robinson, and John Henry Dunn, the receiver general of the province. The name chosen was the "Simcoe & Ontario Railway."[5] The committee began to take action almost immediately; by the end of August W. B. Robinson was writing to Newbigging from his home in Newmarket saying that he felt that the railway could be surveyed for £50. As their surveyor the committee chose Thomas Roy, a civil engineer and one of the most competent men in his field in the province. He was, however, a rather difficult person with whom to work, and on more than one occasion differed strongly with his employers. Nevertheless, his services were still much in demand, for while he was associated with the railway company he was also superintending the construction of Toronto's first sewer system and preparing recommendations for improvements to the harbour.

The instructions the committee gave Roy were very detailed — probably too detailed. He was to survey a route from Toronto to Lake Simcoe, starting between the Don and Humber rivers, running between Markham and the west branch of the Holland River, and terminating at a point on the Holland River where steamboat connections could be made. He was to advise them of any deviation from the line suggested, to be careful to note elevations, names of landowners and types of soil, and to place marks in the ground to show his lines and curves. As if this was not enough supervision, he was saddled with one D. Gibson as his deputy surveyor. The committee, simultaneously, made application to the legislature for an act empowering them to construct either a railway or a canal from Toronto to Lake Simcoe.[6]

It was decided to begin the survey from the north and by Sept. 30, 1834 Roy was at Red Mills near Holland Landing. He was already running into difficulties, not only from the over-supervision from Toronto but also from a lack of funds and inadequate personnel. His reports provide a clear picture of his problems. On Oct. 6 he wrote Newbigging from Newmarket that he was having trouble with the rough land, and

> we are already out of funds and would beg of you to produce us a little for to pay the men at the end of the week - I do not know where to order it be sent unless in the care perhaps to Mair's Inn ... we have only 3 men besides myself Mr. Gibson

having left - any more just now would be a useless expence as the ground is so intricate and wooded, but as soon as we pass Richmond Hill I would be for putting on more hands and finishing it in 8 or 10 days.

He followed this up on Oct. 13, again from Newmarket:

Mr. Gibson left us on last Thursday week and had not returned — he left a young man his apprentice who also left on Tuesday morning without giving any reason so that I have been left entirely without assistance — The young man also locked up the Level — so that I was left no choice but to go on with 2 labourers and to lay out and stake of[f] and measure but the road, and return and level it (a short process) when I get Capt. Bonnycastle's level.

Adding that he was now near the Ridge (Oak Ridges), he closed with a plea for more money. This was to become something of a ritual. Captain R.H. (later Sir Richard) Bonnycastle was the commander of the Royal Engineers in Upper Canada. Later he wrote four works on Canada and Newfoundland which remain invaluable references for anyone studying this period.

On Oct. 28 Roy was able to report that he was at the Ridges and about to move on to Toronto. Gibson and his young man had returned, but he still had received no money. This letter was followed on Nov. 1 by another providing a report on progress to date, including a comment that since the fall of the land from the Ridges to Lake Ontario was 723 feet, the railway would have to descend 33 feet per mile for the 22 miles. He concluded, "I have not been able to pay the men and am now nearly 2 weeks in arrear. Mr Gibson has also asked me for money — please let me have a little and oblige." Money, however, was not forthcoming and by late December the survey had been abandoned after it reached Hogg's Hollow (York Mills) north of the city (which W.B. Robinson looked on "as the greatest obstacle [in the route]").[7] Meanwhile, Gibson had resigned, and Roy discovered that that worthy's surveys were inaccurate:

> I took the leveling books as left by Mr. Gibson ...
> some time ago — to my great surprise I found
> nearly all the levels altered an error of 13 feet
> commencing at or below Yonge St. ... He never
> informed me of any error but when I challenged
> the careless manner in which they were done it
> was taken in bad part.[8]

In spite of his carelessness, Gibson had no compunctions in submitting a bill for £23 for 28 days work at 15 shillings per day (Roy himself received 25 shillings), plus another £9.3.9 for his assistant. Roy accepted his resignation, and told him that he either had to redo the work himself, or get another man to do it at his own expense. In January 1835 with no further progress made, Roy was merely able to report to Newbigging that another six to eight days work would be necessary before any calculations would be done. It was the end of March before a report could be presented to the subscribers. By that time, the committee had paid out £75.12.5 and had only £1.17.5 balance on hand. Until more funds could be raised, no action was possible and during the spring and early summer the project was dormant.[9]

On Aug. 22, 1835 Roy reported to another Court House meeting under Sheriff Jarvis that construction of a railway was possible. This report was accepted on the motion of Dr William Warren Baldwin, and books were opened for subscriptions at Murray, Newbigging & Company. Thomas Dalton, editor of the Tory *Patriot*, printed a stirring editorial:

> Our city is by no means upon the advance ... nor
> can it be kept on the advance, but by the energy
> of the wealthy Citizens. Many towns and villages
> are in rapid growth to the Westward, and all bent
> on advancing their own particular interests, and
> already take away much of the Trade of Toronto,
> for they have their regular importing merchants,
> who are gradually increasing in both number
> and power. Now it is clear in our mind, that
> Toronto must be finally left to take up with such
> portion of Commerce, as her own enterprise
> shall place at her immediate command, and it

will ere long be the route of the trade of the West to Lake Ontario [either] by Toronto, or by the back Lakes to the head of the Bay of Quinte. If the latter route be taken, it will be fatal forever to Toronto. The question is *now* pretty much in the power of our Citizens to solve. If they are first to establish a Route, it will be hard afterwards to change it. Let the matter be considered, *and in time.* [10]

A full public meeting held on Oct. 20 under the chairmanship of Mayor Robert Baldwin Sullivan, Dr Baldwin's nephew, decided to petition the legislature to enact a law setting up a joint stock company, this time for the broadly described purpose of building a single or double-track, wooden or iron, railway from Toronto to Lake Simcoe. Ambitious suggestions were also made for carrying the railway on from Lake Simcoe to Lake Huron, and the meeting finally resolved, on the motion of Solicitor General C.A. Hagerman, that

> the multitude of passengers who would take advantage of such an easy and expeditious communication would render the railroad the most productive in North America. That instead of Buffalo, Oswego and Toronto would be the certain route chosen by all Emigrants to the Western States, and so open the Province, and bring such incalculable wealth into the Colony, as no other public improvement could possibly equal. [11]

The supporters of this extended project felt that such a route would not only become the main line of emigrant transport to the west, but also that the Americans could be persuaded to help build it. The *Correspondent and Advocate* for December 3, 1835 confidently stated that capitalists from New York and Oswego would be glad to take up the greater part of the stock, because "so concerned are they of its importance to their trade and that it would moreover prove a profitable investment."

A typical example of the inter-party cooperation that prevailed during the project is to be found in the composition of the group of men who in April 1836 actually petitioned the legislature for an act to charter the railway. The list read like a "Who's Who" of the Toronto mercantile community, containing names of men of all political affiliations: James Lesslie and Francis Hincks were Reformers; William Henry Boulton and George Cartwright Strachan, Tories; many others, such as Thomas Dennie Harris, were basically men with no particular interest in political matters except as they furthered their commercial ends.

By April 20, 1836 the act was passed to incorporate the "City of Toronto and Lake Huron Rail Road Company." The Lake Simcoe connection had been completely pushed out of the picture and the terms did not even provide for a branch line to that lake. Obviously the Lake Huron faction had the most influence with the legislature despite the resolution of the meetings. The second phase of the operations was now going full steam. The terms provided that "he railway should have full power to "transport thereon passengers, goods and property either in carriages used and propelled by the force of steam, or by the power of animals, or by any mechanical or other power, or by any combination of power which said company choose to employ". [12] The company would have eleven directors, one of whom was to be president, and a capital of £500,000. Money was to be raised by opening subscription books in which individuals would enter their agreement to buy a certain number of shares at a set price. Payment was made in installments called by the directors over a period of time as funds were required. Before the company could be organized £50,000 had to be subscribed. The subscribers then elected the directors who could call for a first payment of ten per cent of the subscription within thirty days. The railway had to be started within three years, and finished within ten, or the charter would become void. The main problem with the system, as will become obvious, was in collecting subscriptions. Many signed in a burst of enthusiasm in the boom times of the mid-1830s and then could not, or would not, pay when depression hit. The directors felt that taking their business associates to court to force payment was just notdone in a small city with an interconnected group of business leaders.

The committee now retained new railway surveyors, Marvin Porter and R. Higham of Utica, New York. These men were also to advise on potential rates of fare. Evidently there had been a quarrel with Roy who had resigned in March and later demanded that his name be vindicated, stating that he had been accused "falsely and dishonestly." He pointed out that he had been circumscribed in his activities by the committee, prevented from completing the survey by lack of funds, and that several of the men were still unpaid. [13]

On July 11, 1836 a public meeting was held in the Court House with King's Printer Robert Stanton in the Chair, and George Cartwright Strachan, a son of the archdeacon, as secretary. The supporters of the Lake Simcoe route were momentarily back in ascendancy, undeterred by the fact that the act made no provision for a Lake Simcoe connection, and on a motion of Sheriff Jarvis and Executive Councillor John Elmsley the assembly resolved:

> That whereas a survey having been made between the City of Toronto and Lake Simcoe by which it appears that a route has been discovered through which a Rail Road can be completed at an expence not exceeding £2500 per mile, and from the nature of the country lying between Lakes Huron and Simcoe, it is believed that equal if not greater facilities are not [sic] afforded for the continuance of the contemplated Rail Road to Lake Huron and an act of Incorporation having been attained [sic] for the purpose of forming a joint Stock Company to carry the provisions of said into effect.[14]

The committee reported that a further £1,000 was necessary for new surveys, and James Newbigging was again appointed treasurer. By July 13 a total of 39 leading citizens had agreed to put up £50 each (again to be credited against future stock subscriptions) and subscription advances of £100 by the Farmers Bank and £150 by the Bank of Upper Canada were promised.

That the first bank was Reform-dominated and the second a Tory fortress again showed how all factions in the city could forget their individual disagreements in the interest of advancing Toronto's prosperity. An analysis of the 39 individuals further demonstrates this cooperation. On the Reform side there were both moderates like Issac Buchanan, George Percival Ridout and the wealthy John Elmsley; more radical were brewer

Joseph Bloor, miller James Hogg, and William Ketchum who fled to the United States after the Rebellion. The Tory group was comprised of such affluent members of the City Council as George Taylor Denison and future Mayor George Monro, as well as several minor government officials, including Hugh Carfrae and John Beikie. At a higher level it included Provincial Secretary Duncan Cameron, former mayor and Executive Councillor R.B. Sullivan, Legislative Councillors William Allan and Joseph Wells, and William Henry Draper, member of the House of Assembly (MHA) for Toronto and a future government leader and chief justice of Ontario. Finally, there were many merchants of no particular political affiliation: hatter Joseph Rogers, builder John Ewart, undertaker John Ross, retired general merchant Alexander Wood, silversmith William Stennett and, of course, James Newbigging. In the end, some of the gentlemen must have lost their enthusiasm because the papers later noted that only £1,500 had been paid by some 29 subscribers.[15]

Although there were still some disagreement on the exact route, the Lake Huron supporters were again in control. On Aug. 2, 1836 the *Patriot* reprinted a statement from the *Courier*, based on the authority of one John Smyth of Toronto, quite possibly the eccentric local poet, who does not seem to have played any part on the committees. This claimed that the best route was from Toronto to what is now Southampton at the mouth of the Saugeen River on Lake Huron about sixty miles north of Goderich. From there, branches could be run south to Goderich and east to Penetanguishene. There was also talk of other branches to Caledon Township in Peel County and to the Head-of-the-Lake (Hamilton). Others, who prevailed, preferred the mouth of the Nottawassaga River running into Georgian Bay, ten miles east of Collingwood, as their terminus. They argued that, although the mouth of the Saugeen River was protected by an island, Nottawassaga Bay was preferable as it had a depth of fourteen feet at the bar. In addition, they felt that an easier passage could be made from it to either Goderich or Michigan.[16]

The proprietors estimated that £250,000 would be required for construction. This could be raised by a stock issue of which a third, or £85,000, could be sold in Canada, a third in England and a third in the United States. On Aug. 23 the *Correspondent and*

Advocate quoted an article from the *Albion* which strongly backed this plan, saying "we are of [the] opinion that the amount of stock will be taken in Upper Canada in three days and that it will be immediately at a premium." To inaugurate the formal sales campaign, a meeting was held at the City Hall (on the site of the present St Lawrence Market) on August 24, under the presidency of John Elmsley. After the preliminary report of the engineers was made public, £15,000 was subscribed within a few minutes. The *Correspondent and Advocate* confidently asserted that reaching the total of £50,000 required by the act would take only a few days. William O'Grady, the editor, added:

> We are greatly deceived if this stock will not prove to be one of the most profitable investments in British North America. Persons diametrically opposed to each other in political feeling, have but one opinion on the subject, more especially as it is distinctly understood that our precious Government are to have no concern in it. There can therefore be but little, if any doubt, of its success. [17]

On September 7 he continued:

> Labourers and Mechanics should take stock in this road were it but one share (£12.10) each. The whole would not be called in for two years, and in the mean time they would be aiding in opening for themselves a source of employment which would enable them to pay their instalments and to subsist their families.

In spite of this backing, the subscription was not an immediate success; it was the next spring before the company could be organized. In the interim a new committee composed of Elmsley, Newbigging and "McGaulay" — presumably John Simcoe Macaulay — was set up to supervise the second survey, which was to be paid for by the subscriptions promised earlier by the thirty-nine gentlemen.[18]

This survey had already begun, for on August 19 R. Higham, who was in charge, gave Secretary-Treasurer Newbigging a receipt for $600 (he was billing them in American money) on account of "Disbursements & Services in surveying a rail Road route from Toronto to Lake Huron." At the same time the remaining debts to Roy and his crew were at last paid off. By October 19 Higham was able to report to the committee that the survey was completed to Nottawassaga Bay, and he "finds that a good and safe harbour for vessels drawing nine feet of water can be made at the mouth of the river at a moderate expense." On the same day he also wrote Elmsley from the steamship *Traveller* saying that he was returning to the United States to fulfill certain engagements, but he would return to terminate his measurements at Nottawassaga as soon as possible. He thought his surveying parties would be finished that week and on his return he would "run another line from the west side of the City to intersect the main line." He finally gave an ominous warning of increased costs. This missive was followed by payments totalling $1500, and then, to defray the expenses paid out by the treasurer, a special meeting of the committee was held at the Commercial News Room, which was a library and meeting place kept up by the merchants in the City Hall. It decided to call another 12 per cent of the subscription from each participant.

In spite of these payments the survey still was not rapidly completed. On December 28 Higham wrote from Utica advising Newbigging that he would not have the finished report until January 15, since he had broken his leg. At Newbigging's request he added some suggestions for a revision of the charter that would allow the company to acquire property directly along the line, which would greatly increase in value when the railway was completed. The report, dated at Utica Feb. 1, 1837, was finally delivered to a meeting of the committee at the Court House on February 11. At the same time, Higham presented maps, estimates of cost, and his account showing a balance of £731.5.0 in his favour. This meant that another 30 per cent had to be called in on the subscriptions. A week later the public and others were invited to City Hall to see the report, with its proposed alternate routes.[19] In it Higham approved the Nottawassaga River, anticipated to be the site of the future great city of the north, as a suitable harbour, and stated that, if required, connections could be made with Lake Simcoe. To keep down costs he recommended timber viaducts and estimated a total expense of from £210,681 to £304,112 for the east line. The continuing enthusiasm of the committee can be seen in two of its draft petitions. One, addressed to new Lieutenant-Governor Sir Francis Bond Head, requested land grants on both the east and west sides of Toronto so the railway at the terminus would form a loop around the city. The other, directed to the legislature, requested the power to construct a branch of the railway to Lake Simcoe and the right to navigate that body of water (either by steam-propelled boats or by barges), and the right to raise money by mortgaging any completed sections of the railway or any of its properties.[20]

Other citizens still remained less hopeful for the prospects of a railway using the direct Lake Huron route. One of them was, not surprisingly, the dismissed engineer, Thomas Roy, who wrote to both William Henry Draper, the MHA for Toronto, and the City Council. His attack is well worth examining; it represents the criticism of an intelligent man, with a very sound understanding of Toronto's metropolitan position. He began by pointing out that Draper had just supported a new act pledging £100,000 of the province's credit for the construction of a railway directly from Toronto to Lake Huron, and then further stated that it was "a measure which I conceive in its ultimate results must produce the most fatal effects upon its [Toronto's] prosperity and sink a great amount of capital without even the most distant probability of remunerating the shareholders or the province." He continued, noting that he had made a survey to Lake Simcoe and recommended an extension to Lake Huron, but that this idea had been thrown out by a new committee and now Lake Simcoe, "the source from whence all the immediate remuneration to the shareholders would be derived, was left out altogether." [21]

Roy then explored the potential benefits of the proposed Lake Huron route. A railway, he believed, was good for the farmers only if they had to ship their produce over twenty miles. Taking this factor into consideration, Roy maintained that for the first forty miles of the planned route it would be cheaper for the farmers to ship to ports along Lake Ontario once roads were developed. Then, just at the juncture where shipping via railway would be economical, the line entered the glen of the Nottawassaga River with the Oak Ridges between it and the agricultural area of Lake Simcoe, and the Blue Mountains to the West. "I forbear to make any comments; judge for yourself what traffic is to be expected here." He continued: "the end of this glen reaches to Lake Huron from whence vessels drawing 5 feet of water can enter the mouth of the river in ordinary seasons — Such vessels may enter the river, but it is very difficult indeed for them to leave it again as the prevailing wind is from the north and blowing directly into its mouth."

His conclusion was simply that, even when the area was settled, the proposed route would not provide enough traffic to keep an engine going twice a week. As for Michigan trade, better routes were being built. In response to the idea that mineral resources might be developed along the route, he countered that the Blue Mountains and the surrounding area were mainly formed of limestone, which lacked minerals. Next, he added a description of the metropolitan position of Toronto at that period that cannot be bettered today:

> Let us next consider the ruinous consequences which will ultimately result to the city of Toronto by adopting this line of railway. The excellent harbour formed by York Bay is decidedly the greatest natural advantage which the City of Toronto possesses — it has no navigable river stretching into the interior of the country to enrich it with its commerce, nor does its position on Lake Ontario give it very decided advantages over other Towns which possess Harbours less spacious and commodious — neither does it command by its situation the commerce of the interior on the East or on the West — but as the country has become settled, it has obtained an ascendancy in the north — from these circumstances it must be obvious that the commerce of the city of Toronto must increase as these northern counties are settled, if she opens up and maintains her lines of communication and by liberal and judicious measures secures their traffic, and that the commerce of this city must dwindle into insignificance if she wantonly throws away to other places these advantages

which circumstances rather than nature has bestowed upon her.... at present, Toronto is the commercial emporium of this district. To secure and perpetuate this intercourse was the contemplated object of the proposed railway which I laid out.... The injurious consequences which will result to the city of Toronto arise from this circumstance. That a better and cheaper line is found by which the Lake Simcoe countries, the Balsam Lake countries and Sturgeon Lake countries can be united by one railway to the good Harbour [i.e. Port Hope or Cobourg] on Lake Ontario, (but not the city of Toronto) — and raise up an important Town so near as to be a destructive rival.

Finally, Roy concluded that he feared that a short railway might be built connecting Lake Huron with Lake Simcoe, and that it might ultimately become part of a railway connecting the Ottawa River with Lake Ontario — but not at Toronto.

From these causes I fear the most ruinous consequences will result to this city, her hold upon the interior of the country will be broken up, not by what she has done — but what she has omitted to do — view the different effects if a railway has been constructed to Lake Simcoe — from the first day of its opening it would have been in full trade forwarding goods and produce to and from all places to which the navigation of the Lake and its rivers extend — it would also have [the line] as a grand trunk passing through the ridges from which on their northern side branches would have diverged westward to Lake Huron and eastward to the Balsam Lake and to the Ottawa and would have firmly established the City of Toronto as the grand commercial emporium on the shore of Lake Ontario.

Roy also noted that the inhabitants of the Simcoe area were considering making other connections with Lake Ontario by railway as Toronto was by-passing them.

He was not the only one critical of the direct Lake Huron route. Thomas Sutherland of Moore Township, the founder of one of the first settlements on the St Clair River, wrote Newbigging on March 17, 1837 suggesting a completely different plan; Toronto should run its railway not northward but rather westward to connect with the planned London and Gore Railroad (Great Western) at Hamilton. Otherwise, he warned, that city would replace Toronto as the metropolis of the province.[22]

Newbigging, however, had no qualms. On April 1 he wrote to Higham enclosing a copy of the new act of the legislature (7 William IV c.60), which Roy had attacked so strongly. Under it, the company could borrow the £100,000 from the government, the terms specifying that as soon as it had spent £12,500 it could borrow £37,500, and from then on it could have an additional £3,750 for every £1,200 spent, until the £100,000 limit was exhausted. The rate of interest was to be 6 per cent, and the loan was to be paid in 20 years. In addition, the act gave the railway the right to hold up to 600 acres of land at each station, and, as the petition had requested, to construct a branch line to Lake Simcoe. Newbigging felt that the company could borrow whatever other monies it might need at 6 per cent and that, with a total subscription of £60,000 on stock, it would have to call in advances only of 15 per cent in order to be able to expend the judicious sum of £60,000 for the first summer's operations.

Newbigging reported himself particularly pleased with the clause of the new act allowing the company to hold land adjoining each station house. Writing Higham on April 1, he said:

> It seems to me that this positively places beyond
> a doubt the work being a profitable one, from
> Toronto to Nottawassaga the road does not come
> near a village, and I fancy at least six may be
> located, in addition to the town of Nottawassaga,
> by the same of the lots in which would yield
> nearly a sufficient sum (making the lots in each
> payable by installment) to pay the interest of the
> £100 for the first 12 or 15 years.

He again painted a picture of immigrants and goods flowing to Michigan and of future railway connections with the United States, and he noted that the line would be completed before any railways now built from Hamilton to Chatham, and would be well established before they could rival it. His enthusiasm was typical of the unbounded hopes of the period. Newbigging tended to be over-optimistic — as some of his firm's activities in the Simcoe area indicated — yet no less an authority than Captain Bonnycastle agreed, telling a company delegation that their project was "one of the surest means of making this fine harbour the permanent seat of the principal City of British Western America."[23] The only hint of troubles to come was the familiar comment in Newbigging's letter than he regretted he was unable to send Higham more money at that time.

Meanwhile, subscription books had been sent out, and subscriptions for stock were being received. By April the necessary £50,000 required before elections could take place had been raised; Sheriff Jarvis, as chairman of the managing committee, called a meeting at the Court House, and a president, vice-president and nine directors were chosen. William Allan was elected president, J.S. Macaulay vice-president, and the nine directors were Legislative Councillor George Crookshank, John Elmsley, Sheriff Jarvis, James Newbigging, builder John Ewart, James M. Strachan (another son of the archdeacon), William Ketchum, hardware merchant George Percival Ridout and Judge George Ridout. Newbigging had subscribed for 150 shares, and Macaulay and Elmsley for 100 each, placing them among the most important backers of the company. Allan, who received the most votes as a director, was supported by the holders of 928 voting shares, Elmsley, the lowest, by 346. Allan's election as president may seem surprising for he had played only a small part in the enterprise. He was, however, the financial genius of the ruling Family Compact, and one of the two or three richest men in the province. He had been president of the Bank of Upper Canada, and became the first governor (president) of Toronto's first local insurance company in 1834. His acceptance of the railway presidency was regarded as a real coup by the shareholders.[24]

The new directors calculated that £230,000 would be needed to complete construction. As £55,000 had been subscribed, and £100,000 promised by the government, it seemed that only an additional £80,000 at the most would have to be raised. Their ambitions, and their confidence in their project, are shown by the fact that they appointed subscription agents in Cornwall,

Prescott, Brockville, Kingston, Newmarket, Barrie and Penetan-guishene, in Upper Canada; Quebec and Montreal (Peter McGill, president of the Bank of Montreal, who personally subscribed to 125 shares), in Lower Canada; New York and Boston (the British consuls); Utica, Oswego, Rochester and Ogdensburg, New York; Green Bay and Milwaukee, Wisconsin; and Chicago. Presumably, these were all centres which the directors felt would benefit from the railway's operations. Several nearby towns such as Hamilton, London, Port Hope and Cobourg, which the directors possibly saw as rivals, were not solicited. The books were to be opened on May 8 and the results returned by the agents by the 28th of that month.[25]

The directors also began to prepare the way for the construction of the railway along the lakefront in the city itself. On April 27 James Newbigging, as a secretary of the City of Toronto & Lake Huron R.R. Company, made application to Mayor George Gurnett of Toronto "for a plan of the vacant ground and Water (lakefront) Lots at the disposal of the Corporation, and [to see] whether they are willing to yield any and what portion to the Rail Road Company."[26] As the water lots were under the control of the provincial government, the municipal government was merely able to promise cooperation and record its interest.

By this time, disturbing reports were beginning to come in from the agents. Just as the company was planning to start construction the panic and depression of 1837 struck the entire continent. The height of speculation in the United States had come to an end in 1836 and by May 1837 every bank in that country had suspended specie payments. Soon there were rising demands that similar action be taken in Upper Canada. With England in the same predicament, and indeed with the whole world plunged into a major economic depression, expansionist projects would have to wait. The effect on the subscription can be read in the letter Quebec agent James B. Forsyth wrote to Newbigging: "I rec'd yours of 22nd April with the Subscription Book for the Lake Huron Rail Road Co. which has been open at our office, but not a single share has been taken, nor do I see any chance of you getting any subscribers here such is the scarcity of money and those having it feeling no anxiety to invest it in any public Improvement."[27] Most of the subscribers were from Toronto; but there were a few from Montreal, some from Albion Township and a few more — possibly still hoping for a Lake Simcoe route — from North Gwillimbury.

With such a negative response even the most enthusiastic board of directors should have postponed construction. But this did not happen — Newbigging continued corresponding with Utica to get the operation underway. The proponents of a Lake Simcoe route had not given up either, for on June 8, 1837 the official *Upper Canada Gazette* announced that Sir Francis Bond Head had appointed Hamilton Hartley Killaly, a civil engineer who was later chairman of the Provincial Board of Works, to survey a route between that body of water and Toronto. But with no money neither project could go ahead.[28]

In July there was a new election of directors, the only change being the substitution of George Munro for John Elmsley. The declining interest is shown in the number of votes exercised, for this time Allan and four others led the poll with 221 votes each (well under the lowest number a few months before), and George Munro at the bottom was elected with only 131. The financial report was far from encouraging. The call of 10 per cent on the stock subscription had collected only £1,745. As the initial survey bill was £1,512.10.6, and there had been other expenses, the treasurer reported that he had only £44.19.6 in his hands. Nevertheless, Vice-President Macaulay issued an encouraging report to the shareholders on the eve of the new directors' election:

> considering the difficulties in money matters, the first installment had been so far well paid and they [the directors] felt satisfied that the public confidence in the success of the undertaking is so great, that a slight relief in money matters will enable the company to proceed rapidly with this great undertaking. ... Under the circumstances they cannot but congratulate themselves and the Stockholders upon the happy commencement of a work of such benefit and Interest to the City of Toronto and to the Province of Upper Canada in general.[29]

This brave but mendacious declaration was followed up by an announcement calling for tenders for the grading and bridging of the first seven sections of the railway, stretching to Black Creek, to be completed by May 1, 1838. The tenders were to be submitted to the engineer's office at the Market Buildings by July 28, 1837. Yet the month end, not surprisingly, failed to show any financial improvement. Finally, in early September, Allan and Newbigging admitted the truth. The £150,000 anticipated was a vision and no more; the first installment that should have brought in £5,000 to begin the line was only partly paid, and all their efforts to raise this amount — required by the act before construction could begin — had proven to be in vain: "Longer time was given, this not producing the wished for result, further indulgence was offered, and it was agreed to take notes of hand at three or six months that the advances might be less burdensome, but nothing availed, and instead of £5000, barely £2000 have been received." Some subscribers, they continued, had pleaded disorders in the money market, and some people of large property had not paid; but in spite of this they had not taken legal action since "such proceedings are exceedingly disagreeable, and not only tend to cause delay, but injure the prospects of the company." They concluded that all that could be done was to hope for a more auspicious season in Upper Canada.[30]

Even the lack of public support failed to bring the operation completely to a halt; negotiations were continued for control of the water lots along the lakefront, and small payments were dribbled out to Porter and Higham as long as funds remained. As late as January 1838 their firm drew up plans for the first three towns to be built on the line: on the Humber River; in the north part of Albion Township; and in Tecumseh Township beyond the swamp. On Feb. 9, 1838 Newbigging died suddenly and George P. Ridout became the new secretary. The financial statement shows that the amount paid out to date was £2,324.11.1. When the stockholders met at the Court House on Sept. 3, 1838, the report was hardly a cheery one. Times had not improved and, although the directors advised that they had managed to get the first section ready to let the contract, they also had to state that "the original subscribers who had last year failed to redeem their pledges, still continue in default." Allan, Macaulay and much the same board were elected, but for all practical purposes operations were at an end.[31]

In March 1839 Porter wrote Allan from Geneseo, New York, enquiring about £23 which remained unpaid. He was advised that the directors would have it brought to their attention. In

May he tried again with no more success, and then there is a total break in the company records until March 7, 1841, when Porter once more asked for his money. Allan responded on April 17: "there has been no Board of Directors chosen, or any business done by the Rail Road Company since long previous to the time of your sending the Note. I have no power or authority over any of them — I presume if ever the Company does revive or make any more progress they would provide for this note." Not only had the finances run out, so had the time limit provided for the start of construction under the act. Toronto's first railway venture was at an end.

The scheme was revived by William Allan and others in December 1844, when business conditions had improved. With the help of government assistance under the Railway Guarantee Act of 1849, construction was begun at Toronto in October 1851 and the line was opened to Aurora in May 1853, Allandale (Barrie) in October 1854, and finally connected with Collingwood in June 1855. The route was thus a logical combination of the Lake Simcoe and Lake Huron schemes, joining Toronto to its agricultural hinterland by the most direct route and connecting it with the Lake Huron trade. Simultaneously, other revived railway schemes opened connections from Toronto to the east and west, and one of the greatest boom periods in the city's history began.

The survivors of the original enterprise may have taken this as proof that they had been right all along in their plans. Even if the panic had not intervened in 1837, however, it is doubtful if the railway could have been built even as far as Lake Simcoe. Costs would probably have proved too great for the fledging city, and the government was not yet ready to intervene with financial aid of the order needed. Nevertheless, the fact that the idea was carried to such lengths shows the ambition of the city's merchants to expand their trade by improving communications, and their statements demonstrate that they had a good idea of the importance of the metropolitan hinterland they were attempting to open up, as well as not unreasonable dreams of wider commercial domination in the more distant future.

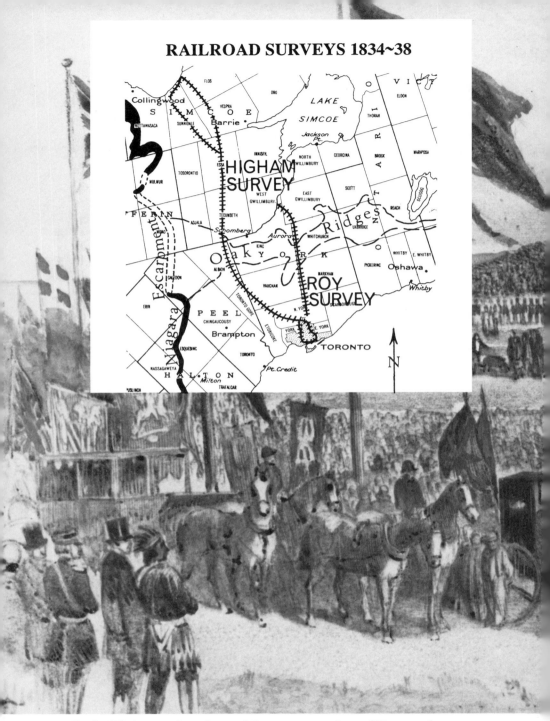

RAILROAD SURVEYS 1834~38

Lady Elgin turning the sod for construction of Toronto's railway, 1851.

NEVER DESPAIR

Metropolitan Toronto Library

73

William Lyon Mackenzie, from a portrait by J.W.L. Forster.

Part II: The Most Controversial Torontonian: William Lyon Mackenzie

Evaluating William Lyon Mackenzie has always been a problem. While he was well known, vociferous, and colourful, he was not the only Reformer who fought to end the rule of the Family Compact of Upper Canada, that alliance of local Tory groups which, for so long, ran the affairs of the colony. Further, after 1828 the lieutenant-governor of the colony, instructed by a more reform minded Colonial Office, was eroding the Compact's power well before the ill-planned and unsuccessful Rebellion of 1837 plunged Mackenzie into exile, and wiped out the fortunes and in some cases the lives of his followers. Thus, to the probable benefit of the moderates on both sides, he was outside the province when Great Britain—in a logical continuation of earlier attempts at reform—reacted to the rebellions in Upper and Lower Canada by uniting the two colonies into one new province. This was a move that abruptly undercut the position of Upper Canada's extreme Tories, just when they thought that they had won the contest and consolidated their hold on power.

Mackenzie was still in the United States when the British Whigs decided to grant internal self-government to the colonies and Robert Baldwin and Louis-Hippolyte LaFontaine formed the second responsible colonial government in 1848, a few weeks after the same process had taken place in Nova Scotia under equally moderate leadership. British North Americans had thus come to govern themselves by evolution not revolution. The Rebellion of 1837 in Upper Canada was simply that: a rebellion. The very term denotes that it was not successful. The right to govern ourselves was attained by moderates in Great Britain, the Maritimes and the Canadas working in somewhat uncoordinated concert. It would have come in much the same way if Mackenzie had not attempted his uprising.

Yet changes in constitutions and governments provide only dull facts and hardly stimulate students, literary and media figures, left-wing historians and provincial ministries of education. The last group sometimes appears bound and determined to impose an heroic, American-style revolutionary framework on our peaceful course of evolution. To these groups, evidently, non-violent, gradual change must seem almost a shirking of social responsibility. It is not heroic, not freedom-loving, to have the right to govern ourselves granted by the colonizing power. We have gained the same rights as Americans without killing anyone in the process. This makes poor fare for mythmakers.

Thus they all fall back on Mackenzie. He was a blaze of colour, he did set off Ontario's only rebellion, he left quotable opinions on almost every subject in his newspapers, and he was elected first mayor of our largest and richest city — and the first incumbent is about the only mayor who ever gets remembered, even when he is completely faceless. It is not surprising, then, that the historical and literary writing on Mackenzie has developed a split personality. As a result, for practical purposes, today there are really two Mackenzies. Evaluating Mackenzie is a constant source of controversy, and will continue to be so.

How has this come about? In gaining his place in history Mackenzie was lucky in a variety of ways. The consummate stupidity displayed by many of his Tory opponents, particularly in breaking up his press in the type riot of 1826 and in expelling him repeatedly from the House of Assembly in the early 1830s, made him a martyr in the eyes of many people and gave him a vast amount of publicity. Beyond such contemporary events, however, the historic Mackenzie was fortunate in that such a large number of his personal papers survived, including almost all his newspapers. He also had an admiring son-in-law, Charles Lindsey, another journalist and a radical in his youth, who produced a monumental two-volume biography based on Mackenzie's own stories and writings in 1862 only a year after the latter's death. It became the basic primer in the onwards-and-upwards atmosphere of late Victorian liberal Ontario. Finally, Mackenzie was lucky in his grandson, William Lyon Mackenzie King, who during his long career as prime minister did all he could to advance the fame of his grandfather.

Literary figures in the late-nineteenth century generally followed Lindsey, and the legend became established of the fearless and indomitable Reform leader who became a highly successful mayor of Toronto and whose necessary rebellion, even if it failed in the immediate instance, set off a chain of events which culminated in our right to govern ourselves. The first break in this tradition came just after 1900, when William

Dawson LeSueur was asked to write a new biography of Mackenzie for a series on Canadian leaders. Using the original documents he came up with a thoroughly unfavourable interpretation, but protracted litigation in the courts by Mackenzie's descendants prevented the manuscript from being published (it finally appeared in 1979).

The legend remained undisturbed until 1927, when Aileen Dunham in her thoroughly researched *Political Unrest in Upper Canada* provided the first historically sophisticated overview of the colony's politics. She completely demolished the view that Mackenzie was the leader of the Reformers, that he had a coherent political philosophy and that the Rebellion was necessary. Her interpretation was confirmed a quarter of a century later by Gerald M. Craig in his classic history, *Upper Canada: The Formative Years*, and has been supported by most subsequent scholarly inquirers, including Ronald Stagg and Colin Read, who have studied the Rebellion in its Yonge Street and southwestern manifestations. This did not mean that favourable biographies based on Lindsey had ceased to appear, or even that he was downgraded in school texts, but rather that a consensus on his place in history was developing among most non-leftwing historians.

My own entrance into the fray came through researching Mackenzie's mayoralty for my doctoral thesis, and discovering that the documents did not support the view that Mackenzie was an eminent success during the year that he held the reins of municipal power. This study is reprinted in one of the following chapters. Two others deal with specific incidents in his career that throw light on his character: the story of the York (Toronto) riots in 1832 and his actions when faced with a strike of his own printers in 1836. The last chapter in this section presents my conclusions on his career and contributions. The interpretation in the article on Mackenzie's mayorality has been energetically—to say the least—attacked by Paul W. Romney in a 1975 article for the *Canadian Historical Review*. Romney, who has written other articles on Mackenzie, takes me to task for both errors and omissions; for my part, I feel that his own error and omission rate is quite outstanding, especially for a critic. However, that is for a fuller reassessment of the Mackenzie legend that I am currently preparing.

For those who wish to look further into the life of Toronto's best-known citizen the original Lindsey biography is easily found, and there is also William Kilbourn's *The Firebrand* , a 1956 study based heavily on Lindsey. Lillian F. Gates *After the Rebellion: The Later Years of William Lyon Mackenzie*, also a favourable interpretation, appeared in the spring of 1988. On the other interpretative side, Ronald Stagg and the writer have prepared the article on Mackenzie for Volume IX of the *Dictionary of Canadian Biography*. A more extended account is David's Flint's *William Lyon Mackenzie: Rebel Against Authority* (1971).

In conclusion, what is the popular view of Mackenzie today? The sesquicentennials of the incorporation of Toronto in 1984 and the Rebellion in 1987 have brought forth a rash of articles and celebrations which have kept his name before the public. There are plays, novels and even a puppet show honouring him, while the school curricula are again being revised to include a strong section on rebellions. Yet, if one can judge the reactions of university students to his deeds, he remains a vague figure, often mistaken for the explorer Sir Alexander Mackenzie or a prime minister (either his grandson or Alexander Mackenzie). Does this demonstrate that the differing interpretations are having an effect, or just that the curriculum for today's younger generation is as soporific as ever? But, to look at the other side, no one seems to have heard of the Family Compact—so how can you have a hero when his opposition and their policies are forgotten? Still, possibly Mackenzie qualifies as something of a current Canadian hero just because of the mere survival of his name, even if so many are unsure of exactly who he was. Regrettably, mere survival of the name is pretty good for a Canadian hero.

Chapter 4

The York Riots of March 23, 1832 [1]

The rapid rise and increasing militancy of the Reform party in Upper Canada in the late 1820s inevitably resulted in the rallying of those conservative forces who believed their own way of life to be threatened, or felt that the maintenance of the British connection was endangered. The leaders of the Family Compact were, in their own minds, administrators, not politicians. Consequently, the formation of an anti-Reform party, when it came, was largely owing not to those notables themselves, but rather to generally prosperous citizens of much the same economic and social class as the group who led the Reformers. After the Reformers' brief period of power in the House of Assembly from 1828 to 1830, this opposition began to coalesce more rapidly, goaded on by William Lyon Mackenzie's constant barrage of resolutions. By 1832 the two factions were on the verge of a head-on collision aross the province. York — or Toronto, as it was soon to be renamed — was the scene of a major confrontation on Friday, March 23, which took place at a public meeting called by Mackenzie. There both groups fought for ascendency and the town was shaken by a series of riots, which, for the time being at least, left the Tories politically in control.

In the months preceding this event the Tory majority of the Legislative Assembly had been attempting to gag Mackenzie, who was one of the two members for the County of York, by expelling him from the House. This was to prove to be a course of action which merely strengthened his hand. The first expulsion took place on December 12, 1831, by a vote of 24 to 15. But, to Tory disgust, when the by-election to fill his seat was held on January 2, the occasion turned into a personal triumph for the little Scotsman. He saw his only opponent retire from the race at the end of an hour-and-a-half with one vote to his own 119, while he himself was escorted from the polls by a procession of 40 sleighs and was presented with a gold medal by his supporters. The Tory party in the Assembly was, however, anything but defeated, and, like the contemporary Bourbons, had not learned anything. On January 9 they used Mackenzie's election address — which had been headed "impeachment or public accusation against the lieutenant-governor of the province and the advisors of the Crown" — as an excuse to expel him again, this time for the full duration of the Parliament, as "unfit and unworthy." The result was a third election, which began on January 30, and this time the undaunted Mackenzie secured a total of 628 votes against the combined 119 for his two rivals. As in the case of the destruction of his printing press some years before, Tory stupidity was Mackenzie's greatest asset. As the House was now prorogued he was unable to contest the ruling expelling him for the full parliamentary term, and the battle for the moment switched from the Assembly to the newspapers and to public meetings around the province. [2]

To many — including the Tory portion of the assemblymen — Toronto seemed to be a veritable hotbed of radicalism, and there even were suggestions that the capital be moved to a safer place. This attitude was clearly expressed by John Carey, editor of the recently defunct *Observer*, writing to Louis Walsh at Vittoria on January 19:

> Parliament will be prorogued on the 24th. A motion will be made for the removal of the seat of government; & yesterday the parliament house, which cost already £8,500 was abandoned. A sum of £3,500 was called for in committee of supply to complete it, & it was kicked out by a large majority! The Solicitor General opposed the grant for reasons that he would not explain. I suppose the lowering attitude of the York folks & the insulting menaces of the people towards the Lt. Gov. and the Legislature contributed to the rejection of the motion.[3]

Any possibility of losing the proud title of capital of Upper Canada was guaranteed to spur the conservative element in the city to action — if any spurring was needed at this date — and on March 6 a group of the local Tory leaders met to decide upon measures necessary to counteract the growing reform menace. Under the leadership of Dr William "Tiger" Dunlop, Thomas Carfrae Jr and George Gurnett, the editor of the *Courier of Upper*

Canada, they soon set up a General Committee and prepared an address to the king expressing the loyalty of the city. Then, joined by another committee representing the Catholic Tories, who had prepared a similar address, they collected signatures. Both groups presented their declarations to Sir John Colborne, the lieutenant-governor, on March 22, for forwarding to the king.[4]

Meanwhile, Mackenzie reacted to the Tories' flurry of activity with the assertion that these committees were using strong-arm methods to collect signatures. He called for a public meeting to reaffirm the Reform resolutions he had had passed at a meeting the previous summer and again at his re-election on January 2. On March 15 this announcement appeared in his *Colonial Advocate:*

PUBLIC MEETING
OF THE
INHABITANTS OF YORK
TO EXPRESS THEIR SENTIMENTS
ON
THE STATE OF THE COLONY
AND
THE CHARACTER OF THE GOVERNMENT
York, March 12, 1832.

The undersigned respectively request the inhabitants of the town of York, His Majesty's faithful subjects, WITHOUT DISTINCTION OF CREED OR COUNTRY, to meet at the Court House on Friday the twenty-third instant, AT NOON, for the purpose of expressing to His Majesty's Government THE SENTIMENTS OF THE CAPITAL OF UPPER CANADA on the present state of the Colony and the character of its government.

This was signed by some seventy Reformers including Mackenzie; Jesse Ketchum, the other member for York County; Dr Thomas D. Morrison, later third mayor of Toronto; James Leslie, Mackenzie's affluent patron; and William Cawthra, who was to become the richest man in Ontario.

The conservatives, worked up to a fever pitch, accepted this challenge with alacrity, and, urged on by the Tory press across the province, gathered their forces to seize control of the meeting. The *Patriot* in Kingston, for example, republished Mackenzie's announcement on March 27 (actually after the meeting was over), and added a postscript:

> We see that the above is a challenge from the Mackenzieites, and if there be life or spirit in the town, it will be met openly, and the faction will be extinguished at once. The requisition is for the inhabitants of York, "the capital of Upper Canada" — confine it to that — let no man but an inhabitant of the town vote, and let all vote — let every man be registered on the yeas and nays — let all who do not attend be called on — and the Government will be supported and the Mackenzieites put down ten to one.

As for the York Tories, they flooded the town with handbills headed "General Meeting" and calling on all who were loyal to come forward and put down the "demagogues." Gurnett's *Courier* threatened that "we most assuredly would not ensure the leading revolutionary fools a whole skin, or a whole shin bone in their shins, for the space of fifteen minutes." The authorities, who were all Compact appointees, failed to take steps to prevent violence, either by swearing in special constables or by other means, even though, with both sides marshalling their forces for a showdown, there was obviously going to be major trouble.[5]

There are several newspaper accounts describing the action on March 23, as well as a lengthy description in the diary of Mackenzie's friend James Lesslie. All of these narratives stress different parts of the fracas, and all leave out inconvenient details. In fact the "disgraceful riots," as Mackenzie was to dub the event, are fully as illustrative of the low level of newspaper reporting of the era as they are of its violent politics. The two principal accounts appear in Gurnett's *Courier of Upper Canada* on March 24, and Mackenzie's *Colonial Advocate* on March 28. Other useful shorter descriptions occur in the *Canadian Freeman* for March 29, and the *Christian Guardian* for March 28. The first was an Irish Catholic paper, edited by Francis Collins, who, although a staunch reformer in outlook, was even more anti-Mackenzie than the *Courier* because of his attacks on the Catholic Church and Bishop Alexander Macdonell.[6] The Methodist *Christian Guardian*, edited by the Reverend Egerton Ryerson, gave what is probably the least biased account of the events, but also, unfortunately, it is the shortest one. Besides, its reporter, who signed himself "An Eye Witness," wisely hovered on the edge of activities and so missed many of livelier episodes. Fortunately, in spite of the many disagreements among these sources, there is a sufficient measure of agreement to permit reconstruction of the meeting and its aftermath.

From the very first it was a Reform catastrophe; Gurnett triumphantly headed his report: "Total overthrow, and utter prostration of the Ryersonian Revolutionists in York" and "last dying speech and confession of Wm. L. Mackenzie."[7] Mackenzie's best effort at a reply was the caption "The Progress of Misgovernment." The Reformers had carefully prepared their forces, and as the Kingston *Patriot* had foreseen when it demanded that the voters be limited to the inhabitants of York itself, Mackenzie probably brought in his supporters from the countryside to back his motions. Gurnett claimed in the *Courier*:

> Every wheel of their well organized political machine was set in motion to transmew [sic] country farmers into citizens of York. Accordingly, about nine in the morning groups of tall, broad-shouldered, hulking fellows were seen arriving from Whitby, Pickering and Scarborough, some crowded in wagons and others on horseback, and Hogg the Miller headed a herd of the swine of Yonge Street who made just as good votes at the meeting as the best shopkeepers in York; notwithstanding these preparations, however, they were most triumphantly routed, horse, foot and artillery.

What Gurnett fails to relate is that the Tories were taking similar and more effectual steps to prepare for the meeting. In view of what happened, the actual size of the Reform forces must have been much smaller than the report suggests.

The other anti-reform or rather anti-Mackenzie account in the *Canadian Freeman* painted exactly the opposite picture of the strength of the radical forces and then went on to describe Mackenzie, who had been beaten up at Hamilton on the 19th:

> About noon, little Mackenzie, accompanied by Mr. Hogg, the miller, approached, followed by about a dozen or two, chiefly boys ... Mackenzie's face exhibited evident marks of the rough handling he met with at the Hamilton meeting — the right eye was neatly blocked up, and a narrow strip of court-plaister extended over the nasal organ, like the finger post of a turnpike, as if to say "let those who follow this course look out for broken heads!"

At that time public meetings were held in front of the Court House, which stood in the centre of the east half of the block bounded by King, Toronto, Adelaide (Newgate), and Church streets. The whole area except for the Court House and the Gaol, which balanced it on the west side, was open ground. Proceedings began at 11 a.m. when the flag of the steamboat *Canada* was hung over the steps, and by noon the two parties had gathered and begun the meeting by taking issue over who should be elected chairman — the Tories nominated Dr William Dunlop, the Reformers, Jesse Ketchum. As the crowd was unable to come to any decision, the supporters of Dunlop moved to the east of the Court House, and those of Ketchum went to the west between that building and the Gaol. According to the *Courier*, this division made it obvious that the reform element comprised less than a third of the total, and that three-quarters of these were not from the capital but from the surrounding countryside. Conversely, both Mackenzie and Lesslie claimed that their supporters numbered at least two-thirds of the total. Sheriff Jarvis, who was hardly an unbiased moderator, proclaimed Dr Dunlop chairman. This decision was, however, probably a fair one, for, as we have noted, the poor showing the Reformers made in the following fracases would indicate inferior numbers. With the matter of the chairman settled, the meeting then proceeded to elect two secretaries representing the two loyal committees (Catholic and General), completely ignoring the opposition in their selection.

The agenda was then attacked with vigour. Dunlop read the notice from the *Advocate* convoking the meeting and Carfrae moved a resolution that the sentiments of the inhabitants of the town were expressed in the addresses which had just been forwarded to the king. This was adopted by an "immense majority" and the Tories, after moving thanks to Dr Dunlop, carried another motion to adjourn. Mackenzie summed up their activities by saying that they accomplished their purposes in ten minutes, without an attempt at discussion, and, he presumed, "to their entire satisfaction."

The events of the day now appeared to be over, and many went home, but the main performance was yet to come. The radicals, piqued at having their show stolen by the conservatives, made the mistake of attempting to hold a meeting of their own right under the Tories' eyes. Moving beside the Gaol and setting up operations in a wagon, they began, to quote Gurnett, "doing the despicable mummery of resolving their old string of grievance resolutions." Mackenzie in the *Advocate* differed, of course, writing:

> Those who were dissatisfied with the election of Dr. Dunlop by the majority, as chairman of the whole, peaceably and quietly removed to a distance, procured a farmer's wagon and placing therein a table and two chairs elected Mr. Ketchum, member for the county, their chairman, and chose Dr. Morrison to act as secretary. Mr. Ketchum addressed the people at some length and with good effect; he was repeatedly cheered. He strongly recommended moderation, good order, and the practice of great forbearance towards political opponents.

The accuracy of this statement is rather to be doubted, and in any case Ketchum would have been better advised to recommend they go home. With the Tory meeting ended, many of the

King Street East, Yonge to Church Streets, looking east from Toronto Street, 1835. From left to right: Jail, Fire Hall, Church Street, Court House, St. James Anglican Church.

potentially more inflammatory elements found themselves with
nothing to do. Naturally, as Mackenzie said, "they next set about
carrying on offensive operations against the party which had
succeeded." What happened is generally clear from all accounts,
but it is uncertain which individuals were responsible, or how
many participated. Mackenzie followed Ketchum as speaker,
even though he was still in pain from the beating at Hamilton,
and was only able to begin after receiving a glass of wine and
water. It was at this juncture that the first riot broke out between
the two factions. The *Canadian Freeman*, in the least accurate
account of the day's activities, claimed that the trouble began
when its reporter tried to ask a question and was only saved
from a beating by Mackenzie's bullies, who included young
Ketchum, by the intervention of some Irish lads "ripe for frolic
and fun." Then, according to that paper, a rock was thrown at
either their reporter or the Sheriff — it landed between them —
and the Tories swung into full attack, or as they claimed,
defence. Gurnett gives a somewhat different story of how the
battle started, stating that the reform meeting evoked a reaction
from some twenty or thirty Irish lads who had been goaded by
Mackenzie's attacks on Alexander Macdonell, the Catholic
bishop. These apprentices

> dashed into the middle of the Yonge street mob
> [the Reformers]; seized the wagon and galloped
> off with it; Patriots and all! to the utter consterna-
> tion of the Yonge streeters; who seemed petrified
> with astonishment; and to the infinite amuse-
> ment of the multitude. The wagon orators find-
> ing themselves "Thus unexpectedly in the hands
> of the Philistines, and abandoned by their own
> mob, quickly scattered themselves" out of the
> wagon, some by jumping and some by tumbling
> out, amid abundant salutes of rotten eggs, leav-
> ing poor Mr. Ketchum alone in the wagon.

According to the *Courier*, the wagon was then dragged
eastwards until it was stopped by an obstruction (Lesslie says a
railing) near St James's Church. The frolicksome lads then broke
the chairs and table into bits and beat up two or three Reformers.
Mackenzie escaped through a yard to safety.

Mackenzie himself, of course, reported the whole incident differently, saying that the Tories began throwing stones and brickbats and that

> they included nearly two hundred persons of the Roman Church supported by the town from the soup kitchen; a variety of individuals holding offices under the government; nearly all the vagrants about the town, (some actually hired for the day at a dollar a head,) official gentleman's servants; all the officers and dependents of the bank and Canada Company that could be spared ... and perhaps 3 or 4 more orangemen; the magistrates and some constables; nearly all the negroes in the town, they having been persuaded that the intention of the reformers was to introduce slavery!!... Taking them as a whole they were the worst looking assemblage, we shall not say mob, we ever set our eyes upon, this side of St. Giles parish, London.

This description was followed by two columns devoted to the details of the nefarious activities of various individuals. Mackenzie, becoming increasingly carried away as he proceeded, launched out on a violent anti-Catholic diatribe, and said further that "many of the assailants had been drinking, insomuch that it was said in joke that whiskey had been mixed with their soup that day at the kitchen." A good portion of the people whom he singled out for castigation were youths, quite naturally, the young Tory bucks had a field day throwing eggs, apples and mud at him — but he also included Sheriff Jarvis and Mr Billings, the treasurer of the Home District. The fact that any Reformers at all lived to tell the tale makes it likely that the *Courier* account is much closer to the truth, and although the conservatives certainly rejoiced at Mackenzie's discomforture, it is doubtful if there was as much malicious plotting beforehand as he claimed.

Thus far the authorities had shown little concern, although many of them were present. As Lesslie wrote in his diary, "the authorities were among the disturbers of the peace and if they did not aid them they did at least give them countenance." After the wagon incident the more responsible elements began breaking up the groups and Sheriff Jarvis begged Ketchum to go home "or he would not be responsible for the consequences." Although Ketchum did leave, Mackenzie and many others refused to follow suit. In order to get the Tories out of the area the Sheriff and the Committee arranged a triumphal march on the Government House, situated at the southwest corner of King and Simcoe streets, then at the west end of the city. This solution gained even Mackenzie's approval; he wrote, "the device was certainly a fortunate one." The conservative faction formed a phalanx four deep, described by Gurnett as including 1,200 demonstrators, and dismissed by Mackenzie as merely "something beyond 400 persons, many of them as ill-looking tattered stragglers as we ever cast eye upon." The procession marched off to the lieutenant-governor's house, gave three cheers there for both Sir John Colborne and the King, and then returned to the Court House via Carfrae's home and the *Courier* office with further cheers at both locations.

Instead of disbanding, the Reformers seized upon this opportunity to start their meeting anew, Mackenzie, in the unkind words of the *Canadian Freeman*, having "emerged from some den or mouse-hole into which he had crushed himself." John McIntosh (relation of Mrs. Mackezie) was elected chairman, the Tory resolutions to the king were condemned, the Reform resolutions were passed again, and the organizers began collecting signatures for their addresses; Mackenzie noted that 438 signed at two tables on Richmond Street, and 100 signed later in the day at Rutherford's store and other places. Then, as the *Courier* put it, they hurriedly adjourned when they heard the sounds of the marchers returning.

Those worthies, on their march back to the Court House, encountered another group of Tory partisans "bearing an effigy of Mackenzie on a high pole, having a gingerbread cake suspended from its neck by a yellow ribbon!" The two groups then merged and carried the scarecrow around the streets for about an hour, pausing, as the *Christian Guardian* noted, in front of Bishop Macdonell's house for three rousing cheers — a clear indication that the Irish element was still active. Afterwards they proceeded to the *Advocate* office, on Church Street just south of King, where they burned the figure in the street. For this portion of the account both Mackenzie and Gurnett are basically in agreement, except that the former did not recognize the scarecrow — at least in print — while the latter failed to mention that it was evidently wearing some of the old clothes of Chief Justice Campbell's grandson. Mackenzie felt this was ample proof that it had been manufactured in the highest quarters.

This gathering of the anti-reform faction in front of the *Advocate*'s building for the burning of the dummy not surprisingly touched off another riot. The Courier blamed the second fracas on the fact that the tricolour was flying from an upper window and the Reformers refused to take it down, while the *Canadian Freeman* went one further and said that it was hung out deliberately as a decoy to cause trouble. Mackenzie described the flag quite differently: "The standard termed tri-coloured is a crimson flag which made out of a yard of narrow silk by the apprentices of the Advocate Office, and used in the procession of the 2nd January. Its motto was "The Liberty of the Press." This would appear to be a more accurate description, and it is confirmed by the *Guardian*. But whether tricolour or not, when the Reformers refused to take it down there were further fights and some windows were broken in the building. In retaliation a shot was fired into the crowd. According to the *Advocate*, "a very trusty and faithful apprentice who has long been in the office fired off a gun loaded with powder to frighten the ruffians and protect his master's property," but the *Christian Guardian* disagreed and asserted that the gun was loaded with type. Whatever the case, fortunately no one was injured, but the shot, predictably enough, drove the attackers to new heights of fury. More windows were broken, and a full scale attack was prevented only by the printers giving up the gun, which was promptly smashed to pieces.

Order was now restored by Captain James FitzGibbon, one of the magistrates of the Quarter Sessions, who was again to come to prominence when Mackenzie attacked the city in 1837. FitzGibbon arrested the man with the gun barrel and took him to jail, thus quieting the situation for the moment, but when he returned — presumably to order the crowd to disperse — the rioters were nearly set off again by Mackenzie's stupidity. Instead of staying out of the way, he met FitzGibbon and demanded that the troops of the garrison be called out to protect his property. FitzGibbon replied, to quote the *Courier*, "I will protect your property, Mr. Mackenzie, without calling the troops

Mackenzie's rescurer, James FitzGibbon.

out, but I recommend you go to your house." Although both newspapers' accounts are in substantial agreement up to this point, the *Advocate* now becomes silent, and we have only the *Courier's* word for what happened next. Evidently an argument ensued, with the two standing in the middle of the mob, and finally FitzGibbon attempted to arrest Mackenzie in spite of his claims of parliamentary immunity. A scuffle then broke out and finally Mackenzie was turned over to some of his supporters who were equally anxious to get him out of harm's way before the Hamilton incident, or worse, was repeated. When they tried to take him home the crowd was so thick that it was impossible to force a passage through and FitzGibbon ascended the steps of the nearby Court House and asked the people to disperse without doing any further mischief. Meanwhile Mackenzie, with more courage — or bullheadedness — than common sense, followed him and while he was trying to calm the rioters kept interrupting with demands for troops. FitzGibbon promised that he would protect him with his life and repeated that troops were unnecessary. He might have added that in any case, even if a messenger could have been sent to call them, by the time the military arrived the mob could have wrecked whatever they pleased. Then he led Mackenzie down the steps, and the mob, either heeding his orders or overawed by his courage, opened a passage and he was able to conduct Mackenzie home safely.[8]

The *Courier's* narrative ends here, but the town was worked up to a fever pitch, the reporter of the *Christian Guardian* noting that Tory mobs prowled the streets all night. Evidently the centre of their activities was the Steamboat Hotel, where, according to an informant of the *Guardian*, £2 worth of whiskey flowed freely. This source mentions no further rioting, but there seems to have been a third outbreak in the form of an abortive attack on the *Advocate* office, which was apparently prevented by FitzGibbon threatening to call out the troops which Colborne now had in readiness. According to the *Advocate*, the authorities of the district had now finally taken proper action; "... three or four Magistrates sat up all night in the police office; Special Constables were sworn in. A voluntary guard of the townspeople watched at the Advocate office and Mr. Mackenzie's house." The silence of the Tories on the subject would seem to support these statements, and the situation is probably well summed up by J.C. Dent's statement that "the town remained in a very disturbed state throughout the ensuing night, and a large portion of the inhabitants did not venture to seek repose."[9]

The Tories and the Irish were triumphant. After listening to Mackenzie for the better part of a decade they had finally gained their revenge and at least temporarily stopped the Reformers' activities. The *Canadian Freeman* gloated that 200 to 300 tickets already had been sold for a grand public dinner at the Steamboat Hotel and noted "we hear it is also in contemplation to transfer the festival of Patrick's Day from the 17th to the 23rd March, in future, in this town." While the delight of the Irish was temporary, the incident had more permanent consequences for the Tory organization. The General Committee decided to put their organization on a permanent basis and by early April had founded the British Constitutional Society, which was designed to bring a united Tory party into being to prevent further reform activities. In both the election of 1836 and the Rebellion of 1837 this organization was to provide firm backing for Sir Francis Bond Head.

As for Mackenzie, his followers were forced to protect his property for some time, and he himself had to retire to the country for a few weeks. Before April was out he had left for England — where he was to remain till August 1833 — in an attempt to effect reform by appeal to the Colonial Office.[10] Possibly the outcome of his meeting on March 23 is rather well described by the little poem with which the *Courier* closed its account of the incident, playing on the Roman custom of awarding a triumph for the greatest victories and an ovation for lesser ones — and the fact that eggs are oval:

> Inprompt on little Mac being pelted by the rabble with rotten eggs.
>
> No more be the Red Wigs's disasters bewail'd,
> A truce to this loud lamentation;
> Tho' to get quite a triumph, he certainly fail'd;
> He assuredly got an ovation

The events at Toronto on March 23, 1832 were a brief incident in Upper Canadian history, but, with the immediately preceding fracas at Hamilton, they highlighted a change in the political pattern of the province. Action breeds reaction, and by his constant flurry of activities Mackenzie had succeeded in solidifying the unorganized Tories and had created an opposing force that was to cost him clearly both immediately and in the longer term. For years the Reformers had been the initiating group in provincial political action, but from now on the Tories were ready to strike back. Unwittingly, Mackenzie was thus something of a founder of the Conservative Party. The incident also says something about Mackenzie's personality, in particular his propensity to rush forth with all the zeal of a Christian martyr regardless of circumstances. He has been called fearless and he was; but foolhardy might be a better description of his behaviour in some of the situations that he barged into. In this regard, the riots of 1832 were a precursor of the Rebellion of 1837.

Chapter 5

The first mayor of Toronto:
A study of a critic in power[1]

In evaluations of William Lyon Mackenzie, generally little account has been taken of the one time he was really in power — the few short months of his mayoralty in Toronto in 1834. His nineteenth-century biographers passed it off with a brief eulogy, and in this century Aileen Dunham and G.M. Craig had no opportunity to examine it in their more extended histories. The result has been that a curious air of unreality hangs over studies of Mackenzie — while his ideas have been examined exhaustively, all too often they have been viewed in isolation from his actions.

Although there were twice Reform majorities in the Upper Canada's House of Assembly, it was only as Toronto's first mayor that Mackenzie may really be said to have had an opportunity to show what he could do as leader of a government. As mayor, within the framework of the Act of Incorporation, he was literally the premier of a responsible government, with an absolute majority behind him, the authority to initiate legislation and public works and to dispense patronage, and, above all, no legislative council to veto his programme. Thus, these few months in 1834 are of the utmost importance in answering the question of whether Mackenzie was just a rabble rouser or whether he was something more — a man who could have set up a successful administration in Upper Canada had the Rebellion of 1837 succeeded.

The 1834 Act of Incorporation which erected the Town of York into the City of Toronto provided that the first municipal elections were to be held within three calendar months from the date it received royal assent; however, Lieutenant-Governor Sir John Colborne promptly called the first elections for March 27, just twenty-one days after he had signed the act. Probably his only thought was to get the new corporation going as soon as possible, because there was so much to be done. Mackenzie, who had recently been elected last warden of the Town of York, saw the early date in another light and claimed that Colborne had called the sudden election at the request of the Tories so that the Reformers would not have time to organize. That his complaint was hardly justified is shown both by the zeal with which the Reform party rushed into the election and by the fact that they were the victors. Having spent at least a decade organizing provincial elections and local demonstrations, the Reformers were a well-prepared group. If anything, the Tories were placed in a difficult position by the early election, because their grass-roots political organization, the British Constitutional party, had been formed only two years before and had never fought a provincial election.[2]

The election that followed in Toronto was naturally characterized by some confusion; there was no experience with the new level of government — Toronto was the first city in the colony — or with municipal regulations and generally the candidates were men who had not already sat in the Assembly. The first civic election contest, and those in the years immediately following, were much more like provincial elections than the non-party municipal elections of today. Both sides, Tory and Reform, though they were, of course, factions rather than parties in the modern sense, produced full slates of candidates, and, although they could hardly be said to have had platforms, divided on reasonably clear lines of principle.

Mackenzie had begun the Reform campaign on March 18, before the election date was set — further evidence that he was ready for the contest, whatever date Colborne decided upon — by calling for a meeting of the "Mechanics and Labourers of Toronto" to be held at the Old King's Bench Court House on the evening of the nineteenth, with the object of forming ward committees and arranging for meetings in the individual wards. There were five of these named for the four patron saints of the British Isles, with St Lawrence thrown in to add a Canadian touch. Each was to elect two aldermen and two common councilmen, the first group requiring higher property qualifications and becoming magistrates on election. Mackenzie also published lists both of those Reformers who were ready to run and of those who declined. Unfortunately for Toronto, the second list included most of the well-known and experienced Reformers who were available: among them, Jesse Ketchum, William Warren Baldwin, Robert Baldwin, and Dr John Rolph (who was to change his mind). The list of available candidates, who were, according to Mackenzie, "the professed friends of peace, quietness and order, the frugal husbandmen of public money," included several men of wealth, but few who had had much experience with politics in an elective capacity. Mackenzie's former business partner, James Lesslie, was one, as were the wealthy merchant Joseph Cawthra, the well-known city doctor Thomas D. Morrison, and Mackenzie himself.[3]

The Tories, too, were holding meetings and selecting candidates; a printed handbill listing their potential nominees included such leading merchants as George Monro and Thomas Carfrae Jr as well as such wealthy landowners as John Elmsley and Colonel George T. Denison. Dr Rolph was listed as an approved aldermanic candidate for St Patrick's Ward — the handbill saying that he was the only man of ability among the Reformers, a tribute hardly likely to enhance his support in the Reform party. Mackenzie, naturally, thought little of the Tory nominations. In his *Advocate* of March 20 he listed the candidates of the Tory or "spendthrift" party and added that he "should be very sorry indeed to see any of that elected under the charter. Even a sprinkling of men of their principles might be very injurious." He also claimed that Dr Grant Powell would be the mayor if the enemy succeeded although it seems more probable that Dr Christopher Widmer was the Tory favourite.

In Toronto's early years, elections were normally held in taverns, one being chosen for each ward, except for St David's Ward, where they were held in the Court House, and St Lawrence's Ward, where, except for the first civic election, they were held in the City Hall. For the first election, the locations were selected by the provincial executive and the returning officers by the sheriff; afterwards they were chosen by the retiring City Council. Consequently, elections moved from tavern to tavern depending upon whether the City Council was Tory or Reform. The selection of the taverns for the 1834 election was rather surprising, for the proclamation, signed by Robert S. Jameson, the attorney-general, and Duncan Cameron, the provincial secretary, both of whom would have qualified as leading members of the "reptile crew" in Mackenzie's eyes, named taverns which were owned by men of both political affiliations: Edward Wright, the proprietor of Wright's Inn, was even a Reform candidate. Mackenzie was to hold his organizational meetings for the wards at the polling stations themselves, while the Tories went elsewhere.[4]

The returning officers, selected by Sheriff Jarvis, were also divided in their allegiances; James Hervey Price, the returning officer for St Patrick, was to be appointed city clerk by the Reform victors, but John H. Spragge, named for St Lawrence, was a Tory, as was William Hepburn for St Andrew, who was also the deputy clerk of the Quarter Sessions for the district. Without more evidence to support such a supposition, it would be too much to say that in view of the Reformers' complaints Colborne probably ordered moderation in the appointments. But there was certainly a remarkable lack of governmental effort to control the elections — especially when one considers that both the bars and the voting were open.

The election was a lively one. Though the *Correspondent*, edited by Mackenzie's friend Father William O'Grady, said on March 29 that the Tories employed every stratagem, there is little evidence that they were in a position to do much to influence the results. In the April 3 edition of the *Advocate* which followed the election, Mackenzie analyzed the votes of the leading citizens in most of the ridings. Some of the most prominent Tories, including judges Sherwood, Macaulay and Powell, and Colonel Rowan, Colborne's secretary, did not vote. Though it might well be argued that all these men should have stayed out of politics because of their positions, their abstention indicates that the Tories were not using every stratagem. Moreover, such Tories as Captain Richard Bonnycastle and — Beikie, the clerk of the Executive Council, voted for the Reformer Wright. The pro-Reform Baldwins did not vote, but the professors of Upper Canada College and Archdeacon John Strachan all turned up to vote a straight Tory ticket. In St Patrick's Ward, Mackenzie noted that Dr Rolph was the only Reformer to receive the vote of such Tories as Justice D'Arcy Boulton and Provincial Secretary Duncan Cameron. The leading figures in the Bank of Upper Canada all turned out to vote Tory. John Maitland, the bank messenger, voted Reform. For this indiscretion, Mackenzie claimed, he was dismissed, but there is no other evidence to support the charge. Mackenzie also stated that the bank (one of whose directors, Dr Christopher Widmer, was a defeated candidate) "as a pitiful revenge ... sent a message to this office never again to publish their notices ordered to be published in all the provincial papers."

When the results were in the Reformers had been victors in twelve seats and the Tories in eight. The reasons for the Reform victory were no doubt complex. The city, with its three Reform newspapers had, of course, been one of their centres of strength. Further, that there was a swing towards the Reform party in the province at the time is shown by its victory in the provincial elections during the same autumn. This tendency in Toronto had been greatly accelerated by the "persecution" of Mackenzie in his expulsions from the Assembly, and by the high-handed way in which both houses of the legislature had handled the city's incorporation bill, disregarding the fact that the citizens had registered their wishes in a series of public meetings. Also, the appointed Tory magistrates had hardly been very successful in solving the former Town of York's problems, and some voters may have felt the other side should be given a chance to inaugurate the new government.

The Reform victory naturally was regarded with horror by the Tories. An example is the gloomy opinion given by King's Printer Robert Stanton in a letter to Kingston's leading merchant, John Macaulay, after the newly elected city government had had a chance to prove its worth. Writing on April 16 he remarked:

> but with the fools he has to work with it is more than even Mackenzie's industry can go though he has a majority, but not a working one, they are in fact a set of ignorant fellows, & though they may *vote* for him & his measures, there is not one among them who can *work* for him — the little fellow must sink under the task & we must only hope that the evil is one which will cure itself in time. The character of our city is certainly degraded, & in the mean time we must be content to bear matters as well as we can.[5]

Stanton's assessment of the City Council was excessively harsh. In both Tory and Reform camps there were moderates who were ready to cooperate in managing the government as well as extremists who, by their votes, seem to have been mainly interested in skirmishing with their opponents. Most of the Reformers remained on the City Council only for a brief period;

many were defeated in the 1835 election, and those few who remained were wiped out in that of 1837. Consequently, they may never had the opportunity to develop with experience. On the other hand, it is rather doubtful, considering their actions while on the Council, whether many had the capacity for much development, which was also the case with many of the Tories. There were, however, some able men: James Lesslie and Thomas D. Morrison were obviously in that category, and John Doel, the brewer, and Joseph Cawthra were successful businessmen.

On the Tory side, some of the first Council members were to remain in office for years; John Craig, who resigned in 1849, and George Gurnett, who sat until 1851 and served as mayor in 1837 and from 1848-50, were the last to disappear. The Tory group included two other leading businessmen who were to play a prominent part in the government: Thomas Carfrae Jr and George Monro. Carfrae's career was brief, since he retired to his collectorship of customs after 1835. Monro became mayor in 1841. Another leading figure was Colonel George T. Denison Sr, the first of a family of heavy dragoons which has had more representatives on the City Council than any other. Generally, Craig, Gurnett and Denison were the most anti-Reform in their votes.[6]

With the Council duly elected, it remained to be seen who the members would elect as mayor. The Act provided that all twenty members of the Council had the right to vote for mayor, but only the ten aldermen were eligible for the office. The contest obviously lay between two aldermen, Dr John Rolph and William Lyon Mackenzie. As *persona grata* to the Tories, Rolph could only be suspect to many of the Reform group. Not only had he received Tory support in the election campaign, but the conservative newspapers generally leave the impression that he was "socially acceptable." His equivocal part in the election is typical of his entire political career, because, for all John Charles Dent's efforts in the first history of Upper Canada to turn him into a hero, Rolph remains a figure for whom it is difficult to feel much sympathy. That said, however, there is a fair amount of evidence that in spite of Tory approval Rolph had been promised the support of most of the Reformers and probably of Mackenzie himself. The fact that he so quickly resigned from the Council when he was not elected would support this interpretation for he had apparently run only in the expectation of becoming mayor.

George Gurnett, opponent of Mackenzie and twice Mayor of Toronto.

Mackenzie, on the other hand, was an unquestioned Reformer. The *Patriot*, possibly anticipating Tory defeat, had begun attacking him even before the election. On March 25, it said: "MARK OUR WORDS. If you make MacKenzie [sic] Lord Mayor you brew trouble for the City. If you make him Alderman you brew trouble for the Lord Mayor; if you make him Common Council man, you brew trouble for the Alderman. It would be difficult to see where you could bestow him, and not make trouble for somebody." Such attacks naturally must have played into Mackenzie's hands. They enhanced the feeling that he should receive some compensation for the numerous wrongs he had suffered, especially the expulsions from the House. It is evident, moreover, that Mackenzie wanted to be mayor and did what he could to secure for his election. That he was the last town warden, and did not hesitate to sign himself as such, possibly provided a certain "legitimacy" for his claims to higher office.[7]

Scadding, writing in 1884, declared that the switch of Reform support from Rolph to Mackenzie, as party candidate for mayor, came at a party caucus on March 31 where Rolph was persuaded to waive his claims in view of the harsh treatment that Mackenzie had received. Apparently he bowed to the will of the majority, though he had none too high an opinion of Mackenzie. Scadding further claimed that Rolph decided then to withdraw from the Council and gave Morrison a letter to that effect to be read at the first meeting. This would appear to be correct as far as the course of events went but the date is apparently a little early, and possibly the procedure followed was a bit more blunt.[8] The *Patriot* of April 4 said Rolph had been told that those who were not his friends would have to vote him in. Certainly the Tories were hoping to have Rolph elected by a Tory-moderate Reform combination. To sound him out on that possibility, Carfrae and Monro had visited him on April 2. They stated afterward that "Dr. Rolph expressly declared to them that he would accept the office of Mayor if elected thereto, and that he would be personally present at the hour of election, and authorized the deputation to say so to the members of the Corporation."[9] As this meeting had taken place only the day before the actual election, the Reform caucus must have been held just before the election itself. After he withdrew from the contest at that meeting, Rolph gave Morrison a note stating his intentions to deliver to Carfrae.

When the Council convened for the election at noon on April 3, Morrison gave this note to Carfrae. In it Rolph had stated that "notwithstanding his promise of yesterday, he had made up his mind not to serve in the office of Mayor, but to withdraw from the corporation altogether"![10] The meeting opened with John Doel being asked to preside *pro tem*, and Mackenzie was nominated. The journal of the City Council then merely notes: "On which Debates ensued." But debate was stopped by Morrison reading his letter from Rolph "withdrawing himself from the Corporation, and resigning his seat." This was confirmed by Carfrae, who said he had a similar letter from Rolph. The vote was then held. The results are worth recording, as they show the typical pattern of division during the following year.

Yea - Doel, Turton, Jackes, Drummond, Lesslie, Bostwich, Harper, Wright, Arthurs, Morrison: 10

Nay - Craig, Gurnett, Trotter, Monro, Denison, Armstrong, Carfrae, Duggan: 8

Although Mackenzie could hardly know it, he had attained the highest dignity of political career.

Contested elections provided the first major battleground for the Council. Under the Act of Incorporation, the Council had the right to try its own contested elections, but the Act did not provide any regulations on how this should be done. Inevitably, the confusion as to procedure was compounded by the holy hatred between the two factions. In the 1830s elections were disputed whenever any possible excuse could be brought forward, and soon the Council received petitions contesting elections in three of the five wards. The battles that surrounded the hearing of the first of these were a fitting prelude to the altercations and confusion which were to mark the Council's debates all year. Indeed, Mackenzie and his majority quickly put themselves into the embarrassing position of carrying on in exactly the same arbitrary manner for which they had so often castigated the Tory majority in the Assembly. The only contested election actually to be tried was the return of Tory aldermen Monro and Duggan in St George's Ward. Mackenzie and his

First City Hall, from a drawing by Henry Scadding, c. 1840.

Model of First City Hall and Market.

supporters did all in their power to get rid of the two Tories and to bring in the two defeated Reform candidates.

Hearings began on April 25 with Monro and Duggan sitting on the Council and the petitioners appearing before that body together with a host of witnesses subpoenaed by both sides. Early in the proceedings Mackenzie ordered that the Council chamber be cleared so the matter could be discussed behind closed doors. Gurnett objected, but the room was ordered cleared on a straight party vote, ten to seven. According to the Reform (though anti-Mackenzie) *Canadian Freeman* on May 1, Mackenzie then ruled that Aldermen Monro and Duggan should not be allowed to sit in the Council during their trial and should retire with the ordinary spectators on the closing of the doors. At this, Duggan departed, and he was accompanied by Gurnett, Carfrae and Denison, all exclaiming as they rushed out "that they never saw such high-handed tyranny as was carried on by the Mayor." Monro, however, refused to leave, "stating that he would retain his seat as the legal representative of St George's Ward, unless driven from it by violence." Immediately Mackenzie sent for the High Bailiff, who dragged the alderman out; accounts differ as to whether he was dragged off to the police station, but this seems doubtful. With the rules for such hearings yet to be set, it is difficult to assign blame. Monro was bullheaded perhaps, but, before ordering his ejection, Mackenzie should have remembered his own expulsions from the Assembly and foreseen the political capital that the Tories could make out of the incident.

Even with Monro evicted, the Council was unable to proceed as the returning officer had failed to appear with the poll book, and so the whole process was adjourned until the next day. In the end a scrutiny of the voting was held only at the third session, and after another three days' discussion Duggan was declared unseated and Cawthra declared elected in his place. As another Reformer, Dr John E. Tims, who became one of Mackenzie's closest supporters, had been elected to succeed Rolph, this gave Mackenzie a majority of thirteen to seven.

With this contested election heard, no action was taken until mid-June on the contested elections in the other wards, where Reformers' seats were in dispute. The *Patriot* on June 13 reported that the Tories had tried to force action on the election in St Andrews' Ward, but that just as they were about to gain the support of a majority of the Council Mackenzie told Lesslie,

Tims and Doel to "toodle off." Then, when they had departed, he adjourned the Council on the grounds that a quorum no longer existed. Subsequently, postponement followed postponement, until at last on October 20 the despairing petitioners agreed to withdraw their petitions and the Council accepted the withdrawal. Mackenzie's tactics in the affair were on a par with anything that he had ever accused the Tories of doing.[11]

In its opening day, while preparing to start hearings, the Council had managed to accomplish a fair amount of routine business. At the first meeting on April 8 James Hervey Price, an able barrister and moderate Reformer, was appointed city clerk. He was accepted by fifteen to three, gaining the support of such Tories as Carfrae, Duggan and Monro, and being opposed only by Denison, Gurnett and Craig. The meeting then appointed three special committees. The first was charged to make the arrangements for setting up the city offices in the northwest corner of the Market buildings. This project included the establishment not only of council chambers but also of a police office and offices for the mayor and clerk. The second committee was given the duty of designing the city seal. The third committee, which was assigned the task of drawing up rules for the Council, was able to prepare a report in the remarkably short space of three days. As a result, the suggested forty rules could be read and accepted on April 11. They covered all the regulations for such a body: voting, notice of motions, method of presenting petitions, standing commission and so on. On April 14 the Council set up standing committees on finance, situations (appointments), fire and water, buildings and repairs, streets and roads, harbours and ferries, police and prisons, and, finally, markets. Appointments to the committees were by vote of the Council; generally, two Reformers and one Tory were put on each. Mackenzie became a member of the committees on situations, finance and the markets — the three most important.[12]

In May the City Council completed its appointments and set up its offices. The Committee on Appointments to Office naturally recommended Reformers, and the City Council just as naturally followed these suggestions. Although nothing else could be expected at the period, the results for Toronto were not in the immediate run too satisfactory. The politics of the City Council changed every year between 1834 and 1837; consequently, there was a constant turnover of officials that was hardly good for the city. Fortunately, however, after the first year both the city clerk and the chamberlain (treasurer) remained in office for long periods. For the chamberlain's office the committee had at first picked Matthew Walton, who was duly elected by the Reform majority without difficulty. His tenure of office was very brief, however, for he died in the cholera epidemic only three months after his appointment.[13]

Finding satisfactory offices for the city administration proved to be difficult. The Council had initially hoped to house the city government in the Court House, but its application was promptly turned down by the Tory magistrates of the Home District (which body included Monro and Denison) on the grounds that it would be a great inconvenience. The city then decided to open offices in the Market, and ran into immediate problems because the rooms they planned to occupy were designed for shops or granaries. In order to make the offices usable a considerable amount of remodelling had to be done, and for a time accommodations must have been quite inconvenient and inadequate. Moreover, the more space appropriated for municipal purposes, the less that could be rented out to pay off the debt for Market construction which the city owed to the Home District under the Act of Incorporation.[14]

With the rules of the Council established, quarters acquired and committees appointed, the time had come to get down to major items of business. The Committee on Streets and Roads, which reported on May 20, brought in extensive recommendations for improving the city. These recommendations were certainly sound but represented an outlay of money which the taxpayers were hardly able to afford. Actual accomplishments hardly matched the recommendations; however, in an attempt to deal with the traditional York mud, plank sidewalks were laid on many of the major streets and squared logs were placed at the main intersections. Unfortunately, except for main streets such as King, where four-foot planks were used, most of the planking was only two feet wide. This led to some alleviation of conditions, but on the whole, dirty little York had merely become dirty big Toronto, and the mud problem was to remain for a long time to come.[15]

In terms of legislation, the record of the corporation was none too impressive in view of the large number of problems awaiting the Council's attention. Only nine by-laws were passed, and all of these fell within the brief period of May 10 to June 19, after which absolutely nothing was accomplished by way of legislation. Of the nine, the first established fire regulations and the second and seventh regulated the market and hay sales. Bylaw 3 was concerned only with the duties of the chamberlain. Number 4 provided fines for a variety of offences, being particularly aimed at putting a stop to animals running loose on the streets and people throwing garbage into the streets or harbour. The fifth bylaw provided for a tax on dogs and the sixth for licences for selling alcoholic beverages. Number 8 established a civic board of health, regulated the operation of hospitals, and provided for certain basic sanitary precautions such as draining stagnant water, removing offal and cleaning privies. Finally, bylaw Number 9 regulated the streets and sewers.

This was the sum total of legislation which the Mackenzie mayoralty managed to put on the books. Much of it was to prove inadequate, partly because of inexperience, and had to be redrawn the next year. Yet by the time this first flurry of legislation was completed, the work of setting up the government and much of the work on the sidewalks had been accomplished. During these first three months, though Mackenzie and his supporters had hardly run the city brilliantly, they had at least achieved something, even if they had spent far too much time squabbling with Tory members of the Council. Of course, the Tories were equally ready to quarrel, but they, too, deserve some credit for the legislation and for the handling of the problems of setting up a new government, because they, too, sat on the committees and helped in the drafting.

Though there were still some six months left to run in the first Council's term, its days of accomplishment were over. The tale of the rest of the mayoralty is a dismal account of Reform failure, a failure which to a very large extent can be laid at Mackenzie's door.

Even while the City Council was organizing the government and passing its bylaws, complaints were arising about its administration of the city. Often these complaints were voiced against the whole Council, and not just the Reform majority. By July the Reform-oriented *Canadian Freeman* was accusing Mackenzie and his colleagues of concentrating on the coming provincial elections rather than municipal business. The complaint was a justified one, for Mackenzie editorially and otherwise was showing less and less interest in his civic office and was not providing the leadership the city needed. His publication of the English radical Joseph Hume's famous letter accusing the mother country of "baneful domination" in the May 22 *Advocate* had already set off an unedifying debate in the Council. Meanwhile, some major problems were obviously outstanding. One of these was the city's finances. On May 19 the Council voted a tax for 1834 of two pence per pound assessment, in addition to the rates payable to the Home District. This was only half the minimum tax allowed under the Act of Incorporation, and certainly was inadequate in view of the expenses that lay ahead. Yet people hate nothing more than new taxes, even if they are crying for more services. There was naturally a great deal of resentment, which was fed upon by the Tory Council members. Those gentlemen either absented themselves on the day the tax was voted or hypocritically voted against it. Even though they knew how necessary the tax was, the chance to blame the Reformers for an unpopular measure was too good an opportunity to miss. The consequent uproar was not helped by either the obviously unequal provincial method of assessment, which was beyond the Council's control or the incompetent manner in which the taxes were collected, which was under their jurisdiction.[16]

Borrowing money was still another problem the Council seemed unable to handle. On June 7 the Corporation had authorized the borrowing of £1,000 for road repairs, but the loan was more easily approved than arranged. Application was promptly made to all likely quarters, with negative results. The Bank of Upper Canada refused flatly, the Commercial Bank of the Midland District at Kingston said it wanted no part of the loan, and both the provincial receiver-general and Thomas Clark and Samuel Street, the Niagara Falls financiers, sent their regrets. They can hardly be blamed, for among the Reform members of the City Council, Joseph Cawthra at least could have made such a loan but gave no sign of doing so; and there were others who could have advanced at least a part of it, but didn't. The refusals resulted partly because of the city's high debt inherited from the town and limited taxation powers but the fact that the Council was Reform-dominated was a major factor. Eventually, the city was saved by the new Toronto financial partnership of Truscott, Green & Co., which agreed to assume the entire amount of the loan.[17]

While the financial troubles were developing, Mackenzie was also being attacked for the way in which he was handling his duties in the Toronto Quarter Sessions. The Mayor's Courts, as they were called, were held at the Court House four times yearly in the same manner as the District Quarter Sessions, with the mayor, assisted by one or more aldermen, presiding. For a mayor like Mackenzie who was untrained in law, the court was both a major drain on his time and a political liability; any sentences which he handed down that were too draconic would be used against him by his opponents. In other words, it would have been virtually impossible for him to come out unscathed, which should have made him careful in handing down sentences. Characteristically, however, Mackenzie was anything but careful.

The trials he presided over were largely for larceny, with assault running a close second, but affray, riot, and misdemeanor cases also appeared. As would be expected in a frontier town with large poor districts and many taverns, there was a surfeit of sordid cases. The judgment which got Mackenzie in the most trouble, and became the delight of the Tory opposition, was his decision in the case of Ellen Halfpenny. Described as a "common scold," she appeared before the mayor for drunken and disorderly conduct, was ordered to be put in the stocks, and was then given the job of cleaning prison cells. The stocks in Toronto, which were of the type that confined head, feet and arms, were still standing, though they had evidently not been used for some years. Mackenzie should have known that sentencing a woman to such punishment for what was a relatively minor crime was bound to cause a furor, but evidently he lost his temper.

Thus, by the end of July, Mackenzie was being attacked for failing to get the city government under way, for improper handling of finances and taxation, and for incompetent judgment. Then, suddenly, on July 30, came the first major tragedy in the city's history: the collapse of part of the balcony around the market courtyard during a public meeting, which resulted in five being killed and about fifty injured. The market itself had been built under the jurisdiction of the Tory magistrates, yet as Mackenzie had called the meeting to discuss taxes, he was unfairly blamed by the Tory press. In fact, he was hardly more at fault than anyone else connected with the meeting, and was not even at the second session of the meeting when the accident took place. Other Reformers may have been responsible for chasing some of the Tories to the section of the balcony which collapsed because of overloading; conversely, the Tory forces were struggling just as fiercely as the Reformers to dominate the assembly.[18]

Before the city could recover from this tragedy, fate struck again. The very next day cholera broke out in the jail and the city was suddenly faced with a repetition of the epidemic which had first struck in 1832 with a ten per cent mortality rate. It remained, in 1834, to see if the City Council would be any more efficient in disease control than the magistrates of the Home District had been during the first wave of the cholera. In both years the Boards of Health were faced by an almost impossible problem. There were no sewers or scientific ideas on sanitation; no medical agreement on how cholera was transmitted; the poorer areas were crowded; and many of the populace had an innate suspicion of hospitals.

In 1834 the Tories and Reformers were quickly quarrelling over the best methods of action and there were various changes in the Board of Health because of their disagreements. Mackenzie's part is not completely clear, but he seems to have been guilty of unnecessary interference in the activities of the health officers. Certainly he did not deserve the plaudits given to him by some of his biographers; the real heroes of the epidemic were the doctors and Lieutenant-Governor Colborne, who made hospital accommodation and money available. When the coming of the cool weather brought the scourge to an end it had taken some 500 victims in the city. Most of these came from the poorer classes, though the sickness also carried off some of the more prominent citizens. Lardner Bostwick was the only member of the Council who was a victim; yet Matthew Walton, the chamberlain, died on August 7. City Clerk James Harvey Price and Mackenzie were both taken ill, but recovered.[19]

Bostwick's death meant that there had to be a by-election for a common councilman to replace him in St Lawrence's Ward. Both sides regarded this as a test of popular support for the administration. The Reformers put up Charles Baker, a tailor who was a friend of Mackenzie, and the Tories Joshua G. Beard, who won handily by seventy-two votes to thirty-five. Mackenzie played down the results, saying that both sides had stayed away. Though his prestige might be damaged, he still had his majority, the standing now being twelve Reformers to eight Tories.

Mackenzie was now, however, beginning to have difficulties with his own Reform majority. These had first blown up during the disagreements on the Board of Health and continued over the selection of a new chamberlain. On August 26, the Committee on Appointments to Office, in a report signed by Mackenzie and Lesslie, recommended Andrew T. McCord as Walton's successor and he was duly elected on September 15. Mackenzie, however, changed his mind and petulantly protested that McCord was "personally obnoxious to him." He asked that his name be taken off the Committee on Finance (where he would have to work with McCord) and Lesslie's substituted, announcing that he could not stay on if the Council thought fit to appoint persons contrary to his expressed wish. He further attacked his own followers for not backing him, saying that "such opposition astonished him." In the division that followed both factions split and Mackenzie was removed from the committee only by his own casting vote.

Such activities did nothing to increase the financial community's confidence in the city government, and the Council soon found that Truscott, Green & Co. were demanding payment of the £500 still owing on their loan. The Council found it impossible to raise funds elsewhere to pay this off, and the bankers were willing to continue the loan only provided they were given a new note signed by the entire City Council. The Council agreed to this demand on September 25, although only fifteen members signed.

However, by September Mackenzie's main interest was not finance, or the Council, but rather the provincial election. Unfortunately for Toronto, he so threw himself into writing and speaking in the campaign that the city government was badly neglected. Nominated in the Second Riding of the County of York, he was elected by the overwhelming majority of 334 votes to 178. Then, with the election over, he began to devote much of his time to the House of Assembly instead of city business. He did, however, cease his activities as an editor of the *Advocate* on November 4, turning the journal over to his friend O'Grady of the *Correspondent*, who renamed his paper the *Correspondent and Advocate*.[20]

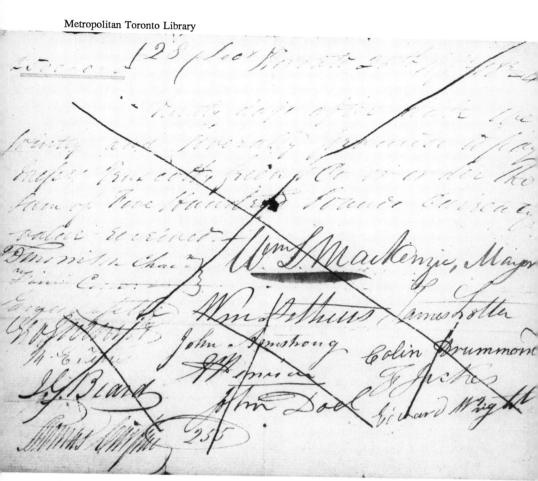

Toronto City Council Papers, September 26, 1834. Note Mackenzie's signature.

In mid-November the City Council met to fix the salaries for the year. The Committee on Finance had recommended that the mayor receive £250, "he being understood to act as Police Magistrate daily," but in the Council this was cut to 100 (which was the minimum under the Act). Most of the Tories present, and Morrison, seem to have been against voting him anything. The main financial arguments, however, arose over the payments to city soliciter Marshall Spring Bidwell, who had been one of Mackenzie's lawyers in the 1826 lawsuit over the destruction of his printing office. When the city was first incorporated, the attorney-general of the province had acted as solicitor and charged £10 for the advice he had to give. In mid-August, however, Mackenzie and Lesslie, as members of the Committee on Appointments to Office, had recommended that Bidwell become solicitor. Accordingly he had been appointed and paid a retainer of £50. The payment was slipped through the Committee on Finance in the absence of Gurnett, the only Tory member, and was not voted by the Council at the time, though the appointment was approved. The Tory *Patriot* in November claimed that Bidwell was an honest man and that he would return the money after he came back from a Florida holiday, but there is no evidence that he did so. What the *Patriot* does not seem to have known is that a second payment of £50 appears in the books under the date September 24. These payments were very high, completely out of line with what the corporation could afford. Further, that the city as yet had no need for a solicitor is shown by the fact that there was no further appointment until Clarke Gamble was nominated in 1840. The whole incident would appear to be simply a barefaced example of patronage to a political ally. Though nothing else could really be expected from either party at the period, the Bidwell case, coupled with earlier appointments, clearly shows that Mackenzie, had he ever been in power provincially, would not have acted very differently from the Family Compact on patronage matters.

Mackenzie also left himself open to criticism by renting one of the granaries in the City Hall as a printing office for his *Advocate* on June 18, for a two-year term, at a rent of £18 Currency per annum. The rent would appear to be reasonable in itself, but he also had the corporation remodel the granary so as to make it airtight and add a ceiling. In this instance, considering the corporation limited funds, he opened himself to charges of using his powers as mayor to his own advantage. [21]

The last great battle of 1834 in the Council chamber came at the end of November over the appointment of a successor to City Clerk James Hervey Price, who resigned on November 12, the Tories claiming that the reason for his resignation was his thorough disgust with Mackenzie. The debate that took place is worth examining in detail for it represents the nadir of the Council's deliberations. The Committee on Appointments to Office, composed of Lesslie and Mackenzie, recommended that one William Thomas Kennedy, an inhabitant of Kingston, be appointed Price's successor. The Tories claimed that they had never heard of Kennedy and that the only reason for recommending his appointment was his backing of Reformer editor ex-Father William O'Grady, Mackenzie's friend, when he had run for election in Kingston. On November 25 Lesslie and Jackes recommended that Kennedy be appointed at a salary of £150 per annum. Gurnett then rose to say that most of the Council had never heard of the man before, and that he wondered if he had the qualifications for office. He further suggested that a Toronto taxpayer should be appointed to the post, and concluded:

> I really think, sir, that it is not decent again to call upon the Council to sanction the appointment of a person who is utterly unknown to the most of us; and of whose abilities to discharge the important duties of the office in question, the members how signed the report had no condescended to give this Council one word of information. I repeat, sir, I think it is indecent to call upon us to sanction the proposed appointment under such circumstances.

Mackenzie broke in: "You cannot, Mr. Gurnett, describe anything which is recommended by Committee of this Council as 'indecent' — you are quite out of order Sir!"[22]

The two then began arguing, and the discussion degenerated with a series of cries of "order, order" from the Reformers, while Mackenzie told Gurnett to sit down. Mackenzie repeated this demand several times, but Gurnett consistently refused.

Then Cawthra added, "Take him into custody! Punish him!" Seizing on the idea, Mackenzie promptly ordered High Bailiff Higgins to do so. Gurnett was taken by the arm and led from the table, and Mackenzie delivered a lecture on "observing strict order — paying proper respect to the chair, and to each other." Reformers and Tories began fighting over whether Gurnett's statement was a violation of the dignity of the Council or not. At last, Carfrae charged that many of the Reformers had been allowed to speak in language ten times stronger and "some of them had conducted themselves in such a way as was disgraceful: did not every person at the board remember one of the members of that party coming to the Council in a most disgraceful state, and yet nothing was done to him." He was then interrupted by further roars of order, but he proceeded to move that Gurnett should be allowed to resume his seat since the proceedings were ridiculous. Dr Tims, who normally supported Mackenzie, promptly brought in an amendment that the whole affair was a misunderstanding and no violation of the rules of the Council had been intended. This sensible suggestion was declared out of order. A vote called on Carfrae's motion went down on pure party lines, six to nine. The *Courier* describes the scene that followed:

> Here Mr. Gurnett took up his hat and was walking out of the Room — when the Mayor called out "Higgins! stop Mr. Gurnett! Bring his to the Bar!" Mr. G. declared he would not stay a moment to listen to the proposed harangue unless he were detained there by violence. Here the constables were ordered to assist the High Bailiff in detaining Mr. G., when the Mayor proceeded to talk for ten or fifteen minutes — but as our back was turned to his Worship during the oration, in conversation with a couple of friends, we did not hear the purport of the Orator's Speech.

The Tories who had voted against the motion then fled the Council chamber, leaving the mayor without a quorum, and the meeting was necessarily adjourned.

Anyone who had played on his five expulsions from the Legislative Assembly for public sympathy as Mackenzie had should have known what the opposition press would do with this performance. The *Patriot*, on November 28, announced that the flight of the Tories was all that had saved Gurnett from the stocks, and the *Courier* on the 27th began its account with the comment that the most indisputable of all adages is that "there is no Tyrant so overbearing and tyrannical — so capriciously and brutally despotic, as your real thorough-going demagogue."

The violence of the meeting seemed to exhaust the Council. From then until the end of its term there was little municipal business conducted. The next five meetings were forced to adjourn because there was not a quorum. On December 15 the Council decided to accept a motion "that the question of the permanent appointment of Clerk of the Council be deferred until after the General Election next month," which is surprising since the Reformers had a majority to back whatever candidate they wanted. It might almost seem that they realized they had little hope for the next election and realized that any nominee who was acceptable to them would be promptly unseated by the new Council.

Although inability to decide on a new city clerk showed the Reformers' complete disorganization by the end of their term, their most damaging failure was their financial policy. Mackenzie and his associates not only failed to establish a financial policy but also never really made any attempt to keep payments up to date, to make sure collections were made or even to prepare proper financial reports. Mackenzie's personal life and business career show that he never was able to keep track of money and, in spite of the fact that there were some very successful merchants on the Council and on the Committee on Finance, his civic accounts were as confused as his personal ones. In part, this was the result of his own philosophy of civic financing. When the Act of Incorporation had been passed, he had strongly attacked the clause allowing future Councils to borrow against five years' revenue, failing to realize that in order to carry out some of the more expensive public works long-term borrowing would be necessary. Here he was merely reflecting in the municipal sphere the same Reform weakness which Aileen Dunham in her *Political Unrest in Upper Canada* has pointed out so clearly in provincial policies: "The reformers failed ... to consider the debts incurred in public improvements are themselves assets, and, if judiciously incurred, ultimately carry their own remuneration. In opposing public enterprise the radicals set themselves against the spirit of the community and consequently suffered in the estimation of the people."[23]

At the end of their term, the City Council was faced with the necessity of paying the remainder of the overdue loan (£500) to Truscott, Green & Co., which had been put off to January 28, as well as an additional £500 due the Home District for the Market construction and other debts. With virtually no cash on hand, all it could recommend was borrowing against the future revenues. In the end the Council was only able to raise £850 from Truscott, which did little but extend the loan under a new note. It left a net additional city debt of £1,727.9.4, a small portion of which was covered by uncollected assessments. The 1835 City Council did what it could to pay the 1834 debts, but it was hampered by necessary public service programmes, and in some cases it felt that the debts represented little more than Reform patronage. Mackenzie did not get his salary until April 15, 1838, when there was again a Reform Council in office. He never did have his full printing bill paid: £17.10.0, the final sum due, was transferred out of accounts payable on February 5, 1838, after the Rebellion had failed.[24]

In spite of the virtual breakdown in civic government, Reform campaigning for the January election in Toronto began as early as November 25. To provide themselves with a platform the Reformers held a public meeting at the City Hall on January 8, ostensibly to draw up a petition for the city to send to the legislature requesting revision of the Act of Incorporation. There were sixteen clauses to the petitions, many of which merely repeated Reform demands made a year earlier when the Act was being debated: secret ballot, direct election of the mayor by the people, revised assessment, different borrowing terms and a more liberal franchise. The Reformers by this time had also chosen their slate, which was very much the same as before.

Meanwhile, Mackenzie himself was conducting a rather strange campaign. After promising to run in St David he evidently changed his mind and held a public meeting on January 5 at which his supporters voted thanks "for the faithful discharge of his arduous duties during the period of his office." The *Correspondent and Advocate* later stated with some disgust that "he told the citizens in the most plain and explicit terms that altho' the liberal party had inserted his name on their ticket, and altho' he was most anxious, that the ticket should carry a majority in the new Council, he felt it to be his duty not to deceive the Ward of St David, and that if elected he would not sit." He also sent out 500 circulars to his friends stating:

CIRCULAR TO ALL PERSONS INDEBTED TO
THE SUBSCRIBER

Sir, — Having retired from the management of a periodical press and resolved to decline coming forward as a Candidate for a seat in the City Council at the ensuing Civic election, I am very desirous of giving my undivided attention to the business of the Country as a member of the Provincial Legislature.[25]

But Mackenzie, unfortunately for his dignity, was too mercurial to stick to his promise of staying out. Very soon the *Patriot* was able to announce that he had decided to run again, and was actively campaigning for his own election, all promises to the contrary. Naturally the Tory press made great fun of Mackenzie's antics. In a probable exaggeration, the *Patriot* reported on January 6 Mackenzie's statement that "I will never be Mayor, Alderman, or Common Council-Man again, so help me God! To this the editor replied: "Electors of St David's Ward! — Will you permit this man to break his voluntary oath! Remember that accessories to crime are as culpable in the eyes of God as the principals."

The Tories also began their campaign early, fielding much the same slate of candidates as they had in 1834. They had every reason for hope, in spite of their provincial defeat a few months previously. The platform the Reformers had brought forward in their petition for a new Act was the same as the complaints they had made a year before, and obviously they had no hope of getting a new Act through the Legislative Council. The complete disorganization of the civic government in the autumn months, the failure to pass a single bylaw since June, and the virtual lack of tangible achievement was bound to play into the Tory hands against the Reformers; especially since the taxes had tripled. Worse, Mackenzie could hardly be considered an asset as candidate for re-election as mayor. He had neglected his civic duties to dabble in provincial politics, and there was no indication that he would not continue to do so. He had not even managed to hold his majority together in the Council, and as a judge he been less than impressive. The failure of the Board of Health during the epidemic could, at least to a certain extent, be blamed on him, and his carrying on in the Council's stormier meetings must have seemed to many to be exactly like the behaviour of the Tory Assemblies in their less responsible moments.

Not surprisingly, then, the municipal voters on January 13 and 14 more than reversed the position of the parties, returning fifteen Tories and only five Reformers. Many of the defeats were of landslide proportions. In St David's Ward, Mackenzie received the lowest vote of anyone running in the riding, 69 compared with 123 for the lowest Tory aldermanic candidate. Toronto had obviously had enough of Mackenzie and his cohorts.

To evaluate properly Mackenzie's career as mayor, one has to go back to his own warning in the *Advocate* of March 20, 1834. There he criticized the Act of Incorporation because it contained "the unnatural union of extensive patronage with legislative, judicial, and executive powers in the same body of individuals, without any adequate check to prevent the natural disposition of man to abuse power for his own advantage." Unfortunately, he failed to heed his own warning when he became head of the city government. His Reform administration of Toronto mirrored the failings for which he had so strongly attacked the Tory-dominated Legislative Assembly and the Family Compact: misuse of patronage, appointment for purely political purposes, and using a majority virtually to maltreat the opposition. His handling of Monro and Gurnett was on the same level as his own expulsions from the Assembly. Anything else, however, was too much to expect, given the vehement politics of the period. Thus, in spite of Mackenzie's innumerable attacks on the system, he can hardly be blamed for his own course, though his actions certainly disprove the contention of those who have seen him as something new and clean in politics. Some modern reformist historious, however, seem psychologically incapable of believing that people act within the framework of their time. Furthermore, Mackenzie must be given some allowance for having been forced to try to set up a new administration with no precedent, inadequate taxation powers, and untrained, and often inept, colleagues, while at the same time contending with the downright hatred of the Tories.

But here the allowance must end. Basically, Mackenzie failed to provide the city with the leadership or programmes that it so desperately needed. Although the voters were fickle, and regularly switched parties every year prior to the Rebellion, Mackenzie's immediate successor, Robert Baldwin Sullivan, and to a lesser extent the next two mayors — Reformer Dr Thomas D. Morrison and Tory George Gurnett — were able to show that it was possible to provide such leadership. They went on to construct the paved roads, public sewers and additional markets which gradually were to make Toronto a much more livable place.

W.D. LeSueur felt that there are people who search for trouble as a hidden treasure and assigned Mackenzie to this class. Here is part of the explanation for his failure as a mayor. Mackenzie loved to do battle, a personality trait that can be admirable in a newspaper editor, or in opposition, but one which can easily lead an administrator astray. Instead of attending to his civic duties, he delighted in warring with his Tory opponents on the City Council — who admittedly reciprocated in full — fighting editorial battles about provincial politics, holding public meetings and passing resolutions. Yet this zest for battle was only partially responsible for his failure to grasp the opportunities at hand. Aileen Dunham has stated that Mackenzie never had a decided policy throughout his life, but moved like a will-o'-the-wisp collecting miscellaneous complaints which happened to be prevalent at the moment. Her interpretation is confirmed by the events of his mayoralty. For all his sometimes penetrating thoughts, the lesson from his administration in 1834 is that he was constitutionally incapable of running the day-to-day business of government, or of organizing his endless schemes and putting them to practical application. Nor could he tell the difference between a reform that was important and one that was trivial. Here was a failing that was again to manifest itself when he bungled the organization of the Rebellion of 1837. That Upper Canada had its difficulties with the Family Company cannot be denied; William Lyon Mackenzie, however, was certainly not the solution to those problems.[26]

The Reformer as strike breaker: William Lyon Mackenzie and the 1836 printers' strike[1]

That Mackenzie exerted a decisive effect on Canadian history can never be denied. But to understand him, and his career, we must stop collecting his best writings, stop stressing the same incidents—such as the destruction of his printing press and his expulsions from the House of Assembly—and try to recreate a picture of the all-round man. To do so, it is necessary to observe carefully the more neglected periods of his career: the formative years before 1824, and the last, sad decade in the provincial legislature when he lingered as a ghost from the past. Even during the years of his greatest influence, from 1824 to 1837, there are many unexplored aspects to his life. Much has been said about his opinions on government, for example, but his blue-stocking moralism and anti-semitism still await investigation. Similarly, his "persecution" as a member of the House of Assembly from 1830 to 1834 has received great attention, but his simultaneous struggle for the reform of St Andrew's Kirk in Toronto remains in obscurity. Yet here is a battle into which Mackenzie threw himself with just as much energy as he did into any political contest. The importance of such incidents may hinge on the light they throw on his apparent inability to restrain himself from attempting to change or reform everything with which he came into contact—a facet of his character, possibly obscured by the constant attention on his political and economic writing, that comes into focus when daily round of activities as a citizen of pre-Rebellion Toronto is examined. To him, it seems, the battle to control St Andrew's Kirk or the York Agricultural Society was just as momentous as the contest for responsible government.

The purpose of this chapter is to explore one of the forgotten incidents of Mackenzie's career—the Toronto printers' strike of October 1836. Mackenzie wrote much on the rights of labour and the part labourers should play in the state, and many authorities feel that his chief objective was bettering the condition of the labouring class.[2] How far he was personally willing to go in forwarding this cause when it was his own printing shop, not the structure of the government, that was involved, has never been considered.

Mackenzie was certainly a Reformer, but equally he was a business man—although hardly a successful one. He started his Upper Canadian career in partnership with the affluent Lesslie family, he was usually the proprietor of his own newspaper, and, in addition, often sold books, stationery and other related items. Certainly he himself belonged to the petty bourgeois class, not the labouring one, and, although he was never to make a fortune, he remained a small independent capitalist during much of his career.

An Upper Canadian printing business in the 1830s did not employ a large number of men by modern standards, but for its time and place Mackenzie's establishment was a considerable one. The question of how he treated his own employees is thus doubly important for it illuminates both his attitudes and the working conditions in the city of the period. When it came to the rights and remuneration of journeymen printers (that is, those who had completed their apprenticeship), was Mackenzie any different from such Tory editors as George Gurnett of the *Courier of Upper Canada* and Thomas Dalton of the *Patriot*? Information on this subject is difficult to find, but Mackenzie's relations with the printers' union and his attitude to the printers' strike cast a clear light on his actual handling of labour difficulties. Writing on the rights of labour is one thing, having a strike in one's own plant quite another.

The period from 1825 to the panic of 1837 was characterized by the formation of many hundreds of local unions in the eastern part of the United States, and not surprisingly, various labour troubles ensued.[3] A similar development took place in Upper Canada where in York/Toronto the first union—the York Typographical Society—was formed in 1832. The reason for the formation of the society was indicated in the organization's minutes:

> Owing to the many innovations which have been
> made upon the long established wages of the
> professors of the art of printing, and those of a

kind highly detrimental to their interests, it was deemed expedient by the Journeymen printers of York, that they should form themselves into a body, similar to societies in other parts of the world, in order to maintain that honourable station and respectability that belongs to the profession...[4]

A few months later, in April 1833, a revised constitution was adopted, the main provisions of which read:

Sec. 6: No member shall engage in any Printing establishment in this town at prices beneath those stipulated, ... viz. 1:15:0 per week.

Sec. 7: Payment shall be weekly. If an employer fails to do this the member shall leave and receive 10s per week for 3 weeks, from the Society, and, if he leaves town through unemployment, he shall receive £1.

Sec. 8: When any member shall work over the usual number of hours (10) per day, he shall receive 10d. per hour for such extra service.

Sec. 11: That on any journeyman refusing to comply with the rules of the Society, those journeymen members of the Society working in that office, shall notify the employer of the same, and shall refuse to work until the said journeyman does comply, or leaves the office.[5]

There were two other articles of note: one forbade members to work in any office where more than two apprentices were employed except in the event of it being the last year of the eldest apprentice's time, while another declared the apprenticeship period to be not less than 4 years. This last was changed to 5 years in 1835.

The 1833 constitution was signed by twenty-five members when it was originally adopted, and by thirty-five when it was amended two years later. In 1835, following the incorporation of the city and the reversion to the original name Toronto, the society changed its name to the Toronto Typographical Society. We know little about the acceptance it received from the various newspaper proprietors in the city except that Robert Stanton, the king's printer and editor of the official *Upper Canada Gazette,* was the first to recognize it.[6]

The high point of the society's existence was a banquet held on Oct. 15, 1833 to celebrate its first birthday. The festivities took place in the Ontario House, at the Market Square at the corner of Church and Front streets, which, under the proprietorship of William Campbell, was one of the outstanding inns in the colony. The apprentices, normally debarred from the trade secrets, were invited, as were three of the chief newspaper proprietors of the city: Stanton, Gurnett of the *Courier* and William Lyon Mackenzie, then publisher of the *Advocate.* After warming up with the usual toasts to the king, the queen, and Lieutenant-Governor Sir John Colborne, the printers were regaled by the two featured speakers, Mackenzie and Stanton. Mackenzie's address was recorded in the minutes as follows:

> He had been at many public dinners but never did he attend one under such feelings of mingled pleasure and satisfaction. When he first embarked in newspaper making there were only a few offices in the province. But now they were increasing so fast and conducted with such respectability that he could not see where such pleasing prospects would end. He was glad to see such a number of respectable persons present, many of whom had worked and some served in his office, and he could not help but feel proud that such happy prognostics augured an increasing and flourishing province. He confessed when he first heard of the formation of the society he was inclined to oppose what in his opinion were arbitrary measures. But since he had investigated the principles of the constitution he could find nothing derogatory to a consistent and moderate policy—nothing that savored of exclusive privileges, but on the contrary arrangements that would secure respectability to journeymen without interfering with the prerogative of the

employers. He should give the society his support so long as its members adhered to the present form of constitution. To the editorial corps this anniversary was a resting place, a sort of neutral ground where the transient unkind feelings that sometimes arise out of party politics could be forgotten.[7]

The hit of the evening, however, was apparently Stanton's talk, though it is not recorded except for the fact that he concluded by stating, "I shall be the last to leave or break up the joy of the evening." About midnight he was temporarily interrupted by the arrival of J. F. Rogers from Hamilton with the announcement that the printers of that city had also founded a union, and the celebration then continued with further addresses and toasts, which soon reach number eleven, "The Press." After this there were nine volunteer toasts, and, as, the minutes recorded "the song and joke flew around without apparent diminution of energy. Ample justice was done to mine host Campbell's wine." Eventually the gathering—a typical soiree of the era—adjourned and the participants stumbled home to nurse their heads and their stomachs.

Despite the evening's success the minutes do not record another birthday party, though the society remained active. Meetings were held regularly, at first at the York Hotel, where the inaugural meeting had taken place, later at the Black Horse Inn on Church Street, and finally at the Infant School on Adelaide (Newgate) Street. The society also drew upon its limited funds to aid members who were in financial difficulty but the fact that a three pound balance in the treasury was considered abundance meant that it was impossible to do much, even with the far greater purchasing power of money in the period. In the fall of 1836 the union was nearly bankrupted by the £3/2/6 paid out to help a sick comrade, James Latimer, for five weeks board before he was transferred to the hospital. Consequently, the financial backing available was hardly adequate when, in late October 1836, a strike was triggered by the rising cost of living created by the boom of the mid-1830s and tales of high wages received in such centres as New York.

By that time there were seven newspapers in the city: three Tory, two Reform and another two that were basically nonpolitical. Longest established of the three Tory papers was the

Patriot, edited by Thomas Dalton, which had begun its existence in Kingston and moved to Toronto in December 1832. Dalton had begun his editorial career as a Reformer, but had gradually become more Tory in outlook and by 1836 was a strong supporter of the Family Compact with a style as monumentally scurrilous as anything Mackenzie had ever displayed. Gurnett, long-time alderman and editor of the *Courier*, had followed a similar career, beginning in Ancaster in 1829 and then transferring to Toronto. Politically, he, too, began as a Reformer, but in Toronto he became a fervent champion of the government. Unlike Dalton, Gurnett was to live long enough to complete the circle and became a Reformer once again! The third Tory paper was the *Albion of Upper Canada*, edited by James Cull, which was still a fairly new venture at the time of the strike. Unfortunately, only the *Patriot* can be used to gain an idea of a Tory editor's attitude to the strike because no issues of the *Albion* survive, and there are no copies of the *Courier* from Oct. 8 to Nov. 9, 1836.[8]

The two non-aligned papers were the *Upper Canada Gazette*, of which Robert Stanton was still the editor, and the *Christian Guardian*, the official organ of the Methodist Church. The first of these was naturally Tory by inclination, and the second, then edited by the Reverend Ephraim Evans, could have no very pro-Reform leanings since the Reverend Egerton Ryerson, the chief prophet of Methodism, had broken with Mackenzie after the union of the major Methodist communions in 1833. Both these journals survive for the period of the strike, but neither makes any mention of the incident. While statements to be found in other papers make it clear that both the *Gazette* and the *Guardian* were affected by the strike, the proprietors evidently carried on with the help of the apprentices and did not consider the whole matter important enough to comment.

The background of the first Reform paper is rather complex. Established in 1832 as the *Canadian Correspondent*, it was edited by William O'Grady, the dismissed Catholic vicar-general of Toronto who had turned to the Reform party and the newspaperman's life. In November 1834, when Mackenzie gave up the *Advocate* to devote all his time to politics, he had turned it over to O'Grady and the combined newspaper became the *Correspondent and Advocate*. The other Reform paper was Mackenzie's new venture, the *Constitution*, which had made its first appearance on July 4, 1836. Both Reform voices mention the strike; Mackenzie has as much to say about it as all the rest put together.

The outbreak of the strike, which took place on October 22, 1836, drew comment from all three of the publishers who did not deem the whole event beneath their notice. Dalton, as a Tory, might have been expected to wax the most indignant at his workers demanding higher pay, but he actually said the least, merely noting that there had been a "tremendous" strike among the journeymen printers of Toronto.[9] O'Grady wrote at greater length, beginning with the terms demanded.

> The Journeymen printers of this City "turned out" on Saturday last for a higher rate of wages than they have hitherto been paid. Not content with 35s. and 10d an hour for extra work, both often making in our office £3 per week for a single printer they demand higher wages, or the New York prices for piece work.[10]

He then pointed out that, though employees were paid at a much lower rate than in New York, "house rent and necessities of life are much cheaper here than at New York." His conclusion was that he hoped that a few days off would teach the printers "the injustice of the proceedings," and that they would then resume work. O'Grady also apologized for the paper being delayed and thus missing the early mails; presumably his makeshift staff were unable to print it in time.

Mackenzie had much more to say in the *Constitution* of October 26, 1836. He began with a history of the union from its establishment in 1832, outlining the terms of employment and the fact that those who did not adhere to the agreement were to be turned out. He also noted "that to enable them [the union printers] to stand against the employers, they were to be supported from the funds of the association." Regarding the limit allowed on numbers of apprentices in a printing house, he stated that Stanton had reduced his number to two as required, but that Dalton had not been interfered with though he had kept no less than five. Moving to his own operation he noted that he employed only four apprentices, though he had kept seven to eight journeymen, and regularly paid $7.00 to $7.50, or even more per week. He than recounted the events as he saw them:

> Late last Wednesday every employee was served with a short of writ signed by no one, but an-

nouncing that after Saturday the wages must be $8, for ten hours, and when I paid my men that evening, they told me that if I did not instantly raise their wages to $8, they would quit to a man on Saturday. I reasoned with them in vain. One of them, Aikman, came up from Montreal with a distinct understanding before he left that $7 were to be his wages for the season, and yet he was among the most decided of the party. I asked them if it was fair to the employer, to combine in the midst of existing contracts to demand wages which would be ruinous, without giving several months notice, seeing that they themselves had fixed the rate of wages. They replied that it was my own fault, that I had taken the contract too low, and that they would have $8. immediately. On this I instantly discharged six of them, and sent notice to the House of Assembly that if the strike continued I could do not more work.

Journey printers need never lose an hour in a year. They walk into a warm and comfortable room at eight in the morning, are attended to by apprentices, and their tools are all furnished by their employers. After 10 hours work, at a species of labour so light and easy that women could perform it better than men, they have their evenings to themselves, and seven dollars in cash punctually at the week's end. Yet with this they are so discontented, that they hesitate not to use their utmost effort to ruin and injure their employers. I told my foreman that if he preferred remaining in a society, combined to injure his employer, and to prevent the young rising generation from learning the trade, I must dispense with his services also, but he disapproved of their unkind proceedings and instantly abandoned the association. But for him and my apprentices this paper would have been the size of a seven by nine pane of glass. This explanation will, I think, satisfy the public sympathy, and will plead my excuse for depriving the writers of The Constitution of the useful quality of news. The workmen in all other offices followed the example set by mine. So there is a general turnout.

Had there been a combination among the employers suddenly to lengthen the hours of labour or to reduce the rate of wages beyond that which the associated journeymen themselves had fixed, the public would have condemned the employers — for the upholding of a fair price for labour is necessary to the well being of a state. It would be well for these journeymen if they would employ their evenings in studying the true principles of economy which govern the rule of wages. Had they so done previous to their present ungrateful movement, it never would have been made. They would have seen that combinations among workmen, intended solely to keep up the rate of wages, are of precisely the nature of combinations among masters to keep up the rate of profits. They are both confederacies against the public, liable to the same objection as monopolies, in which the interest of individuals is sought to be supported at the expense of the interests of the community. Competition is restrained 1st in the supply of labour, and 2nd, in the supply of capital.

Combinations like that of the printers are useful when not carried too far. But, when they begin to foment divisions and animosities in society, when they array classes against each other who could otherwise be united by a common interest, when they attempt to deprive the youths of a city (Toronto for instance) of the privilege of choosing the trade they would desire to pursue, when they attempt to establish a monopoly in the rate of labour instead of leaving it to be regulated by the supply and demand, they become injurious to society; and were all trades and professions to combine like our printers, the effect would be to split up the community into so many selfish and mischievous monopolies, like the guilds and incorporated trades of the 14th, 15th, and 16th centuries.

Upon the principle the journeymen assert, every machine by which their labour is curtailed ought to be interfered with, because it cheapens labour. Yet it must be evident that such a rule generally followed would carry us, (as a Glasgow weaver said to a Committee of the House of Commons) so far that we "could never stop till we came to our teeth and nails".

The works printed by our journeymen are for home consumption. Were they for exportation, like ashes, flour, staves, and etc., such a combination as the journeymen have gone into would have to compete with the products of countries where no such combinations existed. Fluctuations in employment, with high wages to-day and low tomorrow, are not so good as stationary fair rates. Seven dollars to a printer are as good as eight or nine to a carpenter — for the latter has his tools to furnish and often wet days to take off. Not so the printer; he never loses a day.

In this City, within the week threats and intimidation have been held out to journeymen. This is provided against in England by a special statute, by which workmen are made independent of any combination, and allowed to contract to labour where, when and with whomsoever they see fit.

Refusing to work with non-associated workmen by virtue of a concerted act of resistance, seems to me unjust — the lawyers say it is illegal. Waving the view of the case, however, the employers have resolved to employ no member of the obnoxious association until he abandon it, and I am sure that in this instance the public will approve of the decision.

Labour sometimes needs protection — witness the horrible treatment of the factory children in England. There, cruelty and injustice, required to be met by combination — but it is not so here.

If our journeymen could but change situations with the employers for a few short months and contrast the difficulties of the latter with the ease and comfort the former enjoy, we should never again hear of such an ungrateful and considerable proceedings as has occasioned this article.

O'Grady of the *Correspondent and Advocate* was correct in his estimate of the outcome. After thinking the matter over and watching the papers continuing to make their appearance without their assistance, the printers returned by the end of the month. Although O'Grady himself did not consider this event worth recording, both Dalton and Mackenzie commented on the end of the strike. The former was quite generous in his notice:

The Journeymen Printers, having reconsidered their resolution to live idle, have wisely rescinded the same, and returned to their vocations, on condition of a general amnesty, which had been freely accorded by the employers, and the hatchet is buried. Notwithstanding this resumption of their labours, several good Journeymen will be wanted during the season.[11]

Mackenzie, writing on November 2, was less charitable:

The combination of printers against "things as they are," is at length at an end. If all the journeymen were editors, and each had a press of his own, a more resolute, determined, I had almost added obstinate body, would not be found on this continent.[12]

Thus the strike was over in a very short time. Interestingly enough, in spite of the printers' failure the journeymen tailors struck in Toronto before the month was out, on Nov. 17, 1836, demanding a share of the profits. But they evidently met with no more success, and notices of their strike had disappeared by

December 6.[13] Rather surprisingly, the printers' union survived its strike although it was virtually abandoned a year later during the aftermath of the Rebellion. The union remained dormant until February 1844, when it was re-established with its old constitution. Daniel Bancroft, who had been the first president in 1832, then became president of the resurrected organization.[14]

What does this episode tell us about Mackenzie's character and policies? That he had more to say about the strike than any of the other editors whose journals have survived is probably just typical of the man and cannot be taken as significant. What is important are the opinions he asserts. The popular picture of Mackenzie that springs to mind is of a leader who would immediately instantly act to defend the labourer, to extend his rights and to attempt to ensure that he received fair payment for his toil. Yet, when the printers' union was formed, it was the king's printer, Stanton, who first recognized it, and Mackenzie was the one who attacked the workers most vehemently when they struck. His position was that combinations of labourers were monopolies which worked against the public weal, and that if only the workers could change places with the employers they would understand the problems the latter had to undergo. In other words, Mackenzie was no more ready to see the labourers combine to enforce their rights than he was to uphold the monopoly of the Family Compact. Essentially, then, he was very much like the English radicals of the era, who were pro-reform but anti-union. His reaction to the strike provides a case history of a capitalist with labour problems, not that of a reformer leading the workingman on to new rights.

Lillian Gates has stated that Mackenzie had a "decided policy" and that at the heart of this policy was a commitment to the good of the working class. Mackenzie's statements during the printers' strike, however, seem to belie this idea. Possibly we should look in a completely different direction to see what motivated him in his support of labour. It may be that the key is to be found in Craig's statement that Mackenzie "was instinctively suspicious of the great ones of this earth." Mackenzie might demand rights for farmers, labourers and the people generally, but he was simultaneously trying to attract their support in his campaign to overthrow the Family Compact. Only a year later he had no hesitation in lying to his followers in order to lead them into the Rebellion of 1837 or in suggesting that the employees of leading Reform businessmen be used as troops to help topple the government. Still, to say that the destruction of the government, not the rights of the people, was Mackenzie's chief objective, would probably be an over-simplication and lead in the wrong direction.

In a badly neglected analysis many years ago R.A. MacKay stated that Mackenzie was in essence a "journalist in politics" and "a puritan with a mission."[15] Here we may have one of the keys to his actions: he was in essence an inveterate reformer, trying to fix and clean up everything in sight. Nor did the means matter in the attainment of his ends as he saw them. Anything that interrupted his progress towards his mission was evil and had to be fought. He was also highly suspicious of monopolies, and his printers with their union and strike were a monopoly bent on controlling labour and thus had to be broken. There is also a third factor: Mackenzie, for all he proclaimed himself the leader of the oppressed, saw himself as a merchant who had forgone great wealth for his causes, and as a benevolent proprietor. To have his own labourers forming a monopoly and attacking the pay scales of their benefactor, thereby preventing him from bringing his ideas before the people, was guaranteed to trigger an outburst and his personality, his tendency to overkill, guaranteed that it would be a lively one.

In sum, Mackenzie was very much the business proprietor of his era. Though he might defend the worker and support his rights to the fruit of his toil, he also believed that his workers had their place, and that their place did not include telling him how to run his business affairs. Like many later men of his type, he was basically against anything that might circumscribe his activities, be it the government or combinations of labourers.

The incident of the printers' strike of 1836 is a minor one, but it is in such minor, overlooked events of his career that we may finally be able to arrive at a balanced evaluation of Mackenzie. Before we can draw conclusion about his motivations and goals we must see him at home in his day-to-day activities. By this method the historian—with the aid of the psychologist—may be able to come to an accurate estimate of what place Mackenzie really deserves in Canadian history.

Chapter 7

William Lyon Mackenzie: The Persistent Hero[1]

The Ontario Legislature at Queen's Park is surrounded by the usual collection of odd statuary which such structures seem to accumulate over the years, the most recent being the 1940 memorial to William Lyon Mackenzie. There the bust of the little leader, who tried to organize an invasion of Canada from the United States in 1837, stares banefully across the surging traffic of Queen's Park West at Britannia, who stands on guard on top the monument to the Volunteers who died repulsing the Fenian invasion from the United States in 1866. That the twain should thus co-exist, albeit somewhat uncomfortably, typifies the conundrum of Mackenzie's place in Canadian history.

There are several remarkable points about the Mackenzie memorial. Even though he has the founder of the English Sunday school movement for exotic company, he seems rather out of place among the assorted royalties, imperial proconsuls, fathers of Confederation and loyal premiers of our most prosperous province: a jarring note in a tale of empire triumphant. Another anomaly is the inscription, which opens, "to commemorate the struggle for Responsible Government in Upper Canada." Is Mackenzie's bust really the one to accompany this inscription? What happened to the Baldwins, to Lord Durham? Would Mackenzie not better commemorate the Rebellion of 1837? Still the seat of the government of Ontario is surely not the place to commemorate the leaders of unsuccessful uprisings. Furthermore, is it appropriate to have a monument on the west side of the legislature commemorating a local rebel, when, in another piece of sculpture on the east side, Ontario congratulates itself on its noble part in putting down the North-West Rebellion of 1885?

The very contradictions involved in the inappropriate inscription and the curious juxtaposition of the statues exemplify what must be one of the strangest success stories in Canadian history: how Mackenzie became a hero, and why he has retained this distinction in spite of all the calumniators of his name. When John Charles Dent, the first historian who criticized Mackenzie's activities, laid down his pen in 1885, presumably he thought that he had placed him in the correct perspective. But Dent, like many later writers, was wrong. Mackenzie still finds many devotees today; it seems that for everyone who attacks his place in Canadian history, another rushes to his support. The persistence of his aura is as intriguing a mystery as the personality and deeds of the man himself.

When I first began to work on Mackenzie in the early 1960s my objective was merely an examination of his work as first mayor of Toronto in 1834, the only time at which he could be said to have held an administrative office. It soon became evident that as mayor of Toronto he was a disaster; instead of a constructive reformer attempting to solve the problems of the city, the man who emerged from the documents was driven by some inner devil to change everything he encountered, whatsoever it happened to be. True, he fought valiantly to improve the constitution of the province, but he put equal zest into chasing the most obscure will'-o-the-wisps. Some historians have seen him as a reformer, others as a rebel; yet as mayor of Toronto he could best be described as a public nuisance.[2]

This naturally raised the question of how, considering his ineptitude, he ever became a hero in Canadian history. In 1927, Aileen Dunham asserted that "the notoriety which he naturally acquired as leader of a rebellion in 1837 has stamped his importance on the minds of posterity."[3] She also stated that "Mackenzie was the type of man who thirsts for publicity, and who pushes himself forward on every possible occasion."[4] In addition to these facts, Mackenzie left a wealth of material on his activities. Drawing on this material, his son-in-law and first biographer, Charles Lindsey (1820-1908), carefully selected most of those incidents from his career which, until recent years at least, were the only ones that have been familiar to posterity. Lindsey even provided an explanation for those who might dislike the idea of a rebel-hero: although ill-advised, the rebellion both speeded up the process of reform and was more or less necessary before the United Kingdom would grant us responsible government. Does Mackenzie's importance, then, really lie in the fact that he became involved in a Rebellion, seized on any publicity that he could, left us a vast legacy of writings, has a good press provided by his son-in-law and, of course, was first mayor of Toronto?[5]

This chapter attempts to discover why Mackenzie became a hero and why he has remained one, while, on a broader basis, it tries to examine how Canadians have gone about selecting their heroes. To address these issues, it undertakes a preliminary search for the real Mackenzie who seems to lurk behind the legend, together with a discussion of some of his qualifications for the role of a hero in Canadian history. It reflects on the factors, many of them intangible, that have thrust him to the forefront of Canadian history. And finally, by considering the literature on the subject, it investigates the role that historical writing has played in the development of the Mackenzie legend.

In Search Of The Real William Lyon Mackenzie

The first question is what do we really know about the man? To what extent is he suited for the title of hero in the milieu of the late-20th century? Surprisingly, we really know rather little about Mackenzie. Though Canadian historians have tended to beat and re-beat the same paths, and though Mackenzie stands astride one of their longtime favourite obsessions — the road to responsible government — he has yet to be treated to the same searching examination that J. M. S. Careless, for instance, has given George Brown. In 1956 William Kilbourn, in the preface to his colourful biography of Mackenzie that generally follows Lindsey's account, pointed out that in the space available he could present only a "selective account of the events" and that his work was not "offered as a full-scale definitive biography."[6] The vast task of examining all the documents needed to prepare such an extensive, definite work still waits to be done, although light has been cast on many aspects of Mackenzie's activities. David Flint has prepared a short, well-researched account in *William Lyon Mackenzie: Rebel Against Authority* (Toronto, 1971). My own conclusions are contained in the *Dictionary of Canadian Biography* entry on Mackenzie by Ronald J. Stagg and the writer (Vol IX, 1976, pp. 496-510).

To obtain an understanding of the man as well as the hero, it is necessary to divide Mackenzie's careers into five chronological phases: the formative years until he began publishing in 1824; the years of political activity from 1824 to 1837; the revo-

*One of Mackenzie's many early homes, photograph dates from
1885.*

lutionary years, 1837-1840; the later American period to 1849; and the last years until his death in 1861. For the first of these phases, the information available is fragmentary, but what does exist clearly indicates that the Mackenzie-Lindsey accounts of his early life leave out some important facts which point to a more comfortable existence than Mackenzie liked to admit. The last two periods are basically an anti-climax in which he was on the periphery of events. It is thus basically to the second and third periods that we will have to turn to make a preliminary evaluation of the man and his career.[7]

Many aspects of Mackenzie's personality and outlook which the present generation would find unattractive have been consistently overlooked by historians. These are frequently characteristics typical of his class and period which do not today find favour. On the other side of the picture, many of the legends that have clung to his name remain entrenched in the popular imagination, even if they have long been discarded by most historians. In attempting to estimate the direction that a re-evaluation may well take, it is probably these legends that should be examined first.

The most obvious of these fables is the one that he was the "leader" of the "reform party." This is a belief that dies very hard. Aileen Dunham, Gerald M. Craig[8] and others have pointed out that the reformers of the period were far too unorganized to be called a party and that Mackenzie was certainly not their recognized leader.[9] That Mackenzie often had a marked influence on events must not be forgotten,[10] but, as Dunham pointed out, unlike the Bidwells or the Baldwins or Ryerson, Mackenzie "never succeeded in taking the leadership on any prominent issue."[11]

The next most important legend that has gathered around Mackenzie is the tale of the persecutions that he underwent at the hands of the Family Compact in the cause of democracy. This story as told overlooks two facts: first, that he brought many of the attacks on himself by his intemperate conduct; and second, that others were persecuted as badly or worse than he was. Certain incidents which Lindsey stressed are famous: the 1826 destruction of the printing press, and the 1832-34 expulsions from the Assembly.[12] These are reiterated in text after text. Yet they can be questioned. A Tory historian might argue, with considerable justice, that the printing press incident merely proved the impartiality of the Family Compact courts, for Mackenzie was awarded heavy damages,[13] or that Robert Christie should be equally commiserated with for his expulsions from the Assembly of Lower Canada. Further, Mackenzie himself was not above expelling opposition members of the Toronto City Council when he was mayor and had a majority. Finally, if persecutions are to be compared, Mackenzie fared quite well if we consider the case of John Matthews, another member of the Assembly, or his fellow editor Francis Collins.[14]

Another aura that surrounds Mackenzie is that of the fearless newspaper reporter, the man who attacked the government virtually on his own and brought down the Family Compact's vengeance for his daring exposures. That Mackenzie was fearless, or at times foolhardy, is undeniable; moreover, it must be conceded that he was a great newspaper editor of his era. To see him and his fellow journalists in their proper context, however, it is first necessary to realize that the libel laws of the time were very lax, that newspaper reporting was virulent, and that Mackenzie in his virulence differed little from other editors,[15] some of whom, such as Collins, who evidenced no love for Mackenzie, were equally ready to attack the government.

That he could be a hard-hitting writer cannot be denied. In fact, his reputation has probably been enhanced because some of his finest, if most offensive, effusions have been ignored. In this respect, some of Mackenzie journalistic efforts show the extreme lengths to which an Upper Canadian editor could go in his attacks without being sued for libel or closed down by the government. A good example is a diatribe against Lieutenant-Governor Sir Francis Bond Head, who was a well-known author. Captioned "Sir Francis Bond Head and the Eating House Girl," the editorial opened by complimenting the governor on his keen eye for the girls and went on to discuss a comment on a pretty Liverpool waitress which had appeared in one of Head's works: "her stays were tightly laced." After citing this statement, Mackenzie warmed to his theme:

> Now may it please Your Excellency, how could Your Excellency find out whether this languishing flirt's stays were tight laced or slack laced, or whether she actually wore stays, without having some passages with her of a nature too close for

your history of her beauty to mention? Only to think of the old gentleman fumbling about the waiting maid's clothes to ascertain how strait her stays were laced!! [16]

Obviously, the press was far more free than Mackenzie would have had his readers believe, and it would further seem that there was much less bravery required for attacks on crown and government than his supporters would have one think. The comment by Colonial Secretary Lord Goderich that whatever Upper Canada lacked it was not freedom of the press could well serve as an epitaph for all of Upper Canada's newspaper editors.[17]

Goderich's evaluation points of another side to the matter, for it could be argued that Mackenzie may not really deserve his laurels as the most hard-hitting, or possibly the most scurrilous, writer of Upper Canada. My own award in that contest would go to the Reformer-turned-Tory Thomas Dalton — a victory that might well be attributable to a flourishing case of chronic alcoholism. Here is a letter from Dalton's *Patrioit* entitled "A Lover of Upper Canada" which bears all the marks of his literary style:

Mr. Mackenzie knows the tenure by which he holds his popularity. He is the medium through which all the discontented, the splenetic, the malicious, rebellious, and envious can vent their rage and their folly. He is the common sewer into which natural receptacle all the filth and offal of the City are thrown; and from whose mouth it is after due fermentation poured forth a pestiential and disgusting stream ....[18]

Another question closely connected with Mackenzie's editorial career concerns the extent to which he was truly an innovator, a man who presented original ideas. Aileen Dunham stated her opinion on this point very clearly: "Mackenzie was not a thinker but a fighter."[19] Writing a decade later, in 1937, R. A. MacKay, a political scientist, noted that Mackenzie "was not a systematic philosopher, either by temperament or training; he was pre-eminently a journalist in politics."[20] MacKay clearly shows that Mackenzie was eclectic in his use of sources and had files of material ready on almost any topic.[21] Since he would incorporate these gleanings almost verbatim into his journals his own ideas are almost impossible to trace, especially as he either invented quotations or failed to acknowledge their source, depending on his mood.

The impact of Mackay's comments, however, which are buried in the journal of a learned society, has been more than countered by Margaret Fairley's *The Selected Writings of William Lyon Mackenzie* (Toronto, 1960), which is authorized supplementary reading in the Ontario schools. Although the author clearly and fairly states that her collection is "selected," the impression that remains from reading them is that Mackenzie was a brilliant thinker on a vast variety of subjects. Yet the fact is that we have no certain evidence to show how much, or how little, of Mackenzie's writing was in any way original. That he wrote, or borrowed, some magnificent passages cannot be denied; moreover, we must give him credit for complete sincerity in believing that whatever he advocated at the moment was the best policy, and also for an ability to project his thoughts to a large audience. The vast amount of drivel that came from his pen, however, or his excursions into trivia are too easily overlooked.

This leads us to the most important question: whether or not Mackenzie was capable of formulating a policy. Dunham expressed her thoughts simply on this matter: "nor had he throughout his life a decided policy. At any one moment from 1820 to 1837 his writings were but the reflection of the miscellaneous complaints which happened to be prevalent."[22] This was an interpretation that was strongly attacked by Lillian Gates in 1959:

> Not the niggardly question of responsible government, not overcoming the relative economic backwardness of Upper Canada, but the larger question of developing the institutions and resources of the province for the benefit of the common man, that was what mattered. That was throughout his life Mackenzie's "decided" policy.[23]

But the question of responsible government was hardly "niggardly." In fact, the implementation of responsible government was the key that prevented a genuine Canadian revolution, and it set the precedent for orderly colonial evolution, not revolution, elsewhere. Also, despite Gates' assertion, the economic development of Upper Canada was crucial to the colony's growth, and economic problems were completely misunderstood by Mackenzie and the Reformers.[24]

There are still other difficulties with Gates' argument. Can something as vague as the "benefit of the common man" be called a decided policy? Who is the common man? What benefits him? Who decides who he is and what benefits him? In practice, Mackenzie at times carried out policies that almost seem to be the opposite of his expressed support for the common man. When the electors decisively defeated his party in 1836 he went on to rebel against the government they had returned. In a more personal sphere, when the printers of Toronto went on strike in 1836 he reacted more violently than any other publisher, opposing their union as a monopoly and helping break the strike.[25] For all that he has become the hero of the left, at heart he was much the typical nineteenth-century bourgeois capitalist. What we really have in Mackenzie is nothing more or less than what MacKay called a "Puritan with a mission"[26] operating in another guise: in the case of the printers' strike, to prevent the monopoly of the proletariat, not the monopoly of the oligarchs. A mission to slay the imaginary dragon of the moment does not constitute a "decided policy."

A mission, however, does fit with the fact that Mackenzie seemed to have an unceasing urge to reform anything and everything in sight. He simply saw no gradations of importance: all institutions were equally venal, whether it was the government of the Family Compact dominating the province, or a union trying to organize his own employees, or the Tories setting up a horticultural society for the Town of York. The battle for political reform into which this urge led him may have done much to give him his reputation; however, a close study of some of the tangents on which it drew him might do a great deal to put him into perspective.

Another issue centers on how many of Mackenzie's attitudes and outlooks would be appropriate for a hero of today. Again, what would his "unselected writings" do for his reputation? One surprising way in which Mackenzie differed from Brown and so many other reformers, such as James Lesslie, with whom he was so closely associated, was his lack of interest in the social improvement of the poor and oppressed groups. Some of these men, such as Brown, may have been equally anti-union; but on the lists of those who served as patrons and governors of such institutions as the Mechanics Institute, or the Anti-Slavery Society, the Browns and the Lesslies stand out, as do many Tories. Mackenzie is conspicuous by his absence.

An examination of Mackenzie's attitudes to religion, race and colour might also yield interesting results. Basically, he seems to have seen each issue in the light of whether or not the minority group involved supported his opponents of the moment. His railings against the Catholic bishop were equal to those against Strachan, largely because Bishop Macdonell was equally a Tory. The Blacks fared little better, since as refugees from slavery, they too tended to support the government. Mackenzie noted:

> The coloured people of Toronto and its vicinity, have addressed His Excellency, and offered to form themselves into a corps to assist in putting down the Canadians of the sister province, or the reformers here, if they don't be quiet. The blacks and the tories know that monarchy is honour personified.[27]

Jews were another of Mackenzie's phobias, and he did not fail to excoriate them when Sir Francis Bond Head was lieutenant-governor. Referring to Bond Head and his civil secretary, John Joseph, he ended an article: "Never before were there so many emigrations. Even the plague called the cholera was less depopulating than the 'bread and butter' baronet of the city whigs. O, but what we lose in Christians we gain in Jews!"[28] Although such attitudes may have been common at the time (and Mackenzie was ready to use any possible needle in an attack), they are not the attitudes that one would expect in a man who has often been cited in the 20th century as the epitome of reform.

One of Mackenzie's attitudes was rather amusing: although he claimed to be something of a reformed roué, he often went to the other extreme and became guardian of the Toronto's morals. When a group of players wished to visit the city, he wrote:

As to the player people they generally pretend to begin at 7 but in reality commence at 8; they exhibit lewd and profligate scenes, sing questionable songs and repeat double entendres. From 8 until 11 or 12 the citizens are enticed into the theatre, dissipation encouraged, strumpets enriched, profligacy of manners extended, and late hours made fashionable.[29]

Then there is the question of how far Mackenzie's activities can be related to his expressed theories. The answer, as we have seen in the case of the printer's strike, is that there was very little connection between the two. For example, Mackenzie has been particularly commended for his constant attacks on corruptibility in office; indeed, from his railings on corruption in others he has gained a halo of incorruptibility himself. Gates felt that his basic concern was not what form of government was best, but which people were best fitted to administer that government to the public advantage.[30] Yet all this overlooks the fact that it is rather difficult to be corrupt when out of office. As mayor of Toronto, his only real tenure of power, Mackenzie applied the same methods of patronage distribution for which he had criticized the Family Compact in their administration of the province. Although nothing else could really be expected of him, considering the politics of the period, this is not what the myths that have grown up around his name would lead us to believe.[31]

At the same time Mackenzie's use of his authority as mayor to maltreat the opposition ran strongly counter to his own complaints of persecution, while his demands that his dignity be recognized in the city court could as well have come from the Tory judges of the Court of King's Bench.[32] In fact, his performance as mayor epitomized everything he had flung at the Tories. Former prime minister Pierre Trudeau has stated "the Mackenzie rebellion in Upper Canada was a clear struggle for democratic self-government."[33] But on the basis of Mackenzie's mayoralty record, it might be argued that the Rebellion was little more than a struggle between the "ins" and the "outs," with the results suggesting the "ins" had the greater support. Further, Mackenzie's total failure as an administrator again says much in argument against any claims that he had a "decided policy."

Such are the examples to be drawn from the 1834-1837 period. What of Mackenzie's activities in the period after the Rebellion disturbances had died down? In 1862 Charles Lindsey, in his 800-page study, devoted only 30 pages to the years after Mackenzie was released from jail in 1840. Gates's equally long study covering these years, *After the Rebellion*, has just been published. What does it show us? To me the events recounted just confirm my own reading of the documents, though Gates and I would not concur on the interpretation. The later Mackenzie was much the same as the earlier one, except that his characteristics were sometimes exaggerated by age. While Mackenzie lived in the United States, from the end of 1837 to 1849, we find a familiar pattern: constant unsuccessful attempts to publish a newspaper, opposition to the government of Canada, and for the United States itself, first growing disillusionment and then hostility. Also, the old ability to rake over scandals is shown in his exposé of the New York customs operation and his life of President Van Buren.[34]In his last years in Upper Canada, from 1849 to 1861, we again find the same attempts to edit a paper and the same "je suis contre" attitude. The Ministerialists — the old Reform group — are in power, the Clear Grits, the future Liberals, are forming to the left of them, and off to the left of the Grits is Mackenzie. In 1851 he finally did help bring about the resignation of a government leader: not John Strachan, not John Beverley Robinson, not even William Henry Draper, but Robert Baldwin, the first co-premier under responsible government — the very man who had allowed Mackenzie to return from exile and keep his property.

Why Mackenzie?

With these disabilities, how did Mackenzie manage to become a hero and how has he maintained his reputation in spite of so many attacks? Of the factors that catapulted Mackenzie into the role of hero, several are purely fortuitous, but they cannot be overlooked in attempting to analyze his place in history. Take for instance his size. Does the off-cited fact that he was a little man fighting a big oligarchy help his reputation? Here we have one of the questions with regard to which the historian will have to receive assistance from the psychologist.
    The most important of these fortuitous circumstances was

simply that Mackenzie came at the *right time* to gain a reputation. He flourished during a period when Upper Canada was growing up and demanding change, though what changes and what direction these changes would take was yet to be decided. His talents fitted well with the political exigencies of the moment. In a period of slow political evolution, or of more stable economic development, he would have made little mark; however, the absence of any real political parties, coupled with the obvious need for some sort of reform, left the way open for a man who was essentially a demagogue-editor.

The second major fortuitous reason was simply that he supported what future generations saw as the right side; he favoured a new structure of government, and selections from his voluminous have writing have been used to support the case that he favoured all the changes that were to come about. Whether or not he initiated or understood these changes, or whether he advocated other changes that never took place, was irrelevant. To later generations, he could easily be put forward as the champion of the right to govern ourselves: Responsible Government. Thus Mackenzie fits in nicely not only with the "onwards and upwards" interpretation of history, so popular with nineteenth-century Canadian historians, but also with the theories of those who, from a more leftist interpretation of history, are today looking for heroes. As A. G. Bradley remarked in 1923, "many Canadian writers, inclined to judge every period by their own, seek to justify Mackensie [sic] in the fact that all he contended for was ultimately granted."[35] Thus it might well be argued that his "cause" won, even if he personally lost, and that he was carried along with it to posthumous victory.

Coupled with these factors is the inborn need for heroes in any nation, men whose exploits can make its history more readable and who can provide its students with someone with whom to identify. This is particularly true in a nation that is growing up from colonialism and is under the shadow of a larger neighbour whose heroes could be adopted all too easily. Herein lies one of our greatest problems. Our real heroes, the men who made the nation, are not heroic in the classic sense of leading armies across their neighbours' territory, controlling the seas to advance the commerce of their native land or precipitating the nation into independence through rebellion. We have almost no native military heroes, particularly after the end of the

French regime. As Ramsay Cook put it, "what heroes there are are nearly all French, thus making English-Canadian hero-worship difficult."[36] Sir Isaac Brock may shine forth — although much less so than he did in the nineteenth century — but more recent generals, such as Sir Arthur Currie, have had little popular impact.

The problem of finding a focal figure, nevertheless, remains, for this "blood and thunder" type of hero is the one for whom so many people search. J. R. Colombo in *The Mackenzie Poems* says that Canada has far too many "pale faces"[37] (among whom he lists Sir John A. Macdonald) and needs more heroes like Mackenzie, Papineau and Riel. If setting off an unsuccessful rebellion which led to many people being killed and the lives of even more disrupted is the criterion for becoming a hero, our ancestors were very lucky that we have so few. We are lucky, too — with more ancestors killed in rebellions many of us would not be around. Colombo's complaint, nevertheless, does underlie the fact that, for those who glory in violence, we lack a certain colour in our history, a problem that has again been well expressed by Cook: "Our orderly growth from 'colony to nation' has deprived us of the heroic events out of which nationalist myths are made."[38]

Constitutional evolution, unlike revolution, does not create a lively story. Our vast array of lawyers may have created the nation, but how do you make a constitutional decision colourful? ("Tennant vs. The Union Bank of Canada" hardly grips the student as it did the constitution.) How do you explain to the average student the subtle differences between representative and responsible government? As their answers to final examinations clearly demonstrate, even many university students are never able to differentiate. Thus, although the blame may be partially attributed to poor teaching, or the strange curriculums set by departments of education, some of our most "heroic" figures, in terms of genuine national progress, will probably always be lost to us. The Baldwins and Sir Louis-Hippolyte LaFontaine will certainly never occupy a place in Canadian history commensurate with their contributions to Canadian development.

As a result, we have had to fall back on various expedients. In English Canada, especially when we were more colonially minded, we could simply adopt the great heroes of Britain and wallow in their glories, or adulate the deeds of the proconsuls who came to govern us. As we have evolved, however, these men have become more and more unsatisfactory; though some of them such as Durham and Elgin still are usually ranked as heroes in the textbooks — and rather deservedly so — the majority of them can hardly be accepted by more than one part of the nation. The public school curriculum in the past attempted to make heroes out of the fur traders and explorers and as a result the students were dragged through fur traders and explorers *ad nauseum*, up one river and down another, until they may well have come to detest Canadian history. Some of these men can well be made into heroes; others — their number is overwhelming — are best forgotten.

In our attempt to find heroes of physical action, we are now trying to create a multicultural folk picture of pioneers developing the land. Insofar as this brings the social ways of the past to life it can be good. Individuals in this category, however, are hard to come by; it is doubtful whether such heroes as Laura Secord should be greatly stressed. Above all, it is easy to fall into the trap of adopting American folk heroes — statues of Paul Bunyan and his bright blue ox were once put up at the Canadian National Exhibition! If we turn to this type of expedient we might as well fold up our tent. To all this must be added the complication of bilingualism; there are so few heroes on whom our two linguistic groups can agree. Champlain is acceptable, as are a few other figures of the French regime; but since that period few names stand out, Elgin just possibly being one. The result, in English Canada at least, has been the creation of a sort of joint hero figure rather unique in history: Wolfe/Montcalm, Mackenzie/Papineau, Baldwin/LaFontaine, Macdonald/Cartier and King/Lapointe. Here we can discern a pattern into which the subject of our examination fits rather nicely.

Another result of the shortage of heroes has been the tendency to fall back on the leaders of rebellions; it is here that Mackenzie, Papineau and Riel shine forth, deservedly or not. Possibly if we had had more insurrections they would be less charismatic. But again there is a conundrum in Canadian history; we deify the loser, not the victor: Mackenzie not Sir Allan MacNab, Papineau not Sir John Colborne, Riel not Sir Garnet Wolseley. Possibly, this comes about because we like to see our history as a tale of advance to democracy and self-government:

the loser is apparently the harbinger of the future, the man who in the long run proved to be right. Possibly we react this way because it is generally the "native" who is being trodden down. Or possibly both factors enter into the interpretation. Colombo's statement that "Mackenzie has a larger claim on the contemporary Canadian imagination than Canadians are inclined to give him credit for"[39] has a ring of truth. If English Canada needs heroes Mackenzie is ready and waiting.

The final element among the intangibles that have affected Mackenzie's place in Canadian history is the part played by his namesake and grandson, William Lyon Mackenzie King. What role did the prime minister play in sustaining his ancestor's reputation? That he saw himself as the vindicator of his grandfather certainly goes without question. Twenty years ago Ramsay Cook put this rather succinctly in a review. "W. L. M. King's whole career might well be seen as an exercise in clearing the name of William Lyon Mackenzie, the rebel leader of 1837."[40] In addition, it could also be argued that King made good use of his ancestor's reputation whenever it would advance his own ends. The steps he took would be a study in themselves, and involve some difficult questions, such as his exact role in the suppression of W.D. LeSueur's unfavourable biography, or the psychological significance of his naming a new federal building in Toronto the Mackenzie Building.

The Historical Writing

Such are some of the characteristics of the man that tend to be overlooked and some, at least, of the less tangible factors that have led him towards adulation. It remains to say something about the historiography behind Mackenzie's rise to prominence. It may be questioned if this is really necessary; Kenneth N. Windsor and William M. Kilbourn have provided us with an excellent examination of Canadian historiography which very clearly shows us the effect of the "onwards and upwards" or Whig interpretation of Canadian history on the reputations of Mackenzie and his contemporaries.[41]

What may still be done, however, is to examine two very important problems which fell outside the realms of those who have already surveyed this subject. The first of these is the question of the availability and readability of material on the subject of Mackenzie and the Rebellion. The story of the development of historical writing shows us what was written, but the influence of the various books on popular opinion is another issue. The second problem is the influence of a type of writing that falls outside the scope of the surveys already made: the textbook, the teachers' manual and supplementary school reading. In studying such material it is necessary to remember that what is negative is as important as what is positive: the bad press the Family Compact has received is indirectly a major boost to Mackenzie's reputation. The scope of this paper will hardly permit a detailed analysis of either of these problems; however, some relevant cases will be discussed.

The question of the comparative sales of Canadian history books and the extent to which they influenced public opinion cannot be answered with any certainty. Naturally, any figures on sales are difficult to obtain. Yet, to note the earliest histories, the ease with which Lindsey's 1862 *The Life of William Lyon Mackenzie* is still to be found, and the relatively low price it commands in the second-hand book market, indicates that it must have been a very popular work. Also, it has now been reprinted. J. C. Dent's *The Story of the Upper Canada Rebellion* (Toronto, 1885), which did not appear until the Lindsey work had dominated the field for twenty-three years, sells at double the price.[42] In addition, although Dent is generally seen as the first detractor of Mackenzie, he was hardly unsympathetic to the reform group.[43] If we look at his long influential *The Canadian Portrait Gallery* (4 vols. Toronto, 1880-81), copies of which are still quite numerous, we will find a biography that is far from unfavourable.[44] It closes with the comment that "among the names of those patriots who have manfully and conscientiously struggled for Canadian freedom, few deserve a higher place than that of William Lyon Mackenzie."[45] As for readability, it seems hardly likely that large numbers of people waded through the two heavy volumes of Dent's *Story*. The same may be said to an even greater extent about William Kingsford's *The History of Canada* (Toronto, 1887-98). Whatever their historiographic importance, the ten volumes in this set can hardly have been very popular reading. Thus it may be safely concluded that, on the subject of Mackenzie, Lindsey held the field until at least the end of the century.[46]

If we approach the problem from another angle, Mackenzie's reputation cannot have suffered from the almost complete neglect of his rivals. Although the *Dictionary of Canadian Biogra-*

phy has done much to fill the gap, this neglect has continued to this day: there are still no full biographies of Bidwell, LaFontaine or Maitland; Sir John Colborne was covered in an obscure work in 1903; Robert Baldwin had to wait until 1933; Sir Francis Bond Head until 1958; and William Warren Baldwin until 1969. Extended biographies of William Henry Draper, Robert Baldwin and some other pre-Confederation premiers appear in J.M.S. Careless' *The Pre-Confederation Premiers* (Toronto, 1980). Bishop John Strachan did have his biographer in 1870, his successor Bishop A. N. Bethune. Short modern biographies of Strachan are: J.L.H. Henderson, *John Strachan* (Toronto, 1969) and David Flint, *John Strachan: Pastor and Politician* (Toronto, 1971). Chief Justice Robinson's life was written by his son in 1904, and a modern biography *Sir John Beverley Robinson: Bone and Sinew of the Compact*, by Patrick Brode came out only in 1984. Finally Paul Romney's new *Mr Attorney* provides a strongly critical interpretation of Robinson at the same time that it gives a decidedly favourable picture of Mackenzie. The first overall attempt to sort out the personnel of the Family Compact came only with Allison Ewart's and Julia Jarvis's article in the *Canadian Historical Review* in 1926, which has still really not been followed up. The only contemporary of Mackenzie who has received profuse biographical attention is the Reverend Egerton Ryerson, and it is his work for the church and in education, not his rivalry with Mackenzie, that is stressed.[47]

The same problems of wide influence and circulation of pro-Mackenzie works, coupled with comparative obscurity for anti-Mackenzie studies, may be found in later historiography. The first attack on the Reformers in general, all agree, came with David B. Read's *The Upper Canadian Rebellion of 1837* (Toronto, 1896). Any adverse influence on Mackenzie's reputation that may have come from this work, however, was more than balanced by two pro-reform series that appeared in the early years of the century. The first of these was George N. Morang's "The Makers of Canada," which included the old Lindsey biography revised by Mackenzie's grandson, G. G. S. Lindsey (1860-1920), as *William Lyon Mackenzie*. By 1910 the series had sold 2,500 sets and become a basic reference in the public and school libraries. It still lurks as a standard source on student essays.[48]

At the same time that Lindsey was being re-issued, and the Tories ignored, Baldwin and LaFontaine, Mackenzie's rivals for the title of father of Responsible Government, were lumped together in a single volume by Stephen Leacock, with Sir Francis Hincks thrown in for good measure: *Baldwin, LaFontaine and Hincks*. When the series was revised in 1926, and the separate Lindsey volume finally dropped, Baldwin and La Fontaine suffered the ultimate indignity of having Mackenzie foisted on them and made first in precedence: *Mackenzie, Baldwin, LaFontaine and Hincks*.

As Kenneth Windsor has said, the "Makers of Canada" may well have been a great liberal achievement[49] but the "Chronicles of Canada" series, which followed in 1914, was just as important in carrying the Mackenzie banner. Although it lacked a biography of Mackenzie, W. S. Wallace's *The Family Compact* (Toronto, 1915) neatly and ably catalogued all the sins of that coterie. The "Chronicles" took its place in the library beside the "Makers," and both were approved for supplementary reading by the Ontario Department of Education.

For later works, the story has been much the same up to recent times. For instance, Aileen Dunham's *Political Unrest in Upper Canada, 1815-1836* (London, 1927), the first modern history of the early province's politics, was published in the far from popular — in fact, in Canada quite obscure — Imperial Studies Series; the unsold stock of this series which was blitzed in 1940. Conversely, Margaret Fairley's above-mentioned *Selected Writings of William Lyon Mackenzie* has also been approved for school reading.

The most important molders of public opinion, of course, are the school books: the texts, the supplementary readings and — in the background — the guides, instruction pamphlets and curricula for teachers. This is a topic which lacks extensive historiographic analysis, and is so vast that more than a few comments are precluded. For this reason it may be best to limit the scope of these remarks to a short discussion of school books in Ontario — partly because so many texts have originated there, and partly because the system in Ontario has been so controlled that a fairly exact analysis is possible. Textbooks in Ontario have been authorized from 1846, and, since 1888, *Circular 14, Textbooks* has been an annual publication of the Department of Education. It is thus possible to tell, without much difficulty, exactly which texts have been authorized for nineteenth-century Canadian history, a subject which has generally been concentrated in the senior years of public school.[50]

The first history text about Canada made its appearance in 1865 and from then until 1960, when the system became more liberalized, only thirteen Canadian history textbooks in all received the Department's imprimatur, some of them combining English history. The maximum number ever authorized at any one time was four (during the years 1904 to 1910). Supplementary books were also authorized under this circular; some of these have already been noted. Naturally, as time passed, the books approved came to be greatly influenced by the current "onwards and upwards" theories of history. The fact that the government of Ontario has been generally Tory since 1905 made little difference, for the Whig theories on our advance from colonial status had become a part of the accepted national folklore. Just as obviously, the authors needed heroes with whom the children could identify, and the younger the children the greater the need. The result was a certain Whig-Hero approach which formed a major theme in most texts and fitted in well with the Department's sometime stated purpose "history may be made, in several ways, an important factor in producing intelligent, patriotic citizens."[51]

Before examining a few samples of the texts, some comments should be made on the problems of these books and what could go wrong with them generally. With regard to the facts of Mackenzie's career, the old texts were usually not too bad, nor was their interpretation often as bad as one might fear. The real trouble began with the emphasis, which was totally misleading; it was here that the effect of Whig-Hero syndrome easily led to poor work. Another factor that militated against the productions of sound historical analysis was the necessity of pleasing the government. If the authority who will authorize the text has definite ideas, they have to be pandered to, or no listing on *Circular 14* and no royalties.

The earliest authorized texts were the *History of Canada and of Other Provinces in North America* (Montreal, 1866) by J. George Hodgins, Egerton Ryerson's deputy, which held sway from 1865 to 1877, and the *History of Canada* (Toronto, 1878) by J. Frith Jeffers, headmaster of the Peterborough Collegiate, which followed from 1879 to 1889. In these texts, Mackenzie and the struggle for Responsible Government took up little space; emphasis was still on General Brock and the survival of Upper Canada. As the years passed, however, the more colourful events leading up to the Rebellion began to have their effect and Mackenzie gradually received more emphasis. Most of the texts in the 1890-1910 era continued to focus on Ontario though an exception was *The Story of the Canadian People* (Toronto, 1905) by David M. Duncan of the Collegiate Institute, Winnipeg, which was one of the four authorized from 1904 to 1910. It has a more western slant.

George M. Wrong's *Canada, a Short History* (Toronto, 1921), the sole textbook from 1921 to 1928, is probably the best from the point of view of presenting a fair interpretation of the Compact and of Mackenzie. Wrong states that "there was virtue in the Family Compact"[52] and points out the good qualities of Strachan and Robinson. In his comparison of Bond Head and Mackenzie he is equally fair: "this half comic governor was confronted by a man now in a temper so frantic that his mind was unbalanced."[53] But by the 1920s new ideas were coming into education: a demand for fewer facts, more pictures, easier readability. The result was a change in the style of the texts, which was not for the best in spite of the great ability of some of the historians who wrote them. It is in this period that the Whigism of the "Makers" and "Chronicles" took full hold.

The successor to Wrong's text was W. Stewart Wallace's *A First Book of Canadian History* (Toronto, 1928), which held absolute sway from 1928 until 1950. Although unquestionably one of Canada's greatest historians, Wallace wrote in the era when the Whig-Hero interpretation of Canadian history reached its apogee and many of his chapters are studies of either individual or collective heroes. The group naturally included some who had been Tories in life but had now become absorbed into the Whig myth. Witness the chapter headings in the book's second part,

"British Canada before 1867":

VI   The United Empire Loyalists
VII   The Father of Upper Canada [Simcoe]
VIII   The Hero of Upper Canada [Brock]
IX   The Lords of the Lakes and the Forests [the Nor-Westers]
X   The Silver Chief [Selkirk]
XI   Some Pioneers of Upper Canada
XII   The Little Rebel [Mackenzie]
XIII   The Tribune of the People [Papineau]
XIV   The Lord High Commissioner [Durham]

Yet, in spite of this concentration on heroes and a tendency to wind the tale around incidents, the work is generally fairly balanced.

The successor to Wallace — George W. Brown, Eleanor Harman and Marsh Jeanneret, *The Story of Canada* (Toronto, 1950) — was authorized from 1951 to 1960, along with other less popular books, and long appeared as "supplementary reading." It was not an improvement. In fact, it is an example of how the facts can be correct and the interpretation acceptable (for instance, Mackenzie "was not the only person in Upper Canada who said that things needed setting right")[54] but yet the balance so poor that the student will remember nothing but Mackenzie. Of the nine pages devoted to Upper Canada, two discuss the structure of government, seven the career of Mackenzie. Later, first Papineau and then Howe are compared to Mackenzie, but not to each other. On one page there is a picture of Lord Elgin receiving Hincks, LaFontaine (misspelled) and Baldwin, who are shown as "Reform Leaders." This is the only place they appear in the text! [55]

At the same time the Ontario student was instructed by Margaret Avison's *History of Ontario* (Toronto, 1951), which was the first history of Ontario to be authorized in the province (1952-60). It is remarkable for exhibiting all the defects noted above. Factually, it is wretched: Mackenzie's press was thrown into the harbour, Baldwin was a member of the Family Compact, Mackenzie was mayor of Toronto in 1836. In interpretation it is equally a disaster, and with regard to balance, Bidwell is missing, but two pages are devoted to the legend of Bill Johnson, "the pioneer buccaneer of Upper Canada."[56] Fortunately for later history, Ontario must have given up at Confederation, which is where this work virtually ends.

From the above, one might almost get the impression that as time passed Ontario texts became less satisfactory historically, even if they improved in readability and appearance. This may not be an entirely wrong supposition; certainly there was been no great leap forward. With the present multiplicity of rapidly changing texts it is dangerous to make predictions; however, new interpretations seem to be emerging based on more recent writings. [57]

Before leaving the question of school instruction a short note should be made of another problem faced by the teachers of old: the school inspector. One of the great influences in the spread of the Mackenzie legend must have been James L. Hughes, brother of Sir Sam, who was inspector of the Toronto public schools from 1874 to 1913. He prepared a helpful little guide to teachers telling them how to interpret Canadian history. In discussing the Upper Canadian constitution, this guide refers to the "many grievous abuses" that were the fault of the Family Compact.[58] And for Mackenzie and Papineau: "time has proved their demands to have been reasonable."[59] A study of the effect of the biases of Hughes and some of his successors might well tell us much about the Mackenzie legend.

Conclusion

In conclusion, Aileen Dunham's statement that the Rebellion was basically the making of Mackenzie contains a great deal of truth. Also, he was fortunate in that his papers were preserved and he was so favourably presented to posterity by his son-in-law, Charles Lindsey, and his grandson, Mackenzie King.[60] That Mackenzie was very important cannot be denied; nevertheless, it is regrettable that so much of the research on this era has come to be focused on him personally rather than on his times in general. Certainly much remains to be done on his career before we will fully understand him, but equally a great deal needs to be done on Bidwell and the Baldwins, let alone the Tories. Whatever conclusions such research reaches, however, one fact appears to be certain: Mackenzie will remain the "Persistent Hero" in the popular mind; he and his Rebellion are just too colourful to be shunted aside. What is to be hoped is that with the improvements in teacher training and texts, a better balance can be achieved and his fellow Reformers and opponents given a corner of the stage. At the same time we must not go too far in downgrading Mackenzie's place in Canadian history. For one thing, he does indeed possess many of the characteristics of a genuine folk hero. For another, by leading a rebellion that undercut the influence of the radicals and removing both himself and others of them to a foreign land, he eased the way for the moderates to negotiate Responsible Government. That he will remain the darling of the left is inevitable — in Canadian history the left has very little to cherish. In any event, his remaining a hero is perhaps as it should be: very constitutional, generally peaceful, somewhat alcoholic and quite sexless history needs some Mackenzies to keep it alive in the classrooms. Mackenzie, after all, whatever we may think of his decided, or confused, or puritanical policies, provides us with some of the best fun in Canadian history.[61]

Isabel Mackenzie.

African Episcopal Methodist Church on Richmond Street, April 1913.

Part III: Types of Torontonians

While outsiders long regarded Toronto as the dullest city on God's earth, this characterization could have been applied with equal accuracy to many other Canadian cities. Toronto was not the liveliest city in the country; but most of those individuals who complained about its character, or lack of character, came from cities or the rural hinterlands of cities which seemed to be doing their best to emulate it in all respects. Torontonians, of course, were pictured as being as dull as their city: gloomy Victorians in their voluminous dark clothes heading off to church or a temperance meeting. Although many of them certainly exhibited these qualities, the tale of day-to-day activities in the city was often hardly a dull one.

The legislation that enforced some of the more unattractive features of Toronto's moribund Sundays was finalized only in the Lord's Day Act of 1906, just before World War I — quite late in the city's history. Nineteenth-century Toronto, possibly excepting its closing decades, was usually a lively place. Why else would a Lord's Day Act have been needed? It is true that Toronto had its moral and temperance legislation, its sabbatarianism and its incessantly railing clergymen. Yet how far did the citizens of Toronto, like those of most other places, really pay attention to their moral monitors, except when they were forced to? Legislation may have inhibited the lower class from indulging in some of its favourite activities, but that does not mean that lower class people themselves agreed with the objectives of this legislation. The upper and upper-middle classes, for their part, were willing to see sports prohibited on Sundays provided such regulation did not affect their tennis clubs, boating on the harbour or golf courses. They had no objection to engaging a minister who dispensed hell fire, as long as he dispensed it against others. All in all, while the city certainly had its dull spots, it was generally far less regulated in the mid-nineteenth century than in the early and mid-twentieth.

Toronto, too, has always been seen as an ethnically homogeneous city, a great bastion of the Anglo-Saxon race; its currently much-stressed multiculturalism is a recent phenomenon. Yet viewing Toronto as simply an Anglo-Saxon city obscures the fact that its Anglo-Saxon fathers were, after all, a compound of

English, Scottish (both Highlanders and Lowlanders), some Welsh, many Anglo-Irish, and those relative newcomers, the southern Irish Catholics. These groups — partly because they came to the city *via* two distinct traditions, one British and the other American — more often saw eyeball to eyeball rather than eye to eye. And other races were present as well — Mennonite Germans, a small sprinkling of French-Canadians, Blacks, and, as the years went along, Jews and Italians. Toronto, in short, has always been a city of immigrants, and immigrants have provided a great deal of the force behind its advancement. They have brought a diversity of talents to the city, engaged in a wide range of enterprises while living there, and then sometimes gone on to a variety of achievements in other places.

The following five chapters examine some of the types of people who lived and worked in Toronto during the first century of the city's existence. The chapter on the Carfraes looks at a family that exemplified Toronto's early Scottish settlers, who were so closely inter-connected that the city's ruling oligarchy was at one time called the "Scotch Clique." It gives an idea of the range of activities pursued by Toronto's Scots and the scope of their contribution to their adopted city. The Carfraes show how it was possible for those who started well down in the social structure during the city's first years to build a comfortable place for themselves and grow relatively rich in their new home. Since they also demonstrate how the Family Compact awarded its supporters, their careers help explain that group's long hold on power.

In contrast, the study of the Toronto Black community examines the size, distribution and working conditions of another ethnic group half a century later — but this time one composed not of the well-connected but of refugees from slavery. The Blacks had few opportunities to advance themselves, though a small number became relatively prosperous.

The other chapters look at three very diverse individuals and their activities in the growing town. Hugh Richardson was an English veteran of the Napoleonic Wars who later became a lake captain and helped inaugurate Toronto's steamship era, as well as improve its harbour and water communications. William Hay was another Scottish immigrant, and his rather brief career as an architect in the city was but one step in a saga that wound through many places in North America before he returned home. Finally, there is Andrew Mercer, whose ethnic origins, like much else about his career, remains a mystery. In life something of a recluse, he was to become famous because of a contest over his estate, for by failing to write a will he became an accidental benefactor of his city.

The Scottish Immigrant, The Family Compact, and Vertical Mobility: The rise of the Carfrae Family[1]

The Family Compact, which ran the affairs of Upper Canada in its formative years, has more often been the subject of castigation than rational examination. Even today there is a lack of comprehensive biographical material on such leading members as Bishop John Strachan and Chief Justice Sir John Beverley Robinson.[2] Further, apart from entries in the *Dictionary of Canadian Biography*, there have been few examinations of the lives and activities of its many minor members and adherents, men who sincerely believed that the British connection was the best for the colony, who provided the local support for the Compact across the province, and who, hardly surprisingly, were the recipients of the many government perquisites which were available. It is this group, working just as actively as the better-known reformers, who were at least in part responsible for the remarkable Tory record in the thirteen Upper Canadian elections: 10 clear victories, one minority government and two defeats. Their thirty-six uninterrupted years in power from 1792 to 1828 beats the Ontario Liberals' thirty-four-year hold on power from 1871 to 1905, and comes near the Conservatives' forty-two-year term in office from 1943 to 1985. Whether one agrees with their policies or not, the Family Compact represents a faction in early Canadian politics that merits further attention.

One family that provides two admirable examples of hard-working Compact supporters is the Carfraes of Toronto, whose period of activity practically paralleled the life of the Province of Upper Canada — the first Carfrae arrived with Lieutenant-Governor John Graves Simcoe's Queen's Rangers in 1793, and the last important Toronto male member of the family died in 1841, the year Upper Canada was united with Lower Canada to form a new political unit. Coming originally from Edinburgh, or its seaport Leith, the Carfraes are also typical of the Scottish Tory merchants who played such a large part in the development of Toronto in its early days, organizing municipal activities, undertaking public duties, and at the same time building up solid family fortunes as the town increased in size and wealth.[3]

Two members of the family were particularly prominent — Hugh Carfrae (1771-1839), and his nephew Thomas Carfrae Jr (1796-1841). Hugh, born at Leith on Oct. 22, 1771 to James Carfrae, a nailmaker, and Janet, his wife, whose maiden name was also Carfrae, was the first member of the family to immigrate to Upper Canada, arriving about 1791. His career could have been cited by William Lyon Mackenzie as a superb exemplification of the number of minor posts the Family Compact had available for its supporters: he held over half a dozen different offices at the local or provincial levels, and frequently supplemented his income with small government contracts. A former soldier of the 19th Regiment, Hugh enlisted in the Queen's Rangers on Feb. 25, 1792 as a sergeant and remained in service about two-and-a-half years. He was active in the Queen's Rangers Masonic Lodge, which flourished in York (Toronto) from 1793 to 1799.[4]

The next evidence of Hugh's activities comes on Feb. 28, 1805, when an entry in the *Journal of the House of Assembly* confirmed his position as messenger and firelighter for the House. Service with the Compact offered many opportunities for pluralism, and in April, two months after his confirmation as firelighter, the Court of Quarter Sessions of the Home District appointed him to the high constableship. The court, which also served as the supervising body of the Town of York, consisted of appointed magistrates, or justices of the peace. These magistrates were usually local merchants (many of them Scottish), or connections of leading Compact families.[5]

Hugh held the position of high constable for a year only, and then after the lapse of a year he was appointed gaoler for the Home District, a post he held until 1811. These duties left time for other outside contracting activities. When a fence was needed around the gaol in October 1809 it was Hugh Carfrae who submitted the lowest tender, offering to do the job at a rate of one shilling, ten-and-a-half pence Halifax currency per picket: "each piket to be squared & joined close together and to be placed four feet in the Ground." The Home District provided nails and spikes as well as banding for strengthening the pickets. Carfrae's charge for this job was the considerable sum of £60.15.0. In

September 1810, when it became necessary to erect a pound to contain stray animals, he again submitted the winning tender, agreeing to build a fifty square foot pound opposite the gaol composed of pointed pickets six feet high, for one shilling Halifax per picket. He also agreed to do the work that fall, but would to wait until April for payment, which was to be made with interest.[6]

Possibly these and other extra-curricular duties kept Hugh too busy, for in May 1810 D'Arcy Boulton, the pathmaster or road commissioner for the Town of York, summoned him and several others before the magistrates of the Quarter Sessions for failing to perform the statutory road work required of all citizens in 1809. He protested that he had been called upon to make a financial contribution in commutation, not do actual work, but was sentenced to six days work on the roads, it being specified that this work was to be done on the road leading to the Grange (now part of the Art Gallery of Ontario), Boulton's own house. This entranceway crossed a creek in the new part of town and was presumably waterlogged. Obviously, Hugh's skill as a contractor was well appreciated.

There is little information about his personal life at this period. He had married by 1807 for there is an entry in St James's Church Registers of Hugh and Anne Carfrae appearing as sponsors at a baptism in April of that year. Also, he retained his interest in freemasonry and was present at the opening of the Toronto Lodge in January 1811. In that year he was still receiving his allowance as messenger to the House, but by the next year he had moved on to the more exalted position of doorkeeper and messenger to the Executive Council and doorkeeper to the Legislative Council, again at a stipend of £20 per annum. The position was something of an honour granted to a trusted servant, which would explain why he continued to hold it for the rest of his life when it was not financially necessary for him to do so.[7]

Shortly after these appointments Hugh received another new position with the district government, the minutes of the Quarter Sessions on Feb. 13, 1813 stating

> Mr. Hugh Carfrae appointed by the Chairman,
> and other Magistrates of the Town of York on
> 10th January last as Levying Constable of the

> Quakers, Meninists, & Junkers [sic] Fines etc
> approved of this day in Court, and ordered that
> he be allowed the sum of 12s/6d Pro: currency
> over and above the allowances upon Execution
> on such, upon each Execution so Levied ....

The fines were those imposed upon members of religious groups who refused to undertake militia service. Carfrae also managed to hold yet another position with the provincial government, the *Journal of the Legislative Assembly* for Nov. 17, 1818 noting a payment a £5 to him as messenger to the land commissioners. How long he continued in these posts is not certain, but soon after he also became pathmaster of the Town of York, an appointment he probably held from 1823 to 1830. During these years he was still making extra money from contracting work, for when the town well was constructed in 1823 Pathmaster Carfrae was paid £5.2.4 for putting the flagging around the pump "logs, stone, and workmanship."[8]

Meanwhile, as is the case with so many immigrant families, Hugh's success had attracted two of his brothers, Thomas and John, to York. They became merchants, a potentially very lucrative occupation in the growing community. There is little to record of John, who upon his death in 1824 left a young family which Hugh took under his wing; and there is little more to say about Thomas Sr, who was born in Leith on Feb. 14, 1766 and may have operated a mercantile business in North Leith. Arriving from Edinburgh with his wife, Janet, a son, Thomas Jr, and three daughters, Thomas Sr opened a general store on King Street in 1805 which he operated successfully until his retirement from business in April 1832, his store, located on King Street next to the *Gazette* Office, being taken over by one William Russell in June. The Thomas Carfrae family resided at the corner of Richmond Hospital and York Streets.

Thomas died on Sept. 3, 1834 at the age of sixty-eight, Janet having predeceased him on Aug. 12, 1832, aged seventy-one.[9] His will, written in July 1832, was witnessed by Robert Baldwin, and two other attorneys, John Powell and John Elliott. The executors of his considerable estate were his daughter Johanna Patterson and James Lesslie of Lesslie & Sons, a leading firm of booksellers and druggists. In view of the Carfraes' later Toryism, the political affiliation of the group is interesting, for

Baldwin and Lesslie were certainly reformers, the latter being the great patron of William Lyon Mackenzie, while Powell was a Tory and the grandson of a former chief justice. The picture of a thoroughly politicized Toronto, which arises from the constant activities of Mackenzie, some other reformers and their opponents, obviously did not apply in all quarters. The bulk of the estate was divided into shares, eight going to Johanna, four-and-a-half to another daughter, Mary Berman, and three-and-a-half to Thomas Jr.[10] On the evidence it would seem that Thomas Sr's career, while not a colourful one, was apparently quite successful.

Thomas Carfrae Jr born in North Leith on Nov. 29, 1796, trained as a general merchant under his father, but, thanks to the profits from his father's business and a store he operated himself, he was wealthy enough to be able to devote his life to the far more interesting pursuit of politics. If uncle Hugh's career illustrates the number of minor offices in the gift of the Compact, that of Thomas illustrates both the type of Tory politician who was now appearing to back the Family Compact, and also the undeveloped state of the town and the number of organizations and institutions it was possible for one man to help establish. Like his uncle, Thomas was early interested in freemasonry and in 1825 helped establish the shortlived St George's Lodge, of which he was elected first junior warden. He held the offices of worshipful master in 1826 and 1827, and senior warden in 1829. On April 9, 1826 he married Margaret Jane Brooks, the service taking place in St James's with Archdeacon John Strachan officiating. Thomas Jr and Margaret were to be very unfortunate in their family. They had at least a dozen children; but only four daughters lived more than a few days, and of these Anne Jane died in the cholera epidemic in 1832, aged eight, and Mary died suddenly in 1835, aged five.[11]

It was around the time of his marriage that Thomas Jr first rose to civic prominence. There was no cemetery in the town where services could be conducted by denominations other than the Church of England and the Roman Catholic Church, and Carfrae became a leading figure in the movement to establish a non-sectarian burying ground. In the autumn of 1825 he led a group who petitioned the legislature for an act to enable them to establish a cemetery by private subscription. The act was duly passed on Jan. 30, 1826, and Thomas became one of the five trustees appointed for life to administer the new cemetery, the others being Peter Paterson, John Ewart, Dr Thomas D. Morrison and Thomas Helliwell. The group is again interesting since, other than Carfrae, they were basically reformers in political outlook — a possible indication of some link between political outlook and religious non-conformity. Also, it provides further evidence that political factionalism was then still not the dominant factor in daily life. Their new organization was first called "the York General Burying Ground", then the Toronto General Burying Grounds and is now the Toronto Trust Cemeteries. The trustees purchased a six-acre tract of land from Mary Elmsley for £75 on May 22, 1826. Situated on the northwest corner of Yonge and Bloor streets, it became known as Potter's Field, and was used for burials until 1855 when interments ceased owing to the growth of the Village of Yorkville. Those buried there were gradually reinterred, mostly in Necropolis Cemetery, and the land was sold off in 1876-78. Sadly, the first burial there, on July 18, 1826 was an infant daughter of Thomas, and five of the first ten interments were members of his immediate family.[12]

In 1826 Carfrae was also instrumental in the formation of the first Fire Department, which replaced the bucket brigades that had been used up to that time. The firemen, who were volunteers, were generally younger members of the most respectable merchant and tradesmen families of the town. Carfrae, as the organizer of the department, became its first chief, a position he held for six years. The first fire engine, called the "York," was a handpumper of the goose-neck type which was operated by eight men on each side pumping on a bar, or break, which ran along the side of the engine. It could throw a 5/8- to 3/4-inch stream of water about 140 feet. From 1827 on, it was kept in the first Fire Hall erected on the west side of Church Street between Adelaide and Court streets.[13]

Fire fighting was a lively affair in those times, as an account of a major blaze at the Mansion House hotel on September 27, 1827 shows:

> About half past one o'clock, on Thursday morning, we were aroused by the cry of Fire, and the ringing of the alarm bell. We used all expedition in hastening to the conflagration. Upon arriving at the Market square, we perceived the Mansion-

house Hotel on fire, illuminating the country for miles around; and the destructive element proceeding from it, enveloping the adjoining dwellings! Captain Carfrae and his gallant corps of Fire eaters appeared on the ground in a few minutes. From their cool, steady and bold appearance, a stranger would have thought, that, instead of issuing from their beds, they had sat up all night to be prepared for the awful contest. They were fully equipped, and wanted only a supply of water to enable them to commence operations. This great ally ... was not to be had — the pumps and well containing nothing but air; and we regret to state, that nearly half an hour was consummed, before the spectators arranged themselves in proper order, so as to furnish a supply of water from the bay. The fire-eaters did not remain idle — they judiciously commenced an attack upon two houses, & swept them from the range of the fire. During the time this bold achievement was accomplishing our worthy Judge Macaulay, Colonel Allen, Dr. Widmer, D. A. Gen. Greig, Lt. McNab, Major Warff, Mr. M. Meighen, & W. L. McKenzie, formed, by their great exertions & good example, a line of Bucketmen, extending from King Street to the bay: but the fire had taken so deep a hold on four dwellings before a supply of water was procured, that any attempt to save them would be in vain! Therefore, the company commenced playing their powerful engines on the neighbouring houses, the whole of which, owing to the intrepidity of the fire-men, escaped destruction. Mr. [John Spread] Baldwin's beautiful observatory, corner of King street, was twice on fire; but its value to the town as an ornament, and a feeling of gratitude for the numerous favours conferred on the inhabitants by the liberal owner, saved it from destruction! [14]

As this excerpt shows, Toronto's fire protection, even with a fire department, was far from satisfactory. The water problem could be solved, to an extent, by using the public water carters who, with their large barrels or puncheons mounted on carts, provided much of the city's water supply; but the carters could hardly be expected to attend fires and bring water without pay. Finally, in 1831, arrangements were made whereby the Home District and the Alliance Insurance Company — which was the main company operating in the city and of course an equally interested party — agreed to divide the costs of paying carters who attended at fires. Carfrae then published a notice:

> TO CARTERS!
> A PREMIUM of One Pound Five Shillings will be given to the Carter who shall deliver the
> FIRST PUNCHEON OF
> Water to the Fire Engine — Fifteen Shillings to the Second — Seven Shillings and Sixpence to the third — Two Shillings and Sixpence each for thirteen more; and one Shilling Currency for every Puncheon of Water afterwards; these several sums to be paid by the Treasurer of the Home District, and the Agent of the Alliance Insurance Company, to the parties applying for same, on producing a certificate from the Captain of the Fire Company, or other Officer commanding the Fire Company, for the time being.
> THOS. CARFARE
> Captain Y.[ork] F.[ire] company York,
> 16th August, 1831.[15]

This established a system of water supply which was used for many years; even after the establishment of a water works in 1843, the inadequate supply provided by the hydrants had to be supplemented by the carters' services. The system of bonuses ensured the carters' attendance, but often the race over the rutted roads to gain the premium led to half the water splashing out of the puncheons. Then, too, there were frequent fist fights between carters who arrived in a photo finish. As well as the water shortage, there were perennial problems caused by a lack of cooperation on the part of the magistrates, and by the need for wardens to superintend at fires to see that property was protected and to prevent theft. In an attempt to solve these difficulties a public meeting was held on Aug. 10, 1831 and a committee set up to solicit inhabitants to act as wardens. [16]

Besides fighting fires, Carfrae showed an equal interest in prevention and control. In October 1831 he wrote to the newspapers recommending the system of a Mr Cadet Vaux to extinguish chimney fires, wherein small quantities of sulphur were burned in the fireplace and the resulting gas mixing with the air in the chimney prevented further combustion. By this time he had two fire companies under his command, but because of his health he decided to resign as chief. The reason, as he later explained in a letter to the press on Jan. 2, 1832, was "on account of several late rheumatic attacks with which I have been afflicted, and having been advised to expose myself to the night air as little as possible, I am under the necessity of resigning that honour which you were pleased to confer upon me for six successive years."[17]

In the late 1820s Carfrae had become involved in the problems of the Presbyterian Church in the city, and with his usual energy became a leader in the movement to found a new congregation which was to become the ancestor of the later St Andrew's Presbyterian congregations on both King Street and Jarvis Street. There had been a Presbyterian congregation in the town under the pastorship of the Reverend James Harris since about 1820 (the beginnings of Knox Church on Spadina Avenue). This congregation belonged to the United Synod of Upper Canada, which did not believe in state support of churches. Church of Scotland Presbyterians, who supported a state connection, frequently preferred to worship at St James's rather than be associated with an unestablished church. The split between the two types of Presbyterianism, however, was not complete, for some of the Kirk adherents were members of the Harris congregation prior to the founding of a Church of Scotland congregation. Hugh Carfrae, for example, married his second wife, Anne Lindsay, in Harris's church on Oct. 2, 1829.[18]

The originator of the move to start a new congregation was a wealthy merchant, William Morris of Perth, then a member of the House of Assembly for Lanark County and later a member of the Legislative Council. Under his impetus a meeting held on March 3, 1830 decided to build a church and call a minister. To supervise construction, a board of trustees was appointed which included both Hugh Carfrae and Thomas Carfrae Jr. This group was a typical cross-section of the type of men who ran the local affairs of the town under the Compact: Thomas Carfrae, Alexander Murray, James Newbigging, and James R. Smith, were prosperous merchants; Jacob Latham and John Ewart were builders, and Hugh Carfrae and Walter Rose were minor civil servants. They represented the rising middle class that was making its appearance in the city. Hugh gave £50 towards the construction, proof that his many activities had been quite profitable, for the total subscribed when operations began was only £750. Thomas became treasurer, and it was he who laid the foundation stone in late July. The fact that he was asked is illustrative of the unbounding energy he applied to all his projects. Construction was not completed until the next year, for even after the Reverend William Rintoul had become pastor and services had begun, Thomas Carfrae was still advertising for tenders for completion of the carpentry work.[19]

With construction completed, the new church's course of development was still far from smooth — quarrels between the trustees and the elders were to result in Rintoul's resignation in 1834. Beyond that there was a disagreement between those, led by the trustees, who supported the state connection — after all the very reason for building the church — and those led by William Lyon Mackenzie who opposed it. The contest came to a head over a new constitution, drawn up by Thomas, which was submitted to the congregation at a meeting in July 1834. There the Reform forces were defeated, and Mackenzie, claiming Carfrae had brought in Anglicans and a Catholic to vote in support of his cause, quit the church in disgust. Immediately after this success, on July 21, Carfrae resigned as treasurer, though he remained a member of the church for the rest of his life, sometimes serving on management committees.[20]

Thomas Carfrae next turned his interests to politics. Like many other Toronto Tories, he was thoroughly enraged by the unceasing attacks of Mackenzie and ready to fight back. On March 6, 1832 he was elected chairman of a meeting held to decide what measures should be taken; his friend George Gurnett of the *Courier* became secretary. To counteract Mackenzie's attacks, the meeting decided to prepare an address to the King "expressive of their disapprobation of, and their dissent from, the representations which certain persons in this colony are now making to his Majesty's Government regarding the political condition of this province, and to the disparagement of the Lieutenant Governor thereof."[21] Carfrae, Dr William Dunlop and James F. Smith were appointed a Special Committee to draft the address, and, together with Gurnett, were further appointed to a larger General Committee to receive the proposed address when it was completed. The special committee promptly drew up a declaration listing the advantages of living in the province, including "an almost entire exemption from taxation." The town was then divided into seven sections and canvassers nominated to take around the declaration for signatures. Carfrae, with John McDermot, canvassed the area north of King Street and west of Yonge Street.

This assembly would appear to have been entirely composed of Protestants, but next the Catholic Tories decided to hold a similar meeting of their own and George Gurnett, on behalf of the General Committee, invited them to join, stating "the members of the Roman Catholick Denominations who have called a meeting for a similar object with that of this meeting, be invited to Unite and cooperate with this Committee, should they deem it expedient to do so at their meeting." Between the Catholic Committee and the General Committee 1,618 names were collected which, they claimed, represented nine-tenths of the adult male inhabitants of the town. Mackenzie, naturally, said that the signatures had only been obtained by the use of strong-arm methods. The two committees met at the British Coffee House on March 22 and then proceeded to Government House where addresses were read to Colborne by Dr King for the Catholics, and by Carfrae for the General Committee. The declaration was then duly turned over to the lieutenant-governor to be forwarded to the king.

Meanwhile, Mackenzie's *Colonial Advocate* called for a public meeting on March 23, a meeting which both sides saw as a test of strength. When the day came the Tories quickly seized control, Carfrae read out a resolution favouring the declaration, it was quickly passed and the meeting adjourned. When Mackenzie and his followers attempted to vote their own resolutions, the cart in which they were standing was trundled off by a group of Tory rowdies and they were pelted with rotten eggs.

Delighted with this success, the Tories proceeded to set up another committee, again with Carfrae as chairman and Gurnett as secretary, and sent copies of the address to the various Tory bodies around the province so more signatures could be collected and more addresses forwarded to lieutenant-governor. They also put their organization on a more permanent basis, forming the British Constitutional Society by early April. Their stated purposes were:

> First — To promote, and support, by every lawful means in their power, an indissoluable union between this colony and the British European Empire from a thorough conviction that it is to this union that we owe our present unequalled prosperity, and our prospects of security and greatness. Second — To support the local government of this Colony, so long as it shall continue to exercise its power agreeably to the liberal spirit of our constitutional charter. Thirdly — To exert its energies upon all occasions, to counteract the efforts of any and every faction, which may now, or hereafter exist, whose principles and conduct, may be incompatible with the British form of Government, or dangerous to the peace, and true interests of the people of this Colony. [22]

The declaration included the constitution of the Society, which made membership open to all males over twenty-one, but limited the officers and management committee to persons who did not hold office with the provincial government. This last rule was not strictly enforced: Carfrae later held office while he also held a government appointment. Dunlop became president, and Carfrae was appointed one of the vice-presidents and a member of the executive or steering committee which ran affairs between the meetings and held the real power.

On September 13 the Society had the satisfaction of receiving, via Lieutenant-Governor Colborne, Colonial Secretary Viscount Goderich's reply to their address. It read:

> I have the honour of acknowledge the receipt of your dispatch inclosing an address to His Majesty from the Protestant inhabitants of the Town

of York, in the Province of Upper Canada, and having laid the same before the King, I have received his Majesty's commands to acquaint you that he derived much satisfaction on this proof of the loyalty and attachment of his faithful subjects in that Town.[23]

Politics was not Carfrae's sole interest. Like most of the town's middle class leaders, he was active in the many new societies that were developing in the rapidly expanding town. He had already been active on the Committee of the York (later Upper Canada) Bible Society in the 1820s and in March 1832 he attended the meeting which founded the Mechanics Institute, the ancestor of the present Toronto Public Library. The sponsors of the institute, who met under the presidency of Dr William Warren Baldwin, were Carfrae, Robert Baldwin, T. Parson, Bernard Turquand, James Lesslie and Gurnett — truly — as in the case of the Bible Society also — a cross-representation of the various political groups of the time. The subscription books for the new institute were kept at the stores of Carfrae, Lesslie and J. Cockshutt, and after it was launched Carfrae served as one of the committee members. In December 1832 Thomas also became a committee member of the newly formed Commercial News Room, which was established to provide newspapers and periodicals for the information of the merchants of the city. Simultaneously, he was also active in the militia, as captain of the lst East York Artillery Company, which, like the Fire Department, consisted of respectable young tradesman of the town. [24]

In April 1833, however, Carfrae failed to achieve one of his greatest ambitions when his name was not included in a new commission of seventeen magistrates for the Quarter Sessions of the Home District. In view of his undoubted services to the conservative cause this omission is rather hard to explain, unless it was connected with some disagreements that had occurred within the governing committee of the British Constitutional Society the year before. On April 10 George Gurnett's *Courier* editorialized on the new appointments, stating bluntly that "several of the gentlemen cannot, and many WILL not attend to the duties of the office —." The journal then noted that there were some obvious names missing, especially that of Thomas Carfrae, "a very old inhabitant of the town of York; independent

Thomas Carfrae, merchant, politician, and philanthropist.

in his circumstances, and patriotic in his principles." The editorial added that Carfrae's name had been on the proposed list and its omission "affords but little encouragement to others to imitate his useful and Patriotic example." After saying that the names of two or three respectable mechanics might have been included, it concluded,

> we will endeavour to put our neighbours in a little better humour by referring them to the gratifying fact that this document does not exhibit the name of a single Ryersonian Methodistical demagogue. This Executive has undoubtedly found out the folly of temporizing with this iniquitous band of Rebels, and everybody whose opinion is worth a straw, will rejoice in the circumstance.

How much this article was Gurnett, and how much Carfrae himself, is an open question. A newspaper clipping in Carfrae's Scrapbook at this period, presumably from the *Advocate*, attacks Gurnett violently and then states: "So much for the gross ignorance of the silly Editor of the Courier. But why should we lay the lash thus heavily upon this half reasoning animal, when it is notorious that he never moves nor thinks, but through his quondam crony Tom Carfrae!"

Certainly Carfrae was irritated: when immediately afterwards Colborne appointed him to the Board of Health he declined to accept. Apart from the fact that he felt such a minor post was an insult after being left off the list of magistrates, he knew from experience that serving on the board was a thankless task. Not only did it receive no backing — which had led to the joint resignation of the members the year before — but sanitary conditions in the city were terrible. The same issue of the *Courier* that noted his refusal to accept appointment cited the following example of the many problems requiring immediate attention: "In Teraulay Street [now Bay north of Queen] there are large stagnant pools of water, covered with decomposed vegetable matter, which already send forth most noxious and poisonous exhalations, and many other parts of town exhibit similar nuisances."[25]

In October 1833 Thomas retired from business only a year after his father, giving up his store which was situated on the south side of King Street between Jordan and Bay, wedged in between the Theatre Royal and the Black Swan Tavern. The retirement indicates that he was now in comfortable circumstances. It might also indicate that he was not interested in adapting to the changing business conditions of the period and wished to turn his energies elsewhere.[26]

With the incorporation of the Town of York as the City of Toronto in early 1834, many members of the British Constitutional Society, including Carfrae, involved themselves in municipal politics. The Act of Incorporation had divided the city into five wards, named after the four patron saints of the British Isles plus St Lawrence for Canada. Each ward elected two aldermen and two common councilmen; the former category required a higher financial qualification and aldermen automatically became magistrates for the city. The twenty members elected the mayor from among the ten aldermen.

Carfrae ran in St George's Ward, the area south of King Street and west of Yonge Street, which was to prove a real Tory fortress. At a ward meeting at the Black Swan Inn, with Francis Hincks acting as chairman, he was nominated for alderman along with George Ridout, while John Craig and George Gurnett were nominated for common councilmen. Carfrae was elected easily with forty votes; but Ridout received only two votes, with John Elmsley getting thirty-two. Craig was elected common councilman by thirty-three votes; but Gurnett tied with a Reformer at thirty-one votes each. Gurnett's election was decided only by the vote of the returning officer, a Tory appointed by the provincial government. Overall, the election was an embarrassing defeat for the Tories, who received eight seats to the Reformers' twelve. In spite of their efforts to elect as mayor the moderate Reformer Dr John Rolph, the Tories saw Mackenzie swept into the highest office.[27]

The first Council's course was a stormy one, its debates marked by political clashes and personal quarrels. Carfrae was a leading contestant in its discussions, often crossing swords with Mackenzie, yet in many cases supporting reform measures when he felt they were necessary. At the very first meeting he was elected to three of the select committees set up to organize the new administration: the committee to draft rules of order for the Council's proceedings; the committee to draft a code of bylaws for the city; and the committee for setting up the necessary offices for the city business. Later, when permanent standing committees were set up, he was naturally elected to the Committee on Fire and Water and also to the large committee for licensing "Houses of Entertainment, Beer Houses &c."[28]

From the citizen's point of view, this first Council was a failure. It failed to implement the improvements which the city badly needed and, to make matters worse, raised taxes. The Tories unanimously voted against the Reformers' tax increases, although they realized that increases were necessary, thus leaving their opponents in the position of being held entirely responsible for this unpopular measure. The next election, not surprisingly, was a landslide, the Tories winning fifteen of twenty seats. In 1835 Carfrae again headed the polls in St George's Ward with forty-six votes, but Gurnett, now his running-mate on the Tory aldermanic ticket, was defeated by Reformer Edward Wright forty-three to forty-two. Gurnett claimed that he was defeated because the election for St George's Ward was held in the Greenland Fishery Tavern, at the corner of Front and John streets, whose proprietor was the same Alderman Edward Wright! Elections at that time were usually held in taverns selected by majority vote by the out-going council, so Mackenzie's Reform majority had considerately arranged for their confrère Wright to hold his own election in his own tavern. As there were no regulations forcing the closing of the bar, election scenes were frequently quite lively. In the case of the 1835 polling at Wright's tavern, the Tory *Patriot* of Jan. 18, 1835 described the event:

> It was as notorious as it was disgraceful, that the bar was crowded with electors of the radical party the whole day, and they succeeded in getting several of those who had promised their vote to Mr. Gurnett — and some even who had been on the committee — to join them in their libations, and then actually forced them to the polls, so surrounded by radicals that they could scarcely be said to be free agents. Several votes were also MADE for the occasion and this is so palpable that a scrutiny must infallibly displace Mr. Wright.

The fact that not only Carfrae, but also the two Tory candidates for common councilmen, Craig and Alexander Rennie, were

Greenland Fishery Tavern, c. 1885.

elected at Wright's Tavern would seem to indicate that the radical power in the inn was not as overpowering as the *Patriot* made out. The election, however, was certainly open to question, and since the new Council — with its Tory majority — scrutinized the results of contested elections, Gurnett was, hardly surprisingly, given the seat. Carfrae could now have become the second mayor of Toronto had he so desired, but he declined the office and nominated Robert Baldwin Sullivan, who was promptly elected. In spite of his refusing the mayoralty he was very active on the Council, serving as chairman of the Fire and Water Committee, and as a member of the Board of Health and the Committee on Applications for Office.[29]

Before the year was out, however, a completely new phase opened in Carfrae's life. When George Savage, collector of customs for the port of Toronto, died on September 9, there was a flood of applications for his lucrative post, including that of Thomas Carfrae. Strangely, he did not receive the unanimous support of the Tory press, the *Patriot*, on September 18, backing one Archibald McDonell, who, the editor said, was a suitable person connected with mercantile affairs and "moreover he is one of that class of persons whose claims upon the Government are strong and peculiar being the son of a U.E. who nobly sacrificed fortune to allegiance." Fortunately, Lieutenant-Governor Colborne ignored the United Empire Loyalist claim and recognized Carfrae's more immediate services by appointing him to the post on the same day the *Patriot* editorial appeared. Thomas actively served out of the remainder of his term on the city council, but did not run again in 1836.[30]

His departure did not mark the end of Carfrae family representation on the Council since Hugh, now an old man by the standards of the period, was elected a common councilman for St Andrew's Ward in 1837, a position for which his name had been suggested as early as 1834. St Andrew's Ward, which occupied the area between King and Queen (Lot) Streets to the west of Yonge Street, had a larger number of voters than St George's; Hugh and the other conservative candidate received 114 and 115 votes respectively to their opponents' 52 each. He was re-elected in 1838. In 1837 and 1838 he served on the Fire and Water Committee, and in 1838 he was a member of the important Committee on Appointment to Office. Simultaneously, he was also a member of the Managing Committee of the British Constitutional Society.[31]

In the summer of 1838 Hugh's health began to fail and his attendance at the Council meetings, which had been exemplary in that age of absenteeism, ceased almost completely. Finally, on September 17, the Council passed a motion that "as Mr Carfrae is at present unable to attend to his public Duties Mr Craig be appointed to his stead on the Standing Committee on Fire and Water." The work of the Appointments' Committee being finished, no substitute was named there. During the autumn he attended only the two extraordinary meetings held to discuss the defence of the city in case of an anticipated post-Rebellion American raid, and the special meeting to arrange the elections for 1839.

The Council for 1838 had been elected for a two-year term with the idea that in future only one alderman and one common councilman would be elected annually in each ward instead of two. To implement this system in each ward, the alderman and councilman with the largest votes took the two-year term. The men who had received the lesser number of votes ran in 1839. In St Andrew's Ward both Hugh Carfrae and John Ritchey had received eighty-one votes for the post of common councilman, and Hugh's last appearance at a Council meeting, on December 3, was to vote that his colleague be continued in office the next year. Hugh did not run for council in 1839, and on July 15 of that year he died, aged sixty-nine, leaving Thomas and Robert Carfrae of London, Upper Canada, another nephew, as executors of his estate. He was buried in the cemetery beside St James's Cathedral, probably, in view of the fact that he was a Presbyterian, because of his long connection with the Executive Council of the Province.[32]

To return to Thomas, the collectorship of the port of Toronto at that period was far from being a sinecure. Not only was the port a busy one, but there were constant problems caused by the smuggling of goods from the United States and inadequate facilities for proper supervision. Further, the staff had to be constantly on the watch for deserters from the garrison attempting to flee south. Reporting on these conditions for the House of Assembly in 1839 Carfare stated:

> I do not consider the Revenue Laws are observed as they should be, nor do I think the evasions are in most cases detected. The want that is felt at this Port of a Wharf and storehouse, completely under

the direction of the Revenue Officers, is one cause of this. There is no control over the warfingers in the present system, and goods are frequently delivered without any authority from me; it is also found altogether impracticable to search packages of goods or baggage as strictly as should be done, in the public gaze, on the public wharves.[33]

Carfrae then noted that the main goods smuggled were those prohibited by imperial statute, such as tea and fish oils, and that the purchase of a cutter would be the best way to control offenders. Tea, which was a monopoly of the East India Company and legally sold only at auctions at Quebec, created the greatest problem. Carfrae said that "I should think there can not be less than 3000 chests of Tea annually brought into this Port alone". This statement was more or less verified by Mackenzie, who stated in his new newspaper the *Constitution* that "it is believed that at least one-third of the Teas sold in this city, and the neighbourhood is brought from the United States, contraband."[34]

Mackenzie, of course, loathed both the customs and Carfrae, who, unlike his predecessor, was very strict in the fulfillment of the duties of his office. There was quite probably a certain mutual personal animosity arising from Carfrae's activities with the British Constitutional Society, and the battles he and Mackenzie had fought on the City Council. This meant that both the customs and its keeper were regularly the subjects of Mackenzie's editorial barbs. Today these provide an invaluable source of information on the operations of the port in this period. One clipping in the Carfrae scrapbook, which almost certainly bears Mackenzie's style, reads:

> MORE CHEAP TEA!!! Since our last two fresh arrivals of Tea have come to hand per the Enterprise and Bull Frog; the owners of which vessels supposing that our active and sharp-eyed Excise Officer had got completely supplied last week, would not think of examining amongst Potatoes for TEA, though God knows there is a sufficiency of Potatoes and Sloe-leaves at present mixed up

with the greatest portion of the tea which is now selling in our City. Mr. Carfrae, having made himself perfectly acquainted with the effluvia of Tea, as well as Apples and Potatoes, on going a-board of the above mentioned vessels, immediately proceeded to turn over a quantity of Potatoes, and at once discovered lots of Hyson, Twankay, &c &c. &c. and as is usual in such cases, placed the Broad Arrow [indicating seizure] on each of the schooners; so that if Mr. Carfrae goes on at this rate for a week or two more he will have a very nice little fleet of his own, for the benefit of His Majesty.

The *Courier* for Jan. 16, 1836 noted that two Customs House sales were to be held; the first, on January 30, to consist of the schooner *Enterprise*, the cutter *Bull Frog* and *The Peacock*, another schooner of seventy-five tons burthen, as well as tow boats, chain, canvas and so on. The second sale, on February 1, was to consist of tea, clocks, crackers, "segars" and other smaller merchandise. Such sales were held periodically, and boats could be confiscated, not just when they were found to be carrying contraband, but also at any time within three years after if it could be proven that they had been engaged in smuggling. The collector also could confiscate the smuggled stock of merchants in town, which Carfrae had no hesitation in doing.[35]

Deserters were another recurring problem and, if Mackenzie can be believed, desertions were frequent. An example of Carfrae's involvement is given in the *Patriot* of Sept. 19, 1837: "Mr. Gurnett, the Mayor of the City, a few nights ago, with the assistance of Mr. Carfrae, the Collector of Customs, and some others, arrested two deserters from the Grenadier Company of the 24th Regiment, who had changed dress, and had taken passage in a schooner bound for the United States."

Dealing with smugglers and confiscating ships had its dangerous side; almost immediately after the arrest of these deserters Carfrae came close to being killed on two occasions. The first involved one Michael "Fisty" Masterson, the rather unpleasant ex-proprietor of the small schooner *Christina* which was used largely for smuggling, and had been confiscated by Carfrae.[36] Masterson, who had only one hand, the other having

Customs House, Front Street East.

been replaced by an iron hook, attempted to drown Carfrae on September 23. Three days later the *Patriot* described the incident as follows:

> A notorious ruffian, of the name of Masterson, whose boat Mr. Carfrae had lawfully seized for the non-payment of Lighthouse dues, suddenly seized him around the waist while standing on the wharf, and after a short struggle both went together over the wharf, but in falling, Mr. Carfrae retaining an admirable self possession dealt the scoundrel a blow which sundered him from his embrace, and drove him to a considerable distance from him; by this means he escaped a watery grave. He was encumbered with a heavy surtout, and a good weight of specie, in his pockets, and it was with difficulty he reached the wharf. Masterson is in gaol, to answer for his crime at the Assizes, when it is to be hoped he will be visited with the exempary punishment which ought ever to await resistance to lawful authority.

Not surprisingly, the *Constitution*'s description of the affair, the day after the *Patriot*'s account was less favourable:

> Mr. Carfrae, the collector of customs here, was trying a few days ago to enforce the harsh & cruel law levying enormous customs taxes at this port, when a one handed man pushed him over the wharf, The Collector hauled him in with him, and for a time they were in full communion with the cold water society. The parties went off to the Mayor, and we may easily guess how matters went there.

Masterson was duly tried before Chief Justice John Beverley Robinson in the Court of Oyer and Terminer, and found guilty. However, he escaped before he could be sentenced.

Two days after this unpleasant incident, on Monday, September 25, Carfrae and his assistant, a Mr Stewart, went down to the wharf at night to see whether any persons were attempting to land goods from the US without paying duties and taxes to Sir F. B. Head's government, and found several persons so employed, and also landing teas, and other articles which the Laws of the Treasury forbid us to buy in the United States however cheap. The worthy Collector and his assistant attempted to stop these proceedings and received a severe beating from the persons on the wharf, whose names are not known. They are both greatly hurt.[37]

Fortunately, both recovered rapidly. The attackers were never caught although Sir Francis proclaimed a £50 reward for information on the assault, as well as £25 to any of the offenders (excepting those who delivered the blows) for giving up his accomplices.[38]

In this case Mackenzie showed some sympathy, stating in the *Constitution* of September 27 that

We think that to pay to a government to enable it to subvert the constitution is illegal, and would consider ourselves justified in buying or using articles which had not paid a duty for this unlawful purpose; but Carfrae and Stewart have a very dangerous duty to perform, taking, as they do, a very different view of their moral obligations.

As well as disliking Carfrae, as a person and as a collector, Mackenzie believed that both he and Sir Francis Bond Head were using their power to make personal fortunes out of the customs confiscations. On November 29 he made Carfrae the subject of one of the remarkable pre-Rebellion editorials he was writing in the *Constitution*, any one of which should have shown the Tories that trouble was brewing. "If Mr. Carfrae pays for all he buys at Custom House Sales he and Sir Francis will do well enough after a while. He buys pistols, everything, going ahead of every body. If difficulty should happen, perhaps he had better keep out of the way." As it turned out, it was Mackenzie, not Carfrae, who would have been advised to keep out of the way. The latter had continued his militia activities and by 1837 was the major commanding the First Toronto Artillery Corps (later, the

Royal Provincial Artillery). Aside from parades, the corps only noteworthy activity prior to the Rebellion seems to have been the firing of a ceremonial twenty-one-gun salute in August 1835 when the government gave the city the newly built bridges across the forks of the Don River. On Dec. 7, 1837, however, when the loyal forces marched on Montgomery's Tavern to put down the Rebellion, they were accompanied by Major Carfrae with two field pieces under Captains Lackie and Stennett. On arrival these were ordered to the front and soon drove the rebels out of Montgomery's Tavern. Later, when Mackenzie occupied Navy Island, Carfrae and his Corps were ordered to the Niagara frontier.[39] Evidently Carfrae was somehow injured or took sick on this mission, for on Jan. 2, 1838 the *Patriot* noted that "Our readers will be gratified to learn that Major Thomas Carfrae is convalescent."

Carfrae was busy in many other fields, too. He was finally appointed a magistrate of the Quarter Sessions in 1837. He did not attend the meetings regularly, although he always appeared to support St Andrew's Church in a dispute it was having with the Home District authorities over land. On Sept. 17, 1838 the City Council, on the motion of George Gurnett, appointed him Harbour Master of Toronto, and set up a Select Committee to draw up regulations for this new post, as well as a scale of fees for the duties of the office. In addition to his official tasks, Carfrae continued his connection with the British Constitutional Society, being elected a vice-president in 1838 after some years out of office. He also helped form in 1836 the St Andrew's Society of Toronto, an organization originally intended to assist Scottish emigrants who might need aid. As collector and harbour master he acted as one of the stewards of the Toronto Regattas of 1839 and 1840.[40]

At this time he took his only lengthy trip away from Toronto since he had arrived as a boy about 1805. In October 1839 Govenor-General Sir John Colborne, who had been highly respected in the city while he was lieutenant-governor from 1828 to 1836, made his final departure from the British North American colonies. Both the City Council and the magistrates of the Home District moved addresses of respect, and Carfrae and Mayor John Powell were appointed deputies to deliver these to Colborne in Quebec City. The addresses were read to Colborne and his officers at Payne's Hotel immediately before he embarked. In his reply Colborne promised to encourage emigration to Upper Canada, and stated his opposition to the suggested removal of the government offices from Toronto with the planned union of Upper and Lower Canada. Then, at his request, Carfrae and Powell accompanied him on board his ship, the *Pique,* and were the last to bid him farewell.[41]

These innumerable activities must have presented a severe physical strain which cannot have been helped by the frequent, and equally strenuous, banquets a public figure was expected to attend. A typical example was a dinner held at the Freemason's Arms to celebrate the third anniversary of the defeat of the Rebellion, or as the *Patriot* of Dec. 11, 1840, described the occasion: "in commemoration of the Battle of Yonge St., to celebrate the overthrow of the Rebellion in Upper Canada, and in honour of SIR FRANCIS BOND HEAD." Major Carfrae was president of the feast, where, after an excellent dinner, there were ten regular and five volunteer toasts, each accompanied by singing and speeches. The toasts included the Queen, Sir Francis, his successor, Sir George Arthur, Lord Seaton (Colborne), the various regiments and finally "the memory of those who fell at the hands of the brigands during the late piratical incursions."

After leading such an active life Carfrae, aged forty-four, died suddenly on June 1, 1841, from what the vague medical terminology of the period described as "apoplexy." He was buried in Potter's Field on June 3. By his will, dated Nov. 9, 1836, he appointed Walter Rose, John Ewart, David Paterson and his wife, Margaret Jane, as joint executors of the estate. His wife was given the use of his movable property and real estate during her lifetime, and lived in the house at 34 Scott Street for the rest of her life, long after the area had become a commercial district, and was cut off from the lake by the railroad tracks. Margaret was one of the founders of the ladies' association of St Andrew's Church and played a part in helping to pull it back on its feet after many members were lost when the Presbyterians split over the Free Church question in the mid-1840s. She died on March 23, 1872 at the age of seventy-two.[42]

What do the careers of the Carfraes tell us of the life and politics of Toronto under the Family Compact? Certainly, they demonstrate the strength of the grassroots support the Tories enjoyed in the capital. They show how the Compact could reward its followers, and also prove that the followers could be men of considerable ability and often earned their rewards.

They tell us something, as well, of vertical mobility in early Toronto. The original upper class that arrived with Simcoe or came in the formative years immediately afterwards could stand at the top by just being there. They could watch the province and city grow around them and, almost passively, make their fortune in the process. Those, like the Carfraes, who stood on a lower rung of the social ladder, or who came later, might have to work harder but they could also achieve prominence in a burgeoning metropolitan centre. Lastly, the Carfraes' careers show something of the politization that came to permeate so many facets of life in early Toronto. In the 1820s we see Tories and Reformers and working together to found the various institutions needed in a growing centre. By the mid-1830s the growing politicization of the colony was frequently creating splits right through the fabric of the city, particularly when Mackenzie was involved.

Despite their contributions to their communities and the many elections they helped to win, the Carfraes and their contemporaries, who worked so hard for the Family Compact, have, more often than not, been written off as dinosaurs and consigned to oblivion. Yet it must be remembered that, when Hugh and Thomas Carfrae died, the Tory party in Toronto and Upper Canada was triumphant, Mackenzie a fugitive, and Sir Francis a hero. If the Carfraes could have seen how transient the victory of their conservative principles would prove to be, they would have been astounded and horrified.

The anti-Tory reaction which followed the Union of Upper and Lower Canada in 1841 has treated the Carfraes unfairly. Although the Carfraes were what Mackenzie called "placemen," they earned their places by hard work as well as party loyalty. Like many followers of the Family Compact — which unquestionably had its share of dunderheads — they were men of considerable abilities. Politically they were just as sincere as Mackenzie and the Reformers in feeling that their policies were the best for the country, and they fought just as hard for their principles as their Reformer rivals did for theirs. Their contributions to a developing city were substantial, and are reflected in institutions which still perform a public service today.

Chapter 9

Evolving Multiculturalism: Toronto's Black Community in the late 1840's[1]

Although a good number of early directories exist for Toronto and other centres of the province, it is surprising how little they have been used to reconstruct the activities of the communities they depict, particularly in the pre-Confederation period when other sources are so often unavailable. Admittedly, the directories have their drawbacks: they were issued at irregular intervals, they vary to quite an extent in the information they provide and the order in which they present it, and they are never as complete, or as accurate, as the reader would like. Still, they supply a wealth of information and are often our only source of data.

Toronto is fortunate in having quite a long series of directories beginning in 1833, although up to 1859 they only appeared at rather widely spaced intervals. For the middle years of the century they are particularly important since the breakdowns of the censuses of 1848 and of 1851 for the city have been lost and, aside from the more limited municipal assessment rolls, the directories provide our only detailed source for a study of Toronto between the censuses of 1842 and 1861. This was a crucial period in the development of the city. In the early 1840s Toronto quickly recovered from the transfer of the capital to first Kingston and then to Montreal, or possibly just discovered that it no longer needed to be the capital to flourish. Simultaneously the city absorbed annual hoards of immigrants from the old country, survived the typhus epidemic of 1847 as well as a cholera epidemic and the first Great Fire in 1849, and, finally, swung into a new period of expansion with the opening of the railways from 1853 to 1856. For the years immediately preceding the railway boom, two directories exist, those of 1846 and 1850; it is in them that we find the most complete picture of the mid-century city just before it entered a new economic phase: the era of the iron horse.

One of the many factors affecting the development of the city at this period was the increasing influx of escaped slaves from the United States, for there was a natural migration of these refugees to urban areas. There had, of course, been Blacks in the town from the earliest period, for some had come to Upper Canada as slaves of the loyalists. What this chapter will do is examine the 1846 and 1850 directories, to reconstruct the size, occupations and distribution of Toronto's Blacks just before the arrival of the railways. At the same time, it will demonstrate the values and limitations of these directories for historical research.[2]

An analysis of the Toronto's Black population is possible because these two directories employed the system of putting "(Coloured)" after the names of the Black inhabitants. This invidious distinction had not been used by the three earlier directories—for 1833, 1837 and 1842—and may, in itself, indicate that some prejudices were developing in the city as the size of the Black community grew. After 1850 no directory was published until 1856, and by that time the "(coloured)" was again omitted, possibly because of the influence of the local Anti-Slavery Society which had been formed in 1851. The notation did not appear again. It is thus only in the late 1840s that the directories can be used for an investigation of the Black population without the backing of other sources.[3]

Since they will provide the basis of this study, a word should be said about these two publications before examining the information that they provide. The *1846-47 Toronto City and Home District Directory*, which was published by George Brown of the *Globe*, was the first of many directories issued by that firm. Generally speaking, it is one of the better examples of that class of work for the period, well compiled and reasonably accurate in detail. Despite the fact that the book set a precedent in distinguishing the Black population as a separate group, the Brown family were strong supporters of the anti-slavery movement. When the Anti-Slavery Society of Canada was formed in Toronto both George Brown and his father, Peter Brown, were on its committee, and Thomas Henning, the secretary-treasurer of the *Globe*, became its corresponding secretary. The other directory, *The City of Toronto and County of York Directory for 1850-51*, was compiled by J. Armstrong and published by Henry Rowsell. The latter was one of the leading book and stationary dealers in the Toronto area, as well as being printer to the city corporation for many years. It is less reliable than that of the Browns, but does have one distinct advantage in that, unlike the *1846 Directory*, it lists several Black females who were householders or heads of families.[4]

The fact that these directories are neither as complete nor as accurate as those of today was not entirely the fault of the compilers, for, as Mrs Christiana MacKay stated in the preface to the *MacKay's Montreal Directory* for 1857-58: "It is with the utmost difficulty that anything like accuracy can be obtained among the working classes in the suburbs, the fear of taxation, &c., causing them to give wrong names, and in many instances to withhold them altogether"[5]. Her problem would have applied equally in the compilation of the contemporary Toronto directories, especially in the gathering of information on the Blacks in the city, many of whom would naturally not want their whereabouts publicized for fear that their former masters might cause difficulties. Also, as the Black population was so mobile, it would have been particularly difficult for the directories to obtain anything like comprehensiveness.[6]

One important problem that arises in the use of these books should be noted: that is the question of whether or not the compilers managed to place the designation "(Coloured)" after the names of all those who were Blacks. That they did not is evidenced by the fact that the *1846 Directory* lists thirteen men, who are shown as coloured in the *1850 Directory*, without the designation, and the *1850 Directory* lists seven men, who were shown as coloured in the previous work, as white. Presumably, some were incorrectly shown as white in both directories, but probably those designated as coloured were so in fact. Curiously enough, those shown as white in 1846 included some of the most prominent of the city's Black citizens: Thornton Blackburn, the first man to operate a cab in Toronto, Richard Gray, who owned a provision store on York Street, and James Mink, the proprietor of the Mansion House Inn and Livery Stable. In all there were ninety-three Black men listed in the *1846 Directory* (thirteen as white), and seventy listed in that of 1850 (seven as white), along with six women. The drop in numbers is almost certainly a comment on the accuracy of the two directories, not a diminution of the size of the community, for the flow of immigrants was increasing as the situation in the American South become more tense.

How do these figures compare with other estimates of the Black population in the late 1840s? As well as the nominal listings the directories contain overall censuses of the city, which include women and children who would not appear in the nominal listings. These censuses, however, lack any specific breakdown by race. The *1850 Directory* shows a figure of 726 for all American inhabitants of Toronto, but this cannot be taken as too useful a yardstick since it would include white Americans and exclude Blacks from the West Indies. Further, the figure appears to be rather low, which would fit in with the overall population estimates in this directory. Probably the most accurate surviving statistics are those taken for the interim Upper Canadian census in 1848. These show the Black population at 236 males and 280 females for an overall total of 516. The figure for men is two and a half times higher than the 93 shown in the *1846 Directory*, but when we consider that children would be included, and that there had probably been a slight population increase between 1846 and 1848, the directory figure would appear to represent a reasonable percentage of the adult males then resident in the city.[7]

Population totals, however, provide the least interesting information that can be extracted from the directories. Among the other facts that they present, one of the most significant is the picture of rapid population changeover in the Black community of the city. This changeover, which clearly demonstrates the problems that must have faced the emigrants in relocating in an alien environment, is especially striking when we consider that only the more settled portion of the city's Black population could have been listed in the directories and censuses. The mobility is not surprising, however, considering that many of the newcomers were untrained in occupations that would be useful in a northern city, and that they arrived in Upper Canada under the most adverse conditions. A few years after the period being examined, G. P. Ure, in his 1858 *Handbook of Toronto*, stated: "Many of these poor creatures reached our city in the greatest distress, their immediate wants had to be provided for while employment was obtained as far as possible for those who were able to labor."[8]

Comparing the two lists of inhabitants for 1846 and 1850 to establish the turnover in the group presents many minor problems. The directories, like most works of the period, were none too careful about first names or initials and street addresses usually do not include numbers. In a small city, though, it was not too likely that there would be two inhabitants of the same name, especially if it was not a common one: thus Wm. H. and W. W. Edwoods are surely the same man. Even making these likely combinations, however, and taking individuals listed as coloured in either directory as Blacks, the most startling point in dealing with the community is that of the 93 individuals listed in 1846 only 45 are to be found among the 70 men listed in 1850. Thus, over half the 1846 Black population is not shown as resident in Toronto a mere four years later. Admittedly, there were probably some omissions, but the rapid turnover is confirmed by checking the names back through the various directories to the first one, printed in 1833, and ahead to the *1859-60 Directory*. Of the total of 118 different males enumerated in the two directories, 30 appear only in that of 1846 and 18 only in that of 1850. If we work backwards the directories show just 4 of these listed as resident in Toronto as early as 1833, and another 8 as having arrived by 1837. If we work forwards past 1850, merely 22 of the 70 entries for that year appear as late as 1859.

That there were a few long-term inhabitants is shown by the fact that two of the four who appeared in 1833 were still living in Toronto in 1859: William H. Edwoods and William Hickman, both of whom were barbers. A third long-term Torontonian, Jarrad Banks, a hatter of York Street, must have died after 1847; his widow, Rachel, continued to live on York Street until 1850. Of course, a few of the more settled citizens may have been left off, but not too many could have been missed by several successive directories. One certain omission was Wilson R. Abbott, a native of Mobile, Alabama, who had moved to Toronto by the time of the Rebellion in 1837 but does not appear in records earlier than the *1846 Directory*.

The occupations present no surprises. As one would expect in such an uprooted population, with so few opportunities for training, most of the men did manual work. Breaking the group down into categories is difficult, because, while the *1846 Directory* listed unskilled workers as labourers, that of 1850 either tried to show much more specific occupations, or put in no listing at all. As a result, the first provides occupations for everyone, including thirty-two labourers, while the second shows only six labourers and has nine individuals with no occupation designated. Some of the categories it uses—such as whitewasher, bill sticker and carter—would not, however, call for much training.

In addition, there were several who would be called skilled workers, some of them in the building trade or working as cooks or waiters in hotels or on the boats. The main categories were:

		1846	1850
Construction:	Bricklayers	1	1
	Carpenters	4	4
	Plasterers	1	2
Skilled Tradesmen:	Blacksmiths	3	0
	Shoemakers	2	1
Service:	Barbers	7	8
	Cooks	7	7
	Waiters	3	6

Finally, there were a few storekeepers; the 1845 Directory lists four, that of 1850 five; these merchants included tobacconists, fishmongers and provision dealers. Almost the same figures, three for the first directory and four in the second, applied to innkeepers and restaurant owners. Some of the restaurants had very flowery names, often copied from other cities: Prince Albert Recess, Rescue Inn, Tontine Coffee House and Epicurean Recess. Most of these businesses seem to have been ephemeral. The only substantial Black owned operation was the Mansion House Inn, which, along with a livery stable, was operated by James Mink for many years. Many of the barbers may also have had their own businesses.

At the top of the social order would have been the ministers of the African Baptist and African Methodist chapels. The Reverend Washington Christian of the Baptist Chapel (founded 1826), who was a native of the West Indies, had lived in the city for many years before 1846. He died in 1850, and the directory lists the Reverend Rufus Derby as the Baptist minister. The Reverend James Harper was the Methodist minister in 1846, but no Methodist minister is listed in 1850, although by this time there may have been a second African Methodist congregation in the process of formation.[9]

One of the most interesting points about the Black community was its distribution in the city. The great refugee influx had hardly started to arrive by the late 1840s, but already the Blacks were concentrated in certain areas, generally those which were being developed for the new poor immigrants. To clarify their distribution, it is best to begin by outlining briefly the extent of the city at this period.

Toronto in the 1840s was still fairly small, with some eighty-five streets. The most important of these was Yonge Street, which ran north from the lake to divide the city into two halves. King Street was the main commercial thoroughfare, and Queen Street marked the northern limit of the heavily built-up region until the mid-1840s, when the area to the north up Yonge Street began to expand rapidly. In spite of its small size, the town naturally had many poor areas typical of a rather hurridly built frontier settlement; these were not grouped in one section, but tended to spread around the city and its suburbs. The eastern central part of the town around Lombard (Stanley) Street and the nearby parts of King Street East and Church streets had long been something of a slum, and even poorer shanty areas were to be found on both the western and the eastern outskirts. It was mainly in one of these, that in the far northwest, in which the Black population community was concentrated.

In locating the Black community complete accuracy is impossible as the directories contain only alphabetical entries; no street directory appeared between 1833 and 1856, and house numbers had not come into regular usage except on King Street. Thus, while we can tell what street an individual lived on, we cannot know exactly where that person lived on the street. Roads that crossed Yonge, however, were already designated as east or west, and so it is possible to say in which half of the city a person lived. Also, since the Cane Map (Sir Charles Bagot Plan) of 1842 and the Fleming 1851 map of the city show all the buildings, the growth of the city of Toronto can be charted fairly exactly and areas of dense population identified.

The *1846 Directory* is extremely helpful because it provides addresses for all but one of the individuals listed. The *1850 Directory*, unfortunately, not only lists fewer people but also is less exact in its addresses. As far as it goes, it confirms the facts derived from its predecessor of 1846. Because of the incomplete listings in this directory, it is not advisable to try to make a comparison of the two to attempt to show how the Black community had evolved during the four years which had lapsed.

However, a quite detailed picture of the community as it existed in 1846 can be constructed. The only major change in 1850 seems to be that a few Blacks were moving to the growing Yorkville suburb at Bloor and Yonge streets, a mile to the north.

The first noteworthy fact is that, in 1846, seventy-one of the ninety-three Blacks listed lived west of Yonge Street. Of the twenty-two resident in the east, four lived on Queen Street East and one on Victoria Street, possibly clustering around the African Baptist Church, which had been erected at the intersection of those two streets in 1840. Four others lived on Church Street, a generally poor area not very far away, and five lived on King Street East, the main business thoroughfare. Possibly these individuals and the King Street residents in the west resided at their business premises, for, as noted, many operated barber shops or small businesses. Except for Adelaide Street East, with three listings, no other road in the eastern half of the town had more than a single Black inhabitant.[10]

Within the western part of the city the Black population was to be found concentrated in certain areas. A few Blacks were scattered along the new streets that opened off Queen Street West in the far western reaches of the city, especially Spadina Avenue, and another seven lived on King Street West. The greater number by far, however, lived in the north-central section of western Toronto. This concentration began on York Street, where ten are shown, and adjacent Queen Street West, where another four lived, and spread up Chestnut (Sayer) and Elizabeth streets to an enclave about three blocks north of Queen, where forty-one of the ninety-three Blacks in the directory had their homes. The statistics for this northern area are worth presenting in table form, giving the less complete 1850 figures for comparison:

	No.of Blacks listed	
	1846	1850
North-south streets, running north from Queen west of Yonge.		
1st James	0	0
2nd Bay (Teraulay)	6	2
3rd Elizabeth	6	4
4th Chestnut (Sayer)	9	2
5th Centre	7	7

East-west streets, running west
from Yonge north of Queen.

1st Albert	0	1
2nd Dundas (Agnes)	6	3
3rd Edward	7	5
Totals	41	24

How can this population distribution be explained? Leaving out those Blacks connected with what might be called downtown businesses on King Street (twelve in all), nearly all the rest lived in two areas: one at York Street and the blocks to the north (fifty-five listed), the other around Church/Queen East/Victoria streets (nine listed). These areas do not correspond entirely to the less affluent sections of the city: some of the most thickly populated poorer areas, such as Lombard (Stanley) Street, had no Black inhabitants. Aside from business reasons, one obvious explanation is the location of the churches. We have already noted that a third of the Blacks in the east probably lived near the African Baptist Church, and the Black population on York Street, as well as two groups on Adelaide Street West, may have located for convenience near the African Methodist Church, which had been built on Richmond Street, just east of York Street, about 1833.[11]

Another reason for the distribution was the expansion pattern of the town. In the east, the area south of the African Baptist Church was a well-established neighbourhood by the time that structure was built in 1840, and expansion northwards from Richmond Street East was long blocked by two great estates. Thus, prior to 1850, there was little room for immigrants to establish themselves in this part of the eastern section of the city. In the western part, the story is quite different, for here the estates were being subdivided and the section of Toronto around York Street was not built up until after the African Methodist Church had located there in 1833. As a result, it would have been relatively easy for new settlers to move in around that church, and some did. The more open blocks to the west of York Street, however, were not as available for building as they seemed. Queen Street West was already becoming a major thoroughfare by 1840, though west of York Street much of the open area to its south remained unsettled until after 1850, because of the grounds around the suburban residences of wealthy citizens such as Chief Justice Sir John Beverley Robinson.

North of Queen Street there were better opportunities. Osgoode Hall and its lands blocked direct communication northwards west of York Street, and Macaulay Town occupied most of the area stretching east to Yonge Street; but between them Black refugees, who were looking for a location near their church, would find ready access up Chesnut and Elizabeth streets to the empty lands that were later to become known as "the Ward" (modern Chinatown). This section was just opening up at the time when the large Black influx began, and would have been little favoured by people with money because of its distance from the centre of commerce around the St. Lawrence Market and St James's Cathedral. Even the newer St Patrick's Market, which had been opened on Queen Street West in 1837, was located some distance westward near John Street. However, it is impossible, to estimate what percentage of the population was formed by the forty-four Blacks listed and their dependents; the maps show this section of the city as relatively thinly built up, yet the nominal list in the *1846 Directory* indicates that, like most poor areas, it must have been quite congested.

How long this Black concentration lasted in these few blocks is a question that cannot be answered from the directories, and awaits a complete investigation of the later censuses. It is probable that at least some of the Black immigrants of the 1850s continued to locate there. When the Second African Methodist Church was erected in the early 1850s Chesnut Street was chosen as the site. With the beginning of the American Civil War in 1861, however, the Black migration to Canada was over and with the end of that war a counter-exodus to the United States was to begin.[12]

Thus, the two directories give us a good deal of information on the state of the Black community in the city during a period of rapid change. The picture the directories present is one that hardly contains any surprises, but it fills an important gap in our knowledge of the Black population of the city. Also, it serves as an example of how useful the directories can be in the reconstruction of the appearance of the early towns of Canada and the way of life of their inhabitants. And, finally, it points out that, while the English and Scots held the reins of power Toronto was becoming a multicultural city long before Confederation.

Chapter 10

Captain Hugh Richardson and Toronto's Lake Communications[1]

Among the most colourful figures in the history of the Great Lakes are the early steamboat captains who first established a regular transportation network on Lake Ontario in the decade after the first steamer, the *Frontenac*, was launched in 1817. One of their number, Captain Hugh Richardson, an English immigrant, was long one of the most prominent figures in Toronto, first as an owner-captain from the mid-1820s until the mid-1840s, and then, for two decades before his death in 1870, as the first government-appointed harbour master of Toronto. His role in the evolution of the port was therefore a dual one—for he not only helped set up steamer communication on Lake Ontario, but also, for nearly half a century, played as great a part as anyone in both preserving and improving the harbour of Toronto. In regards his contributions were as significant as those of the railroad magnates who were simultaneously developing their transportation networks, for the harbour was of the utmost importance in establishing the city's position as the great metropolitan centre of the country.

Hugh Richardson was born in London, England, on June 12, 1784, the second son of Thomas Richardson, a merchant in the West Indies trade. Apparently two of Hugh's brothers, William and Richard, also came to Upper Canada, settling in or near present-day London, but another brother, Edward, remained in England. Since legal documents describe them all as "gentlemen," they seem to have possessed some property.[2] The first evidence we have of Hugh's activities dates from 1798, when, at the age of fourteen, he went to sea where he served with distinction in the Napoleonic Wars until 1810. In that year Hugh and one of his brothers were captured by the French and imprisoned, first at Verdun, then at Arras and finally at Paris. With the abysmal record-keeping system of the period, and the intermixing of prisoners of war, debtors and criminals in the same prison, he was not released until 1818, three years after the

Napoleonic Wars were over. Even then he was lucky; some prisoners of war were to remain in French jails until 1821.

Returning to England, he married almost immediately, but was evidently unable to find satisfactory employment. In the spring of 1821, he and his wife, Frances, immigrated with the eldest children of what was to be a large family, settling in the Town of York. Shortly after his arrival he joined the militia and in March 1823 was commissioned captain of the 2nd East York Regiment. The regimental commander was Attorney General John Beverley Robinson, who became his friend and patron. By the mid 1820s he was commending his own ship. He was appointed a coroner for the Niagara District in 1824, and in 1828 and 1830 he received similar appointments for the Newcastle and Home districts, the three together covering much of the Canadian shore of Lake Ontario west of Prince Edward County. One of his more dolorous tasks as coroner was attending to drowned bodies.

Richardson may first have been involved with the building of the *Queenston* in 1825; if so, his active interest was brief, for in 1825-26 he was instrumental in forming the syndicate which built the steamer *Canada*. Constructed at Joseph Dennis's yards on the Rouge River, the *Canada* was a 127-foot wooden ship of 250 tons, with engines built at Hess Ward's Eagle Foundry in Montreal. With Richardson as captain, the *Canada* made her maiden voyage from York to Niagara on Aug. 7, 1826.

No sooner was the ship completed than some of the stockholders attempted to oust Richardson as captain. In 1827 he was forced to make a trip to England to borrow funds to buy them out, his main supporter there being a Mr Bellamy, possibly a brother-in-law, who loaned him £1,000. In Upper Canada he was also assisted by Robinson and Dr Christopher Widmer, the father of surgery in Ontario. Richardson thus gained control and was able to designate himself as "managing-owner." He continued to purchase shares whenever possible during the following years until he had a total of 112, which apparently gave him complete control, although we do not know the capitalization. The result, however, was that he had borrowed too deeply to be able to make a profit. In 1832, when the net profits reached a new high of £1,946.11.1, he reported to Robinson that "sink I often think I shall—founder in the midst of a mine of gold, with a millstone about my neck." By that date he had paid back some £1,040 interest and £300 principal.[3]

Captain Hugh Richardson.

Meanwhile, the *Canada* had settled down to a regular run between York and Niagara (Niagara-on-the-Lake), leaving the former at 7 a.m. and returning from Niagara at 1 p.m. As well as carrying passengers and cargo the *Canada* became one of the first regular mail ships in 1830-31, but Richardson did not renew the contract the next year. The *Canada* also had some adventures, for in 1831 Richardson received a civic testimonial for rescuing the crew of the brig *Prescott*. His activities as captain apparently occupied so much of his time that he was unable to continue as an officer of the militia. When he was promoted to major in May 1830, he expressed a wish to resign from the active militia, and in July 1831 he was transferred to the reserve list. By that time he had commanded the 1st, 2nd and 3rd companies of the 2nd East York Militia Regiment. That he had achieved a certain financial success in the community by the early 1830s is shown by the fact that he was then sending his sons to prestigious Upper Canada College and had a home on Front Street, overlooking the harbour, near that of Church of England Archdeacon (later Bishop) John Strachan. When a collection was taken up in 1835 to present that gentleman with a piece of plate, Richardson was a subscriber.

Naturally, as a lake captain, Richardson took a great interest in the state of the ports at which he touched. In 1830 he suggested building a wet dock on the flat river bank near Fort George at Niagara. This suggestion was one of the factors leading to the foundation of the Niagara Harbour and Dock Company.one of the leading ship-building firms on the lake. At Toronto he displayed great civic consciousness in effecting improvements in the harbour at his own expense. From the time he began sailing the *Canada* until the new city government took over a decade later in 1837, he buoyed and beaconed the harbour. He also kept an entrance light at the Western Gap near old Fort York for some years, until the provincial government provided a lighthouse at the new Garrison Wharf about 1833. Finally, Richardson placed notices in the paper giving warning of dangerous rocks.[4]

To circulate his ideas on waterfront improvement, in 1833 he published a pamphlet entitled *York Harbour* advocating several changes, including the creation of an eastern entrance to the harbour (today the Eastern Gap), and the narrowing of the Western Gap, then the only entrance. That year the province voted £2,000 to build a 700-foot pier at the Western Gap, extending out from the garrison (Fort York). Richardson was one of the three commissioners appointed to superintend the work, sitting with William Chisholm and the surveyor James Grant Chewett. Four years later, when another £1,500 was provided for wharf and lighthouse improvements, Richardson and Mayor George Gurnett were the active commissioners. As usual, costs exceeded estimates, running to £2,375, and they were forced to ask for another £1,000 in 1838. In the same year they recommended that Collector of Customs Thomas Carfrae Jr be appointed harbour master of Toronto. The province did not act at that time, but the city did appoint Carfrae to serve as harbour master for the municipal government. The growing confidence of the provincial government in Richardson is shown by the fact that he was appointed one of the justices of the peace for the Home District in September 1837.[5]

In 1835 Richardson had decided to expand his operations and had purchased the steamer *Constitution*, built at Oakville about 1832, which he renamed the *Transit*. The new acquisition was first put on a semi-weekly Toronto-Port Hope-Cobourg-Rochester circuit in 1835. The next year Richardson sold the *Canada* to some Rochester merchants for £1,400, and they placed her on an Oswego-Kingston itinerary. In 1837 she ran ashore near Oswego and subsequently was broken up. Meanwhile, in 1836 Richardson was operating the *Transit* on the *Canada*'s old Toronto-Niagara-Lewiston route, which he extended to Queenston the next year.[6]

While Richardson was concentrating his attention on his ships and harbour improvements, the political state of the colony was taking an unexpected turn for the worse. The combination of the depression of 1837, the rising unrest in Lower Canada, the existence of some political and economic grievances in Upper Canada, and, above all, the dubious competence of the lieutenant- governor, Sir Francis Bond Head, gave the radicals under William Lyon Mackenzie their opportunity. In early December 1837, Toronto found itself in the throes of a full-scale, albeit comic- opera, rebellion. As a good Tory and supporter of the Church of England, Richardson naturally stood behind the government.

When news of the insurrection burst suddenly on the city on the night of December 4-5, with the frightening possibility that it might fall to the rebels, the *Transit* was one of two ships in the harbour. At Strachan's suggestion the women and children of some of the prominent Tory families, including Lady Head and the Robinsons, together with plate and valuables, were rushed aboard until the danger was over. Later Richardson sailed to Niagara to warn that town. When the fiasco was over he was thanked by Head, and at the end of the next year, when there were attempted invasions at Prescott and Windsor, he was commissioned one of the special magistrates, with powers extending to all the districts of the province.

With the return of peaceful conditions on the frontier Richardson purchased the *Queen Victoria* from James Lockhart of the Niagara Harbour and Dock Company, for £7,000. The funds were loaned by Samuel Street of Chippawa, who was possibly the largest landowner and mortgage holder in the province. Built in 1838 at Niagara, the *Queen Victoria* had operated as a competitor to his *Transit*. Probably Richardson wanted to monopolize the business, especially as the rapidly increasing population and trade at the west end of the lake made expansion of his operations seem feasible. The *Queen Victoria* was placed under the command of his son Hugh Richardson Jr, assisted by younger sons Charles and Henry; she plied from Toronto to Lewiston, New York, and back.[7]

Richardson next had the *Chief Justice Robinson*, a wooden 160-foot, 272-ton, vertical beam steamer, built at the Niagara Harbour and Dock Company in 1841-42. This ship had a snout-like prow designed as an icebreaker, which enabled Richardson to carry on winter service between Toronto and Niagara, though she could not enter the Toronto harbour proper. The *Chief Justice Robinson* joined the *Queen Victoria* and the *Transit* on the Toronto/ Head-of-the-Lake/Niagara River Circuit.[8] Although the finances of Richardson's expanding operation may have been shaky, life aboard his fleet was lively. Richardson held balls on the decks of the *Transit* and on July 30, 1840 that ship and the *Queen Victoria* joined in a gala flotilla which sailed to Niagara to help raise funds for the restoration of the Brock Monument, blown up during the border troubles. The *Transit* also had the honour of carrying Charles Dickens on his visit to Niagara Falls on May 2, 1842.[9]

Nevertheless, troubles were on the horizon. In some years Richardson and Donald Bethune, owner of the Royal Mail line, were able to operate in cooperation, with Richardson monopo-

Steamboat Chief Justice Robinson, *1852, painted early 1900s.*

lizing the Lewiston-Toronto run and Bethune that from Toronto to Kingston. By 1843, however, the two were engaged in a rate war which was complicated when the American steamers plying between Ogdensburgh and Lewiston began touching at Toronto, thus cutting into the Canadian lines' profit. When Bethune tried to reorganize his operations by running his steamers on a Toronto-Rochester-Cobourg run, they were seized by the Rochester customs authorities. In 1844 Richardson, in reply to the American rivalry, transferred the *Chief Justice Robinson* to a Kingston-Oswego-Niagara circuit, thus setting off a rivalry with Bethune which was fatal to both. By the end of the year Thomas Clark Street, Samuel's son, was doubtful that their loan would be repaid. In 1845 Richardson and Bethune did manage to cooperate; but in 1846 they were again at war. In April the *Transit* was severely damaged when she collided with Bethune's *Sovereign* at the entrance to the Toronto harbour.[10] Finally, on Aug. 12, 1846, Richardson was forced into voluntary bankruptcy. His debts of £19,286 were estimated at to be covered up to between 50 and 75% by his assets. James Brown, Duncan McDonell and Thomas Dimmie Harris, who was later to succeed Richardson as harbour master, were appointed assignees of his property and the next year the assets were sold for what Richardson considered a poor price. Bethune purchased one ship; but the collapse of his rival did him little good, for he followed the same course into bankruptcy in 1848.[11]

The next three years were the saddest ones of Richardson's life. Left with little hope of employment and no funds at the age of sixty-three, he could hardly see that he still had a second prominent career opening before him. By 1848 he was in Montreal as captain of the steamer *John Munn*, which had just been purchased by the speculator of that name to ply between Montreal and Quebec City. Unfortunately, rivalry was as acute on the St Lawrence as on Lake Ontario and the *John Munn* was involved in an accident with a rival, for which Richardson was blamed even though his ship's owner was aboard urging her forward. Next he was engaged by the St Lawrence and Atlantic Railway Company, piloting his former *Transit* on what was really ferry duty in the Montreal area, but this work also soon came to an end. After unsuccessfully attempting to be appointed harbour master of Montreal, Richardson finally saw his luck change in 1850 when he was given the newly created provincial post of harbour master of Toronto. As he stated, the office might be something short of an appointment as a harbour commissioner, but he was glad to accept it. The new supervisory, five-man harbour commission, appointed in September 1850, consisted of his former colleagues James Grant Chewett, representing the provincial government; George Gurnett, once again mayor, and Alderman William A. Campbell as the city representatives; and Thomas Clarkson and Peter Paterson acting for the Toronto Board of Trade. Thus Richardson had a board of commissioners he knew personally and with whom he could work easily.[12]

Life as harbour master was not rigorous, and by the 1860s he was receiving the not inconsiderable salary of $1,600 plus $300 for rent of a house. Again he established himself on Front Street and soon became one of the patriarchs of the city. The newly founded Toronto Boat Company (now the Royal Canadian Yacht Club) quickly elected him as honorary member in 1852. He was also to begin the gracious custom, which still prevails in parts of southern Ontario, of presenting a silk hat to the master of the first ship to enter a harbour in the spring.[13]

His immediate objective on appointment was to prevent further deterioration of the harbour, which he felt was in an advanced state of decay and inadequacy because of the growth of the city and its trade, coupled with a continued neglect of necessary public works. From his first report in 1854 on, he constantly stressed the need for improvements and his appeals met with considerable success. At the western end, the Queen's Wharf was improved in 1856-57 and then extended in 1863. The channel at the Western Gap was widened from 260 to 400 feet in 1859 and the depth increased to 13 feet. During the 1860s Richardson was fortunate to have the able assistance of the prominent engineer-architect Kivas Tully as superintendent of works for such projects as the Queen's Wharf reconstruction. The Eastern Gap, which Richardson had advocated in 1833, was finally created in 1858—but by a series of storms, not the ingenuity of man. In the next few years it began to come into some use.

Yet other major problems remained, one of the worst of them being the continued emptying of the city's raw sewage into the bay, a process which had been going on since the first sewers were built in 1835 and was to continue for some two decades after Richardson's death. Richardson attempted to have a new system put in as early as 1865; but the costs, along with the public's apathy about pollution and the widespread disbelief in the possibility of an epidemic, frustrated his efforts.[14]

For the last three or four years of his life Richardson was paralyzed; the last annual report he signed was in 1866. In spite of this, he was allowed to remain as harbour master, although his salary was later reduced and his duties were carried on by James Smith Jr, his deputy. He died on Aug. 2, 1870, and was buried in St James's Cemetery. His wife had predeceased him, dying at the age of seventy-one in August 1868, but four sons and two daughters survived.

Canon Henry Scadding, Toronto's great nineteenth-century historian, described Hugh Richardson as a man of chivalrous temperament, officer-like bearing and high character. Coming to the Town of York when it was a village of some 1,600, he lived to see it grow into a city of 55,000. In that growth he played a prominent role for nearly half a century through his work in developing both the harbour and its maritime communications, a contribution for which his adopted city owes him a significant debt.

Chapter 11

An Ambulatory Architect: William Hay[1]

The nineteenth-century British Empire has now receded sufficiently far into the past that those of us who can remember our grandparents' tales of life under Queen Victoria are numbered among the older generation. As time passes, and legends grow, the pre-1914 world is becoming a magic, golden place, marked by prosperity, overall peace and the general advance of science and technology. It is easy, however, to remember the good and forget the bad: the public health conditions, the primitive state of medicine, the minor wars of conquest and the clashes between empires that broke out regularly.

With the growth of legends there can come a magnification of the distances that separated the parts of the British Empire, scattered as they were across the globe. One can easily emphasize the vastness of the world, the slowness of transportation—especially before the coming of the trans-oceanic steamships and the railways—and wonder how communications were carried on at all. Yet, what we miss is the fact that the Victorians were geared to a much more slow-moving way of life. When they travelled they hardly expected speed; to travel was to rest on a ship, not to tangle with the difficulties of airport and jet-lag. Like us, they rejoiced in new technological breakthroughs which accelerated the pace of travel—witness Jules Verne's *Around the World in Eighty Days*—but at the same time they could still enjoy the forced leisure of a transportation system that moved at what was a more human pace.

Furthermore the transportation delays of the era did not stop large numbers of people from traversing the world to explore its farthest reaches. Some of them went as explorers, others followed the routes of commerce, still others planned to write about their travels, and there were an increasing number of tourists. In addition, there were the many people who moved back and forth in the service of the Queen: the soldiers for the Empire's defence; the missionaries to save its soul; the administrators, lawyers and clerks for its governance; and the Royal Engineers to advance its communications and lay out its towns. As well as these obvious groups of imperial servants, there still others who went forth as individuals to apply some specialized knowledge in the colonies, either as imperial advisors or as fortune-seekers bent on advancing only their own interests. Professionals of all types were at a premium in the colonies and dependencies and in the sometimes exotic countries with which the Empire traded. Yet this wholesale transference of ideas and techniques was far from being a one-way street, for these voyageurs carried ideas from colony to colony as well as back to Great Britain. Toronto and Upper Canada naturally were tied into this pattern and greatly benefited from the interchange of experts and ideas.[2]

Among the professionals, the architects form a group that deserves to be better known. The profession was only gradually evolving as the century progressed. In the early nineteenth century the architect was often basically an engineer or a builder; by the end of Victoria's reign there was a fully developed architectural profession with standards, organizations, and journals devoted to its improvement.

This raises the question of how ideas on architecture were transmitted. There were, of course, the widely circulated pattern books, which showed not only how to build complete buildings, but also details of decoration, sometimes in infinite variety. The prospective client could choose from these, in much the same way as modern shoppers select wallpaper. Over the course of the century, the architectural journals began to appear. These showed the latest ideas and the important buildings that had been recently completed. *The Canadian Architect and Builder*, which began in 1888, was one of the latecomers. Then, too, for the general North American public, which was always eager to be educated on the latest styles from England and the Continent, there were the illustrated magazines, the *Illustrated London News* from 1842, and our own *Canadian Illustrated News* from 1870 to 1883. Here the affluent patron could see the most recent fad and be ready to demand it from his builder. Finally, as noted—and here we must look at the role of the individual—there were the various architects who migrated to the colonies, or travelled around the Empire and brought their training and often the latest British ideas with them.

Many of Canada's greatest nineteenth-century architects fall into this category: Frederic William Cumberland, William Thomas and William Hay, all of whom worked in Toronto, are good examples. Once these men had selected their centre of activities, their influence and practice quickly expanded. Cumberland, the architect of St James's Cathedral, the central part of Osgoode Hall and University College, may have located in Toronto, but he also designed structures in many centres in southern Ontario. William Thomas, who also used Toronto as his home base, designed St Michael's Cathedral and the St Lawrence Market, as well as buildings in centres as far afield as Halifax. William Hay, similarly, had a far-flung Upper Canadian practice. He, however, had a wandering career, not just remaining in Toronto but settling and working at several locations over the course of his activities.

One last preliminary question must be asked—where does the architect rank as an enterpreneur? When one considers the numbers of staff who were even then employed in their offices, the distances that they travelled, the geographical extent of the areas they worked in, and the wide variety in the types of commissions that were each individual took on, the answer would appear to be that they occupied a rather important place. Like the early general merchants and the later wholesalers and industrialists, they did much to extend the influence of Toronto across Ontario and Canada. The amount of wealth these men left behind them is indicative of their success as immigrants. The fine mansions of Cumberland and Thomas still stand in Toronto; Hay's new country home east of Edinburgh, also still standing, is impressive and his estate was considerable. Architects, being professionals, may not want to see themselves categorized as enterpreneurs, yet in the nineteenth century they were definitely just that.

In examining the career of William Hay as an example of the type of architect who flourished in many centres of the Empire we are very fortunate in the amount of information that is available, although there are some considerable gaps. As is the case with so many immigrants who were to become prominent in Canada, the youth of William Hay is rather obscure, although his early career is better known than that of so many prominent

Architect William Hay.

Canadians. Born at Dikeside in the Parish of Cruden, Aberdeen-shire (now in Grampian), Scotland on May 17, 1818, he was the son of William Hay and his wife Jean Alexander. His father was a grain merchant, although one who possibly was not too prosperous, as William Junior was apprenticed as a joiner rather than in the family business. The family were Scottish Episcopa-lians in religion, a fact that was to be of great help to William in his later career, for he was to design many Episcopalian and Anglican churches.[3]

The great turning-point in Hay's career came as the result of an accident, when he fell off a roof and broke his leg. This necessitated a long convalescence and his doctor suggested that he study architecture while recovering. His studies were so successful that he was able to make the transition from carpentry to building and received his first commission, to design St James's Episcopal Church at nearby Cruden Bay, in 1843. The next year he went to Edinburgh as assistant to John Henderson, a prominent architect in that city. There he met Henderson's son George, who was to become his partner many years later. He married Janet Reid (1819-60) on March 3, 1844. Her younger brother, Thomas, became their ward and later made an impor-tant career for himself in Bermuda—another connection which played a role in forwarding William's career.[4]

When his training, or assistantship, with Henderson was completed, Hay found new employment with George Gilbert Scott, later Sir Gilbert, who is today probably the best known Victorian Gothic Revival architect in the English-speaking world. Although Scott's theories are now regarded as dubious and his restorations are generally seen as desecrations, he was then "the" architect, the man who was first approached when a prominent parish needed a church, or an abbey or cathedral required restoration. Scott also had a great indirect and uninten-tional influence, for his restorations to a considerable extent were responsible for the foundation of the English Society for the Protection of Ancient Buildings, which still flourishes today. In his career, which lasted from 1834 until his death in 1878, he built so many churches that even he himself was not certain of what he had done. There is a story—told also about other archi-tects—that, as he was rushing across the English countryside in a train compartment filled with draftsman and assistants, he looked out the window and watched a church go by of which he, for once, approved. Turning to an assistant he asked who had designed the structure and was advised: "but you did sir." Since Hay, like the canny old Scottish-Canadian merchants, was quick to turn connections into commissions, Sir Gilbert was exactly the type of man with whom he needed to apprentice. Scott was of value for the weight that his name as master carried in Hay's future career.

Opportunity soon opened for Hay to do some semi-independent work. In 1844 the energetic Edward Feild became Bishop of Newfoundland and two years later a great fire in St John's burned down the cathedral. Feild, like many of the Church of English prelates of his era, was hardly a modest man. Wanting nothing but the best for his diocese, he accordingly asked Scott to prepare the plans, which he did willingly. Then came the question of the superintendents of the actual construction. Scott could hardly be expected to come to St. John's—in fact no one would have suggested that he make such a pilgrimage. This did not present a problem, however, for at that time it was customary to appoint an assistant as clerk-of-the-works to oversee such tasks. Hay was willing to go and as a result, after touring Great Britain and Ireland to select stone and masons, he sailed for St John's in April 1847. His work basically involved the completion of the nave of the building only, since that was all Feild could afford at the moment. The choir and transepts of the cathedral—which was dedicated to St John the Baptist—were not built until 1880-85, again under Hay's supervision. The whole building was burnt in 1892 in another great fire; however, the walls were so solid that they could be reused and can still be seen today. There is a legend that part of the masonry is Caen stone taken from the ruins of the fortress of Louisbourg.[5]

While in Newfoundland Hay began to take on commissions of his own. He did not build the old legislative, known as the Colonial Building, which is sometimes attributed to him, although he may have undertaken various other government contracts and probably had a hand in the rebuilding of St John's after the 1846 fire. He did design some altar furniture and planned a wooden church for St Francis's Harbour in Labrador, a design which may well have been influential in his later Garrison Church at Toronto. Since Feild was also bishop of

Bermuda, Hay was called upon to advise on the construction of the pro-cathedral at Hamilton, the capital of that colony, in 1848-49, when difficulties were being encountered in carrying out and English architect's designs. Hay was to be a regular consultant in Bermuda for the rest of his life, visiting the island several times—hardly an unsatisfactory way of spending a Canadian or Scottish winter.

With the work at St John's completed Hay returned to Scotland in 1850. During the next three years, William's activities are very difficult to follow. Apparently Scott had no more ready-made commissions, and Hay returned briefly to Scotland where he was the architect of St John's, Longside, in his native Aberdeenshire, completed about 1853. Around this time he is also supposed to have visited both Montreal and Chicago with the idea of establishing a practice. Finally, around 1852, he settled on Toronto. With William Thomas well established in practice in the city and province, and Frederic William Cumberland just going into business in the years preceding, the competition there was fierce. Hay, nevertheless, was quick to make a name for himself and during the next decade built many of the important buildings in the city. Unfortunately, these structures, unlike those of Cumberland and Thomas, are no longer standing.

His commissions in Toronto might best be examined by type rather than chronologically, since his style changed with the whims of his patrons and with the kind of building required—as was common to all architects at that period. He also demonstrated the two most important qualifications for the successful entrepreneur: an ability to keep up with the latest styles which were becoming popular in England, and a thorough knowledge of the most advanced technological improvements.

His institutional buildings were characterized by the use of the Mansard style, with its high, steeply pitched roofs and towers. This style was architecturally up-to-date, having gained great popularity from the fact that the glittering court of Napoleon III and the Empress Eugenie held sway in the Mansard-style Tuileries Palace. The style was also practical, because the high roofs formed an inexpensive upper floor and the towers provided ample space for such practical inclusions as water tanks. Hay's two large commissions of this type in Toronto were the Catholic House of Providence on Power Street and the second Toronto General Hospital on Gerrard Street East, both begun in 1854. They were huge buildings for the period. The Toronto General Hospital was demolished in 1920, after the new hospital was built in the present location. It was characterized by a liberal supply of baths and water closets, as well as air vents designed to carry a flow of fresh air through the building through flues in the walls and ceilings. The similar House of Providence was demolished to build a ramp for the Don Valley Expressway in the early 1960s.[6]

Hay did extensive renovations to the provincial parliament buildings for the return of the Parliament of the United Provinces to Toronto, then the joint capital with Quebec, in 1855. These additions connected the three old 1832 buildings, creating one rather inharmonious block. He also revamped the old hospital as the Executive Council (Cabinet) Offices in 1854-55. Finally, in 1859-60 he built a Venetian-revival town hall for the northern suburb of Yorkville. Thus, in all his projects he showed his ability to adapt to a wide variety of architectural needs.[7]

In ecclesiastical architecture Hay, like William Thomas, was ready to work for any denomination. His church designs, however, were always Gothic, usually Scott's Early English variety, and he wrote articles on correct Gothic church style. In Toronto he prepared a design for the chapel of old Trinity (Anglican) College, which was not accepted, and built a wooden Anglican church for the Garrison, which had resemblances to his Newfoundland plan. As well, he designed a large Gothic Presbyterian Church and the original St Basil's Catholic Church and St Michael's College. The last two structures were to be joined in a planned cloister which was never completed. Today much altered, they are virtually all that remain of Hay's work in Toronto, except for some dwellings.

Outside Toronto Hay had what the *Canadian Architect and Builder* referred to as "an extensive practice" throughout Upper Canada. Some plans survive, and several buildings can be identified today, although others that are not attributed to him probably exist. The Commercial Bank of Kingston, 1853, in the Classical style, is an example of his business architecture, and the Anglican Church of St George at Newcastle, begun in 1857, and St Luke's, Vienna, begun about 1860, represent his churches. He did not build some other structures, such as the City Hall and

Toronto General Hospital, c. 1855.

St. Michael's College, 1855.

the Frontenac County Court House at Kingston, which are sometimes ascribed to him.[8]

It might be asked how a man who apparently had no connections in the city managed to do so well in what was an extremely competitive, although prosperous, period. Cumberland had, after all, married into a family who were leading members of the Family Compact and Thomas had been long established. The answer lies not only in Hay's sheer ability, but also in his amiable personality and in his canny sense of practicality. By 1854 Hay had signed the vestry roll of the prominent downtown Anglican church of the Holy Trinity, where he was later to make additions to the fabric as well as to build a manse for the assistant rector and a house for the rector, Canon Henry Scadding, Toronto's first great historian. Both buildings still survive between the church and the Eaton Centre. In the same year he joined the Mechanic's Institute of which he became a director and vice-president in 1859-61, and he was on the Council of the Canadian Institute, now the Royal Canadian Institute, in 1858-60. He was a member of the Board of Arts and Manufacturers of Upper Canada, and of the Association of Architects, Civil Engineers, and Provincial Land Surveyors of Canada. Clearly, Hay was a joiner who made contacts in many places. He also ghost-wrote the architectural sections of G.P. Ure's 1858 *Handbook of Toronto* , in which he did not hesitate to expand on the beauty of his own work.[9]

His closest association was with the Freemasons, a fact that may seem strange in a man who designed St Michael's Catholic College. Hay must have been a magnificent salesman, and Armand, Count de Charbonnel, the Catholic bishop of Toronto, unusually broad-minded, or some factor existed which now escapes us. At any rate, Hay was initiated into St Andrew's Lodge in Toronto in May 1854—apparently his first connection with Freemasonry—and in 1859 he became Worshipful Master. He also belonged to other similar organizations at a higher level. The 1859/60 directory shows him as the first principal of the St John's Royal Arch Chapter of the Registry of the Royal Arch Chapter of Scotland, as well as a captain of the Geoffrey de St Aldemar Encampment of the Templars. Interestingly enough, William G. Storm, Cumberland's able partner, was also an official of the Templars at the same time. Obviously the Masonic Order was one road to commissions.[10]

By 1860 Hay was nearing the end of his stay in Upper Canada. There are several possible reasons for his decisions to leave. First, the decade of the 1850s had been a time of active building in Toronto and by its end the city possessed enough institutions and new churches to serve its needs for many years. Commissions, especially given the depression that began in the late 1850s and continued into the early 1860s, were obviously going to be thin. As well, Hay's wife died in September 1860, aged 41, possibly in childbirth, an event which may have made him want to break his connections with the city. But beyond these facts, Hay was, as is evidenced by his many moves, a restless man, and he also shared the desire—common to so many emigrant Scots—to return to his native soil. Thus, in the early 1860s, he began to make preparations to wind up his affairs. Probably in early 1862 he turned his practice over to Henry Langley (1836-1906), who had been apprenticed to him for seven years, and Thomas Gundry, with whom he had just recently formed a partnership. The latter was a civil engineer as well as an architect. The Langley & Gundry firm lasted until Gundry's death in 1869; then Langley continued in practice becoming one of the most prominent architects in the province.[11]

After leaving Toronto Hay did not return to Scotland immediately, instead he went to Nova Scotia, where he settled into a Halifax partnership with the well-known Scottish immigrant architect David Stirling, as Hay & Stirling. Their offices were at 160 Hollis Street and Hay himself boarded on Spring Garden Road. He remained involved with Freemasonry in Nova Scotia, and in 1871 was nominated the first representative of the Grand Lodge of Nova Scotia to the Grand Lodge of Scotland. He was also acquainted with the Freemason Alexander Keith, a leading brewer and legislative councillor, and designed his mansion, Keith Hall, in 1863. Since both had Masonic interests, the stonework is lavishly decorated with Masonic symbols. Possibly appropriately, in view of Hay's work on St Michael's, the Keith Mansion was for many years the home of the Halifax Knights of Columbus.[12]

Although Hay appears in the Edinburgh postal directory in 1863 and apparently opened his Scottish practice then, the decade of the 1860s is again a rather obscure period in his career. In 1862, while still in Halifax, he had visited Bermuda in connection with the building of the nave of the pro-cathedral for Bishop Feild and this may have inclined him to further travels. He may have been back in Halifax in 1864-65. There is a legend in his first wife's family that he was employed by the British government to design buildings in many parts of the empire, as well as in England and Scotland. This may explain his absences, but there seem to be no leads that can be developed.When he did finally settle in Edinburgh he became active in Masonic circles. He was admitted to St Mary's Chapel Lodge in 1865 and was a past master of the St Andrew Lodge of Edinburgh by 1873. Hay was long an influential member of the Grand Committee of the Grand Lodge of Scotland, and was the Grand Lodge's representative to at least one major Masonic conference in London. Again, he was also a Knight Templar.[13]

In June 1870 Hay married Jemima Huddleston of Ryde on the Isle of Wight. The daughter of Robert Huddleston, a master tanner, she had been born around 1838 and was to live until 1905. About 1874 they had a daughter Frances Mary, or Fanny. That Hay was well off is shown by the fact that he was able to purchase an estate on the Firth of Forth to the east of Edinburgh at a place called Joppa, which is today part of Portobello. There he erected a large home, called Rabbit Hall, where he was to live for the rest of his life.

In Scotland Hay practised by himself before admitting his one-time fellow apprentice George Henderson to the business in 1878. A son of his old master, John Henderson, Henderson had had a career as wide-flung as Hay's, for he had immigrated to the colony of Victoria in Australia and built many buildings along the south shore west of Melbourne. The partnership between him and Hay was to be both amicable and successful. They constructed a large number of buildings in southern Scotland, including several at Galashiells, Selkirk and Lanark, and did work in Cumberland in the north of England. The most important commission, which Hay received himself in 1872 and was not completed until 1882-83, was the restoration of the interior of St Giles Cathedral in Edinburgh, which was made possible by the donation of some £30,000 by Sir William Chambers. The cathedral, which dated back to the 11th century and had been dedicated in 1243, had been badly mauled by the Reformation and by various restorations in the early part of the nineteenth century. Hay's restoration of the interior, which had been divided into three separate churches, has been generally accepted as quite successful.[14]

Work in Scotland did not inhibit Hay's wanderings. His one-time ward and first wife's brother, Thomas Samuel Reid, had settled permanently in Bermuda, after being educated by the Hays at Upper Canada College in Toronto and possibly staying with Hay at Halifax. In Bermuda he had a highly successful career, marrying into one of the influential families and becoming a mayor of Hamilton and a member of the Legislative Council. In 1882, probably through his influence (for Bishop Feild was now dead), Hay was commissioned to design the Bermuda Government House and a year later he visited the island to advise on the construction. The building was finished in 1892. Hay may have had a role in designing the legislature, or Sessions House, which is in somewhat of the same style. The 1883 visit was followed by an extensive tour of America with his wife and daughter, and on this journey he almost certainly visited Toronto.

Then in January 1884, the Bermuda cathedral, on which he had expended so much effort in erecting a sound structure despite bad designs, was burnt down. A complete reconstruction was necessary. Thomas S. Reid was Secretary of the building committee, and Hay and Henderson were asked to prepare the plans. Construction began in 1885 and after Hay's death three years later the work was carried on by Henderson. At the time as he was designing the cathedral, Hay drew up plans for the large parish church which still stands, incomplete and ruinous, overlooking the old capital of St George.[15]

In the fall of 1887 Hay took ill and he died at Rabbit Hall on May 30, 1888. His will shows extensive holdings of stock and bonds in such corporations as the Bank of Scotland, the Prudential Heritable Property Trust, the Portobello Gas Light Company and the Great Northern Railway. There was also considerable rental income from various properties. In all, the estate, or the part that could be traced (and this omits such real estate as Rabbit Hall), was valued at £7,600, or about $38,000 Canadian at that period. Translating this into modern terms would be difficult; however, Hay obviously had been a fairly successful entrepreneur. He had also been popular: the obituaries stressed his charity, his "kind and genial disposition" and his conservative outlook.[16]

Hay, then, may serve as a case study of the type of entrepreneur who travelled widely in the old empire, with his skills adding something to its beauty and his knowledge of technology making it a bit more liveable. Unlike so many of his contemporaries who settled in one place, Hay had a career that is difficult to follow. Nevertheless, his life points up a fact that is often overlooked: the British Empire was composed not just of officials and settlers, but also of professionals who moved from place to place and helped tie its skeins together with their efforts. When one considers the number of Toronto buildings that which were built by immigrant architects in the nineteenth century—to look at just one category of endeavours—it becomes clear that the city was more than a little benefitted by its imperial connections.

Chapter 12

The Unwitting Philanthropist: The Curious Case of Andrew Mercer[1]

One of our problems with Ontario history is that, while there are all too frequent claims that it is dull, especially in the modern period, at the same time little effort is made to examine the many curious characters who flourished in all walks of life. Yet it is these very characters who provide some of the most interesting sagas in our history. Some of their stories involve legal matters, or, at least a police investigation, for instance the careers of Ambrose Small and Charles Vance Millar, on whom books have been published recently.[2] This is true also of the hero of this chapter, Andrew Mercer.

For the older generation of Torontonians, among whom, I suppose, I must now count myself, the name Andrew Mercer calls to mind a red brick, Gothic fortress, which long rose behind a bleak unkempt yard on the south side of King Street West in Toronto. Forbidding and grubby, the Andrew Mercer Reformatory for Women stood surrounded by factories and railway tracks. It was there, beside the new harvesters for Massey-Ferguson, or Massey-Harris as it was then named, that attempts were made to rehabilitate fallen women — possibly by instilling in them a desire never to return. To an even older, now departed, generation of Torontonians, Mercer was also the founder of the Eye and Ear Clinic at the old Toronto General Hospital on Gerrard Street East. He thus had helped to advance the march of medicine as well as to improve the lives of society's outcasts.

One pictures an aged gentleman, luxuriently bewiskered, somberly attired, kindly and spiritual in countenance, gnarled from his devotion to worthy causes, and the doubtless honest labours that had gained him his hard-earned fortune. Like Andre Carnegie, he can easily be seen as a person who specialized in the moral and medical improvement of his adopted city, which had given him the opportunity to attain his wealth. Unfortunately, as happens all to frequently, the true story is somewhat different; but then, happily, it is also much more entertaining.

Two decades ago, when the *Dictionary of Canadian Biography* was making its first foray into the nineteenth century, there were some leftover Toronto figures whom no one seemed to be interested in writing up. Having some spare time, I offered to help out and thus acquired Andrew Mercer, who, at least, was a familiar name. As the research progressed, the name itself rapidly became all that remained familiar. Most historical figures attain their fame by what they do; Mercer was one of those rarities whose notoriety is entirely based on sins of omission, not commission. As a result of these omissions, his story culminated in one of the most interesting court cases, or series of court cases, in Ontario history, involving many of the leading Torontonians. The Mercer saga itself became entangled with many of the fascinating themes of mystery, as well as of history: a man of unknown origin who rises to wealth, which he does not spend; the reclusive family in a crumbling cottage whose extensive property has been engulfed by the swirl of an expanding urban downtown; lost legal documents of arguable authenticity; missing heirs; trials before the highest courts of the land and even the Judicial Committee of the Privy Council in England. And, finally, some conundrums that have no solution.

What was to become the celebrated case of Andrew Mercer surfaced on June 14, 1871, when such leading Toronto newspapers as the *Globe* noted in their obituary columns that Mercer had died suddenly at his residence, 41 Wellington Street, supposedly aged 90, and that the funeral would be held on Thursday. The *Globe* provided no write-up, for Mercer had not been prominent in the city for years and his affluence was unspectacularly based on mortgages and land holdings. As the same journal was to state later, "the growth of the city brought him wealth."[3] This fact was nowhere more in evidence than at his rather dilapidated cottage, which occupied a roughly 200-square-foot property on what was already prime business land, at the southeast corner of Wellington and Bay, just eastward from the site where the golden towers of the Royal Bank arise today. The journal did not even mention the fact that Mercer was probably the city's oldest inhabitant, although the Toronto papers usually stressed that very point in obituaries of more prominent individuals. Nevertheless, Mercer's antecedents were soon to be a subject of a major importance.

Mercer Cottage, c. 1880.

To establish the origins of the Mercer mystery, or at least to get as close as we are ever likely to come to the origins, we must go back much farther to the muddy town of York at the end of the eighteenth century, when John White, attorney-general of Upper Canada, and John Small, clerk of the Executive Council, quarrelled over the matter of the rather dubious virtue of the latter's wife. The result was a duel, fought in the early hours of the morning of January 3, 1800, which vindicated Mrs Small's honour — probably much to the hilarity of various denizens of York and its garrison — but left the colony short one attorney-general.

Because of the remoteness of the colony, obtaining new professionals is said to have been difficult, even with the ample salaries that were provided. This point may require further investigation, since there seem to have been many lawyers without good posts in England. Whatever the case, Henry Allcock, a judge of the Court of King's Bench who was shortly to become chief justice of Upper Canada, had been a law student at Lincoln's Inn, London, with Thomas Scott, a Scotsman who had gone to that city for his studies and was now seeking a post. Using the old-boy network that has so often played its role in lucrative appointments, he quickly arranged for Scott to replace White.

That worthy received his appointment in April, and at the beginning of September boarded the *Brickwood* at Portsmouth, where, with the French wars raging, a convoy was gathering to sail across the Atlantic for Newfoundland and Quebec City under the protection of His Majesty's Sloop-at-War *Voltigeur*. It departed on the September 4 and finally, on November 14, after what was regarded even in those days as a particularly ghastly voyage, the *Voltigeur* safely led the *Brickwood*, the ship *Enterprise* and the brig *Dauphin* into the harbour of Quebec. On board, along with Scott and a cargo of dry goods, rum and wine, was Andrew Mercer, then aged, by various estimates, from 16 to 22. This will probably remain his first appearance in history, for, despite many individuals' intensive research, no evidence has been found showing where he was born, what his real age age was, or even how, when and why he had become associated with Scott. It might be hoped that the papers of the *Brickwood* could cast some light on his origins, but — a typical frustration for the researcher on Mercer — the ship was captured by a

French privateer on the return voyage and all the papers were destroyed.[4]

Our first and about our only picture of Mercer in his early years comes from a letter which Chief Justice Osgoode of Lower Canada wrote from Quebec to Peter Russell, the receiver general at York, Upper Canada, whom he knew well from his years as a previous chief justice of Upper Canada. Dated January 21, 1801, it states that the new attorney-general, Thomas Scott, "arrived here late in November after a tedious and dangerous voyage of nearly three months," and then adds that he had remained six weeks, staying with Lieutenant-Governor Peter Hunter of Upper Canada, who was resident in Quebec in his second capacity as commander-in-chief of British North America, before departing for Upper Canada. Then Osgoode said: "not having many objects to excite my anxiety I have felt a degree of solitude for an English lad who came out with Mr. Scott and whom I never saw till the eve of his departure." Obviously, Scott was not presenting Mercer to the Lower Canadian establishment with any haste. The question remains: why did Scott bring him out? The general opinion in the early nineteenth century, for which there was never any clear evidence presented, was that Mercer must have been bachelor Scott's illegitimate son.[5]

Once in Toronto, Mercer lived with Scott and for some time acted as his clerk. By 1805 he had moved to an adjacent cottage, while Scott lived with a servant. Gradually they seem to have drifted farther apart, although Scott did get Mercer some appointments. When Scott made his will in 1824 he made no mention of Andrew, leaving his estate to his brother William in County Angus for life and then to the children of Sir John Riddell, who had been his early patron. This seems rather surprising if Mercer was really his son. Later there were claims that Mercer had expressed a wish to be buried near his old friend, but again there is no good evidence for such a statement.[6]

In February 1803 Mercer was appointed junior clerk of the Executive Council, doubtless at Scott's behest. During the War of 1812 his cottage was used by the King's Printer for preparing the *Upper Canada Gazette*, and in 1813 it was raided and the press broken up by the American invaders. Mercer was to keep some pieces to show as souvenirs. In early 1816 he briefly took over the editorship of the journal, but, lacking the necessary assistance, he claimed that it interfered too much with his Executive Council duties and gave it up in February, although agreeing to act as editor until a successor was appointed. By November 1818 he had acquired the principal office which he was to hold for the rest of his life: issuer of marriage licences for the city. Possibly as a result, he surrendered his clerkship in the Executive Council Office in March 1820. The only additional official appointment, which he received in 1833, was as one of the justices of the peace for the Home District, the administrative area which included Toronto. He was renewed in this dignity in 1837, but in 1843, rather surprisingly, he was dropped in the first commission of magistrates after the union of Upper and Lower Canada.[7]

While he was accumulating these offices, Mercer, like most of his contemporaries among the Upper Canadian establishment, was busily engaging in all sorts of other activities. In the War of 1812 he served in the third Regiment of York Militia, first with Captain Heward's Company and then with Captain Ridout's. In October 1812, he became an ensign and was appointed paymaster to the militia of the Home District. At the fall of York to the Americans on April 27, 1813 he was among the prisoners taken, but was paroled on condition that he withdraw from the fighting and played no further part in the hostilities. Not surprisingly, he was also in business. In 1810 he and Samuel Smith Ridout formed a partnership to operate a distillery and general store. They remained in business until at least 1813. The distillery was probably located to the north of the city at Hogg's Hollow, or York Mills as it is now known.[8]

Again, like all his contemporaries in office, Mercer quickly began acquiring land in both Toronto and its hinterland. As early as 1802 he applied for 200 acres and in 1811 for another 600, both of which petitions were granted. In 1814 he was given a town lot, and in 1820 he received a half-acre lot on the east side of Parliament Street to the east of the town. These grants were soon augmented by purchases, the most substantial of which was his property at the southeast corner of Bay and Wellington streets, which comprised 216 feet on the first street and 196 feet on the second. Actually he may have been living there even before he acquired the land in 1827; clear title was not obtained until 1843. In later years he continued his land speculations — the Rossin family are reported to have purchased the land for the Rossin House Hotel, later the Prince George (now the Royal

Trust Tower of the Toronto-Dominion Centre), from him for $20,000. He also began an active mortgage brokerage business, which, along with the issuing of the marriage licences, became his main occupation. Again, fitting in with his general pattern of omission, instead of using his early start and connections to make a fortune he gradually seemed to fade out of the picture as the province expanded. Socially, he seems to have belonged to no organizations. The Harmony Lodge of Freemasons were allowed to use his house for meetings in 1808-12, yet in later years he was not a member. Nominally he was an Anglican, but he seems to have had little connection with the church.[9]

This brings us to the question of his charity, or rather lack of it. After he was safely dead those who wished to indicate that he intended to leave his estate to the crown dwelt long and lovingly on this charity. In 1878 the leading Toronto lawyer and author, James David (later Sir James David) Edgar, who was acting for the province in the matter of its acquiring Mercer's estate, reported to the Legislative Assembly that "he was noted for the liberality with which he contributed to every religious, charitable, or educational object about which he was appealed to." Equally eager to get the property, Premier Oliver (later Sir Oliver) Mowat reported that all "testify that he was a kind-hearted, humane, charitable and generous man."[10]

Yet what evidence did they have of his generosity? True, in 1822 he had been on the committee to build bridges across the Don River and had helped to collect subscriptions. Later, in 1847 — admittedly something of a chronological jump — he was one of a committee set up to consider the formation of "The Emigrant Settlement Society." This, however, was a large committee comprising most of the leading members of the Church of England. Really, the only evidence of charity that can be submitted is his gift of 1,000 acres to help found Trinity College in 1851. This grant deserves investigation; 800 acres were in the Township of Melancton, now in Dufferin County, and the other 200 in Dawn Township, now in Lambton County. These are areas that are noted for their swamps! The confused surveys of Melancton make it difficult to locate properties, but the land in Dawn is rather near the river. Possibly judgement should be deferred; none-the-less, it is rather difficult to accept the official opinion of the Ontario government, which was to be echoed by John Ross

Robertson of the *Telegram* in his *Landmarks of Toronto*, that "he gave a great deal to charitable purpose." Also, his parsimonious, or downright miserly, way of life, which will be commented upon later, seems rather unlikely in a man noted for his generosity.[11]

Thus, by mid-century Mercer was an aging, reclusive man who seemed more likely to fade into total obscurity than to become the centre of a controversy. Then came a sudden change. About 1850 an illiterate, Irish immigrant woman named Bridget, or Biddy, O'Reilly arrived in Toronto from New York, somehow obtained the post of Mercer's housekeeper, and moved in together with her sister, Catherine Smith. On July 25, 1851, Bridget gave birth to a son. She claimed that Mercer was the father and gave the boy the name of Andrew F. Mercer. It seems questionable that the paternity claim was true. Mercer was nearly 70 at least, he had never married and there are no tales of earlier affairs. However, he never denied Bridget's claims that he was the father of the child, assumed responsibility for raising him, educated him in a commercial academy and made him his assistant in issuing marriage licences — a rather ironic touch, even if an unintentional one, considering the circumstances. The domestic arrangement that resulted was a decidedly odd one, for Bridget did not eat with her son and Mercer and — later at least — according to Dr Joseph Adams, the family physician, she slept in a separate room on a different floor.

Whether or not Mercer and Biddy were married was to be the subject of long argument. The servants believed that they were married and always addressed her as "Mrs. Mercer"; however, she "acted very violently if she was not so addressed." On the other hand, no evidence of marriage could be produced when Mercer died, and such leading citizens, as former city solicitor Clarke Gamble, who was the family lawyer, Frederick C. Capreol, the railway entrepreneur, Henry J. Grasett, the Dean of St James's Anglican Cathedral, and Canon Henry Scadding, Toronto's first historian, all swore in court that Andrew and Biddy were not married.[12]

Why Mercer went along with such odd arrangements, especially if he was not the father, requires some explaining. Possibly, he came to like the child and, in view of Biddy's character, wanted to protect him against her. He may also have been deathly afraid of her; as late as 1855 she threatened to sue him for seduction. Certainly, he had little love for her. In a diary headed "Memo of Biddy's Bad Conduct," he catalogued her "mad fits," noting that she broke no less than twenty-eight panes of glass in 1858-60 during temper tantrums, and he added: "I believe her to be bad enough to do anything." The impression left is of a sad, terrorized old man.

There is also a third reason why Mercer may have gone along with Bridget's domination — the gradual onset of senility. William Henry Pearson, the general manager of the Consumers' Gas Company, an astute, if jaundiced, observer of Toronto society, called him "a very kindly old gentleman with a retiring disposition"; the retiring may have been a gradual withdrawal from the world. Definite evidence of senile decay is the mess in which his financial affairs became embroiled over a long period of years. When Mercer died he left mortgages valued at $90,691, including "interest which has been accumulating for periods, in some cases twenty years and upwards." His bonds were worth $2,400, "whereof $1,200 was barred by the Statue of Limitations before Mr. Mercer's death." Promissory notes totalled $14,119, a large portion of which was barred by the same statute during his lifetime. It may well be that for years Mercer was imposed upon by a wide variety of people, and this may help explain the charity claims, which at least in part were made by people who asserted that he never intended that they repay money or mortgages that he had provided for them. Yet if such was the case why did he bother to have legal documents prepared certifying their indebtedness?[13]

Despite his possible senility, or possibly because he was being influenced to do things he no longer really understood, Mercer began making arrangements to provide for Andrew Jr by buying some farm land in Etobicoke, to the west of Toronto, and promising to purchase more. The idea of setting up young Andrew as a farmer itself sounds rather strange, for the boy, raised in the heart of the city, could have had little practical knowledge of farming. Yet, whatever he did for young Andrew, Mercer apparently refused to take any action to make a will — another omission and the one that was to make his name famous.

Afterwards, naturally, there were all sorts of attempts to find out what he had intended to do with his money. The most interesting opinion on that subject came from Edward Wright, by then of Michigan, who was truly a ghost from the past. He had been one of the original Reform aldermen on the first city council in 1834 and was the proprietor of the Greenland Fisheries Tavern, one of the hangouts of the Mackenzie's supporters. Wright, claiming to be a friend of sixty years standing, although he seems a rather strange crony for a protege of a Tory chief justice of the peace, said that Mercer had told him that he had "no one to leave anything to" and that he "would leave his property to the government." If such a statement was made, it may say something about what Mercer thought of the paternity of young Andrew. Possibly, no explanation of the lack of a will is needed beyond the obvious failure of Mercer to take any action in business matters during his last years.[14]

Such was the confused state of affairs when Mercer died suddenly on June 13, 1871. The newly founded province of Ontario, which was already having difficulties in making revenues match expenses, quickly moved in to take possession. Clarke Gamble, one of the leading lawyers in the city as well as a scion of one of the oldest families, had been handling — or not handling — Mercer's affairs and was holding his securities. He immediately turned them over to the Ontario government. He also advised young Andrew that he had no claim as the natural son of an intestate. This may provide another explanation of why there was no will — young Mercer, who had intended to claim, may have thought that he was the heir anyway. In grateful return, the government recognized Gamble as the legal representative of the estate.

Ontario soon moved to take the necessary legal action to assume control. In its last days in office in early December 1871 the basically Tory coalition government of Premier John Sandfield Macdonald, who was also the attorney-general, ordered a commission of escheat, which would transfer the estate to the crown in view of the lack of legitimate heirs. This is interesting since it shows that the Conservatives, had they remained in power, would probably have handled the matter in exactly the same manner as the Liberals, who were about to begin one of the longest tenures of power — thirty-four years — in Ontario's history. In May, with the new Liberal government firmly in the saddle, letters of administration were obtained in favour of new

Attorney-General Adam Crooks. After Crooks's departure from office, Premier Oliver Mowat became administrator in June 1874, when he assumed the attorney-generalship. The Mercers made little protest until March 1873, when Gamble reported that N. Gordon Bigelow, of Bigelow & Hagle, barristers, appeared in his office to ask for the estate papers and express doubts that the attorney-general had any right to take out letters of administration.[15]

Evaluations of the property were now underway. The Bay-Wellington piece of real estate was thought to be worth $44,600 and carried the substantial municipal tax of $339 by 1877. There were also farm lands in the townships of Tecumseh in Simcoe County and North Gwillimbury in York County. There was an account in the Merchants Bank, and stock, or warrants for stock, in such corporations at the Merchants Bank, the Bank of Commerce and the British-American Assurance Company. In all, the estate, despite Mercer's extreme mismanagement in his last years, was worth an estimated $140,000 in 1878.

While these developments were proceeding, admittedly very slowly, the Mercers remained in the house and the son was allowed the rents on the premises which Andrew Sr had verbally contracted to buy for his benefit. Young Andrew also got married and with the old man's miserly hand removed, plus some of the cash available, went on a spending spree. The results were such outlays as $120 for a gun, $150 for furs and $50 for buggy hire, as well as debts of $70 to Dr Joseph Adams for various loans. Although the government described him as "a quiet respectable young man — not inclined to vice of any kind," it also pointed out that he never worked in his father's lifetime because he thought that he would be "well provided for." This is really how Andrew comes through as the picture unfolds — a spoilt, weak, malleable, probably none-too-intelligent young man, pushed along and around by the various individuals who had interests in the estate in one way or another. Not surprisingly in view of his expenditures, before long he was in great want and was after the province for money.[16]

Despite his financial position, for several years he made no claim to the estate, but in late 1874 he asked for $1,000 as a downpayment on the property which his father had promised to provide for him. The government was agreeable, particularly since it saw the grant as a means to get the estate into the hands of the courts for settlement. Thus an order-in-council was passed and Andrew brought in a bill for the claim. In February 1875, as requested, he swore out some affidavits stating that his parents had not married and requesting that the government search for the next of kin. He also swore out an affidavit that

> None of his [Mercer senior] friends or acquain-
> tances had ever heard him speak of his family or
> relations, or of his previous history; that after his
> death his papers had been carefully examined,
> but that they furnished no information as to
> whether he had any relations; and that they gave
> no clue to his history previous to his coming to
> this Province.

The government then brought in a bill to provide Andrew with his $1,000. This included a statement that "the plaintiff's mother was not lawfully married to said Andrew Mercer."[17]

At this point it may be well to summarize the solid evidence that was, and is, available regarding old Mercer's antecedents: that is, exactly nil. Various people made statements, but they could hardly be proven. One William Hill, who had known Mercer for forty-five years, certified that Andrew had said that his mother was Mary Mercer, and that he had no relatives. Hill also noted the general supposition that Mercer was illegitimate. Mercer's only statement (or possibly Bridget's statement) that can be checked appeared in the census of 1861: Andrew Mercer, 77, single, born in England. This last point was to become one of the main controversies, for if there was to be a family there had to be some agreed place of birth. As Mercer had come from England, there had been some idea that he was English: yet, since he came with Scott, there was a counterclaim that he was Scottish, although Scott could easily have picked him up in England when he came down to study law. Some said that he came from Sussex.[18]

Unfortunately, the name Mercer itself is little help since it is an occupational name meaning a dealer in textile fabrics. As such, while not common like Smith, it is still reasonably frequent in both England and Scotland and there is no reason why one Mercer should be related to another. Hill, in his evidence, seemed to think that Mercer might have come from Sussex, but regrettably, as any researcher who tries to trace Mercers in Sussex will quickly find, there are lots and lots of Mercer families noted in both the modern east and west divisions of that county.[19]

Mercer's birthdate is another problem. His tombstone showed 93, which does not agree with the census statement, which would indicate 87. Genealogical research turned up an Andrew Mercer born at Currie in Midlothian, Scotland, in 1778, a date which fits in nicely with the 93. This has tended to be accepted as the same Andrew without any evidence. Further, the 1778 somehow got coupled with Sussex. And Andrew is hardly a rare name in either southern Scotland or southern England. Just to confuse the issue further, there was another Andrew Mercer who had immigrated to Toronto — an alcoholic upholsterer, who could possibly be confused with him by hopeful relatives. By 1871 this man had been dead for some years. Really, there is nothing concrete to be said about Andrew until he stepped off the ship at Quebec City. Thus, when claims to the estate came in, there was nothing for the government to go on in testing their legitimacy. From Ontario's point of view, this was extremely satisfactory, it meant that the whole case for relationship had to be proven *ab initio* [from the beginning] by the claimant and that could only be to Ontario's advantage.[20]

After the agreement of February 1875 the government duly advertised in Canada, Scotland and England for heirs and several claims came in, the advertisement in the *London Times* attracting the most attention. Clark Gamble, who was sent to England to investigate the claims, found that, except for one, all they did was "write stating they think they are the heirs, without attempting to trace their rights or forwarding any shadow of evidence." The one exception, Robert D. Mercer of Spittal Square, London, presented himself as the sole surviving nephew, sending certificates of marriage, baptism and so on. The Ontario government, not surprisingly, wanted more. Before long the government said that he was the only claimant who had not withdrawn. Nevertheless, although the government claimed that there were few other attempts to gain part of the estate, one P. Byrne was paid $289.33 for making inquiries in Scotland as late as April 1877, and about the same time payments were made to both a London law firm with the delightful name of Messrs Bischoff, Bompas & Bischoff for acting as solicitors to the Ontario attorney-general and also to a commissioner in London for taking evidence. These costs amounted to nearly $100 in all. One is left with the distinct impression that the whole case was not quite as open and shut as the province wished it to appear in the Sessional Papers presented to the legislature.

During all this time young Andrew had been a model of rectitude in keeping out of trouble. With him out of the way and only Robert Mercer making claim, it looked as if the estate would quietly revert without difficulty to the crown, which was now beginning to put it in order, making sure that no further debtors escaped under the statute of limitations. Then came the bombshell. In June 1874 young Mercer, or Biddy, retained a certain Patrick McGregor as their lawyer. Next a law student, Richard D. Reynolds, who may have worked for McGregor, came up with a will dated only a week before the elder Mercer's death. Reynolds, who collected stamps, claimed that he had been rooting through the elder Mercer's law books to find law stamps and what should fall out of *Tomlin's Law Directory* but a six-by-two inch piece of paper, on which was written in pencil, in a shaky hand:

> June 7, 1871, In Case I should die before my son should return or before I have time to make my will, I wish James Smyth and Charles Unwin to have my estate divided among my wife and son.
> Andrew Mercer [21]

The find was timely, for the law library of Andrew Mercer Sr had been promised to a "certain person" the very day in May that the will was found. Despite its importance, which should have surely struck a law student, Reynolds claimed that he was so surprised he put it in his pocket and forgot it for some time. Finally, however, he said he gave it to young Andrew. This will had a limited value: it could cover only "personality" (personal property), since any will transferring real estate required two witnesses. Still, it did provide executors, who could make a claim, and it acted as a curtain raiser for an even more important revelation: Andrew Mercer Sr, it suddenly was revealed, had not been guilty of any omissions after all — not only had he left a will, but he had also married! This intelligence, together with the announcement of the will, was suddenly dropped on the unsuspecting Mowat government in August 1875.

On the June 25, 1851, only a month before Andrew Junior was born, Bridget had taken the train at the Bay Street Station and gone to Weston. There she picked up a stagecoach to the Gore of Toronto Township, where she got off only a half-mile from the church of a Father O'Reilly, whom she persuaded to accompany her back to Toronto to perform the marriage. Altogether quite a feat for a woman eight months pregnant.

Armed with this evidence, apparently provided by Biddy, the Mercer executors applied to the York County Surrogate Court for the probate of the will. The case was contested on suspicion of forgery by the crown and then, in September 1875, transferred to the Court of Chancery of Ontario, which at that time heard cases of contested wills and such matters as legitimacy. The order for trial was issued in October and provision made for the evidence on both Andrew's legitimacy and the validity of the will to be heard simultaneously. This joint case was entered as *Unwin vs. Mowat* after Charles Unwin who became the executor and the attorney-general. The matter was still further complicated, however, by the claim of Robert Mercer of London, England, or *Mercer vs. Mowat*, which was tried simultaneously.

The hearings opened at Toronto on January 13, 1876, with vice-chancellor Samuel Hume Blake presiding, and continued on four later days. Blake should not be confused with his more famous father, William Hume Blake, who had also been vice-chancellor, or his brother, Edward Blake, the former Liberal premier. He was far being from the only luminary at the trial: Andrew Junior was represented by Charles Moss, a young lawyer who was to eventually become Sir Charles Moss, chief justice of Ontario. Biddy was represented by the somewhat mysterious Patrick McGregor, Robert D. Mercer by Mr Small, possibly a scion of the old Family Compact clan and and thus related to the good lady whose vindicated virtue had led to Mercer's arrival in the first place. Finally, the attorney-general's barristers were the already noted James David Edgar, the Liberal politician who was to become Sir J. D. Edgar, speaker of the House of Commons of Canada, and Christopher Robinson, a son of Chief Justice Sir John Beverley Robinson, who was never to become a "Sir" because he and one of his brothers, John Beverley Jr, could never manage to come to an agreement with Queen Victoria on the order in which way they were to be knighted.

There were two points to be established in the trial: Was the will genuine? And was the petitioner the lawful son and heir-at-law of Andrew Mercer Senior? The testimony on these two points intertwined, as did the claim of **Robert Mercer;** but to make sense of what happened, it is necessary to try and treat each separately. A host of witnesses appeared, including what must have been the complete complement of the oldest male inhabitants of Toronto — regrettably the ladies seem to have been completely left out. Included were the already mentioned William Hill and Edward Wright, as well as another ghost of the long-passed Rebellion, John Montgomery of Montgomery's Tavern fame, who sent his evidence by affidavit because at eighty-seven he was too old and frail to attend.[22]

To discuss the will first, both the executors named admitted that Mercer had never asked them to serve. Further, the handwriting experts certified that the calligraphy was not the same as that in Andrew Mercer's letters. Andrew Mercer Jr distinguished himself by refusing to enter the witness box and by walking out of court when he was required for examination. He was obviously in a complete panic. The marriage evidence was rather more spectacular. The Mercers got off to a good start when one Charles Mulholland said that Mercer had recognized young Andrew as his son long before his death and had also admitted to the marriage. More important, Catholic Archbishop John Joseph Lynch of Toronto verified that the writing in the register was that of the now deceased Father O'Reilly. The crown, however, was able to produce Father Griffin, who had taken over the Toronto Gore parish in 1870. He had to admit that there had been eight priests at the Gore between himself and O'Reilly, since it was a sort of missionary parish, that the books had not been locked, and that it was the only entry that he had seen where there were no witnesses mentioned. His first knowledge of the event had come, he said, when Andrew Mercer Jr and a lawyer had come to see him about it during the previous August.

There was a great deal of confusion over the testimony which was presented. Were the witnesses dead, or had there been none? Why was there no wedding ring? Where was the certificate, or lines, that Bridget said she had been given by the priest? Why did the relevant page differ from all the others in the register? Why was the ink fresh when it was supposed to be twenty-five years old? Why was the writing unusually heavy for just two entries, one of which was inked out? Biddy made a poor witness. She had no explanation about why she went all the way to the Gore of Toronto when she attended a church in Toronto itself. Then came the crown's attack. How had she taken a train from the Bay Street station in 1851 when there were no trains from Bay Street until 1853? Further, her stagecoach schedules and routes were wrong, and her distances at the Gore mixed up. There was no stage in 1851 anyway. Also, a hotel at which she claimed to have stopped did not exist, and the priest's house was not next to the church, but half-a-mile away. As noted Andrew fled when called to the witness stand. The evidence was completely damming and the judge rejected the claims of Biddy and Andrew Jr.

When it came to the case of Robert Mercer the appellant received short shift. Various senior citizens, especially William Hill, certified that Andrew Mercer had just said that "he had no relations." Edward Wright was apparently particularly telling in his evidence, but it is uncertain what he said. Not surprisingly, the Richard Mercer claim was also rejected. The decision leaves one a bit uneasy, particularly considering Wright's politics. He had had his way paid to come up from Wisconsin with an attendant provided to look after his wants at the considerable cost of $250 to support his old Liberal party.

In handing down his decision on the will and marriage Vice-Chancellor S. N. Blake waxed eloquent:

> the fabrication of the former [the will] was so far plausible that, at first, some of Mr. Mercer's friends were deceived by it; and the fabrication of the entry was so nearly successful, that those having the custody of the register at the time of the trial, were led to think that the entry was genuine.

After such a hearing one might reasonably expect that perjury and forgery charges would be laid, as well as some investigations regarding disbarment for at least one of the lawyers. Surely neither Bridget nor Andrew Jr. would have had the ability to set up such a complex plot themselves. Certainly, the public was suspicious. According to the *Globe* on November 15, 1875, Andrew Jr had reportedly signed a bond agreeing that he would give his lawyer $20,000 if he got the estate. Yet there was no investigation and the Mercers received a more than generous settlement. It may be that Mowat and his cabinet were just tired of the whole case; it may be that they felt that still more problems would be created if the dispute was not dropped; it may even be that they had something of a guilty conscience themselves on the matter.

For Bridget, Premier Mowat recommended that, though she had apparently got control of some $12,000 of Mercer's money by dubious means, she be allowed to keep it. In view of the forgeries and her cruel treatment to Mercer, however, no further grants could be recommended. The income from the money she had was estimated as $800, which should have been more than sufficient for her needs. As for young Mercer, the government pointed out that, while he was a party to the conspiracy, a "humane and liberal view should be taken," although "it would be contrary to good morals and to public policy to recognize the right of an illegitmate son to the estate as if he were legitimate." The government, however, agreed that Andrew should receive a settlement of $30,000. This was to be broken down in three sections: $5,000 to cover his debts and costs with anything left over to go to him; completion of the purchase of land in Etobicoke as planned, or alternatively $10,000 in property or cash; and finally, $15,000 in stocks or securities.

With the rest of the money the government decided that it would be able to go ahead with some public works. J. W. Langmuir, the inspector of prisons and public charities of Ontario, had long been recommending the construction of several institutions which were designated with customary Victorian frankness: a training school for idiots; a hospital for inebriates; a industry reformatory for females; and an eye and ear infirmary. He particularly stressed the last two and it was on these that the government elected to proceed. In February 1878 Mowat recommended that $10,000 be spent on a provincial eye and ear infirmary in connection with the Toronto General Hospital and $90,000 on the Andrew Mercer Reformatory for Females, which was to be run on similar lines to the institutions at Penetanguishene. These expenditures, Langmuir felt, would not only be "a noble and permanent benefaction of a Provincial and undenominational character, but a lasting monument to the memory of the deceased." Accordingly, the $10,000 was paid to the hospital for the Andrew Mercer Eye and Ear Infirmary, and the reformatory, erected at a cost of $106,000, was ready by 1880. As the reports noted, "the Modern or Gothic style of architecture has been adapted, which will have very little of the gloomy prison-like aspect," a statement that could only have been regarded as more than slightly ludicrous long before the institution closed in 1969.

With distribution agreed upon, the actual transfer of funds made and construction underway, it may have seemed to Mowat and his government that the case was at last settled. The estate was finally declared forfeited to the crown in September 1877, when the last outside claims had been disposed of. In March 1878 the various terms of distribution passed the legislature as the first statute for the 41st year of Queen Victoria. It merely remained to move the Mercers — who had received nearly all of their grant — out of the cottage. Then, much to everyone's surprise after the generous settlement, Bridget refused to move. She claimed that she was a widow "entitled to reside on the said land until the value of her dower shall have been ascertained and paid to her." This might seem comical, but yet another problem now arose: the Dominion government claimed that Ontario did not have the right to escheat estates under the British North America Act, and therefore such estates were a federal prerogative. Since the Ontario and Dominion governments were already virtually at war over the boundary between the province and the federal territories, and Liberal Mowat and Tory Sir John A. Macdonald were continuing to carry on a longstanding personal feud, any new cause of provincial-federal altercation was naturally going to be taken up, especially when it involved a potentially significant source of revenue. Both governments were in agreement, however, that the real test in any further court case concerned the right of escheat; evicting the Mercers was only a question of who had the right to evict them. Thus, while the actions were taken in the Mercer's name, they were really constitutional cases: Ontario vs. the Dominion.

The new hearings opened in the Ontario Court of Chancery in September 1878, and the vice-chancellor decided in favour of Ontario in January 1879. The federal government then took the case to the Ontario Court of Appeal in March 1880, only to be defeated again. However, when the Dominion took a further step and appealed to the Supreme Court of Canada in November 1881, the federal cause was victorious, despite Quebec's sending a lawyer to concur with Ontario's position. Ontario could not allow this decision to stand and the whole affair was carried across the ocean to the highest imperial court of appeal, the Judicial Committee of the Privy Council of England, where in July 1883 the battery of legal talent included Premier Mowat himself, and Zebulon Aiton Lash, who became one of Canada's leading commercial lawyers, active for the Dominion. Lord Chancellor the Earl of Selborne upheld the original decision in favour of Ontario.

Meanwhile, Mowat had continued undaunted with his building programmes and was attempting to collect Mercer's debts. The difficulties he faced can be shown by the example of just one mortgage. Among the people who had not paid was a no less distinguished legal figure than John Godfrey Spragge, chief justice of Ontario, who "alleged that Mercer did not intend to make him pay." When in 1883 Mowat ordered suit, just before the mortgage was outlawed by the Statute of Limitations, Spragge declared mis-service of the writ. Poor Mowat was reduced to threatening a fine; but, as he wrote to Sir Alexander Campbell, the federal minister of justice, "it is very awkward to do that against the head of the judiciary and therefore it has not yet been done."[23] In the end Spragge apparently paid only the principal of the mortgage, without interest. By November 1883 the Mercer property was finally surveyed for sale. Shortly thereafter the Mercers were gone and it was divided into building plots. The case was over, however, hopeful would-be heirs were still hiring genealogists to search for a relationship at least as late as the 1930s.

There is a sequel to the story. When Mercer died, the Ontario government had him interred in a large $12 plot in St James's Cemetery beside the road that winds between the mausoleums and memorials of the Family Compact. Over him was planted a very large red granite obelisk which gave his name, and the inscription advised that he was "A native of England." There he still lies in solitary splendour. Twenty years ago problems arose: the obelisk, possibly because it was a government contract, was beginning to tilt dangerously. Thus, while researching Mercer for the *Dictionary*, I suddenly received a phone call from a gentleman in Toronto who identified himself as an employee of the Ontario Cemetery Board. Was it correct that I was the expert on Andrew Mercer? I supposed so. Good, then could I tell him why St James's was claiming that the government had to go to the considerable expense of putting new foundations under the monument? Surely they had no legal obligations? I explained that for $140,000, less legal fees and payments of course, they should repair the tombstone. The gentleman sounded very sad when he hung up.

The government of Ontario is a body that honours its obligations. If you go to St James's Cemetery to commune with the Family Compact you will find that the obelisk stands nicely upright on a new firm foundation. Yet there is still one last mystery, the part of the inscription showing his place of origin has been carefully, and neatly, chiseled out, obviously by expert hands. Who ordered it? Why is it erased? These are just two more questions in the Mercer's saga. And they are two more mysteries that probably cannot now be solved, just as the various attempts to find the Mercer lineage have met with no success. Andrew Mercer must rest in limbo and the Province of Ontario remains his legatee.

Wyld-Darling Building, which replaced Mercer Cottage, north-east corner Bay and Wellington, following the 1904 fire.

Part IV: Disasters and Recoveries

Disasters have always been a favourite theme in urban history, as can be witnessed by the innumerable books on the destruction of Pompeii, the great fires of London and Chicago, and the San Francisco conflagration and earthquake. Disasters are also a favourite theme for students selecting topics for papers in urban history seminars; there is always a plethora of candidates ready to investigate any one of the above incidents. Yet, while urban disasters have an innate interest, the most memorable thing that emerges from the studies of such events is the way that humanity sets itself up for a rerun. The ancient Pompeiians did not know that Mount Vesuvius was a volcano until it was too late. Today's residents have no such excuse — modern Naples and its suburbs contain two million people within the limits of the fallout area that could be covered by the next eruption. The government says that they will be evacuated! Similarly, Winnipeg, Edmonton, and London, Ontario, for years did little to control delelopment on their flood plains, and finally acted only against considerable oppostion. And today, metropoli like San Francisco and Mexico City could do far more to prepare for the next earthquake.

Preventive action is particularly necessary because disasters frequently tend to be sequential. Witness Lisbon in 1755: earthquake, fire and then tidal wave. Fortunately, a prospering city, with a good economic base and a flourishing hinterland, can rise above even a sequence of disasters, as London, England, did following its plague and fire in 1665-66 and later its devastation in World War II. For a city in economic difficulty, however, a disaster can speed up or even render irreversible a gradual process of decline.

Toronto has been fortunate in having both a second economic base and, because of its place in the developing central province of the nation, a constant stimulus to growth. At the same time, its geographic situation has shielded it against most disasters: it is far from earthquake zones of any intensity, it is sufficiently elevated that it avoids extensive flooding, and it is too northerly to experience frequent violent storms. It has had its share of disasters, such as the cholera epidemics of 1832 and 1834, the Spanish influenza in 1919, the *Noronic* fire with its huge loss of life in 1949, Hurricane Hazel in 1954, and the CPR derailment and fire in 1983. Yet most of these either have been an inevitable local manifestation of global events, such as the epidemics, or had become rather muted in their threat by the time they hit the city. Hazel, for example, had lost much of its force before it swept through Toronto; in fact, the weather office claimed that it was no longer a hurricane, a statement which those of us who remember the storm find hard to believe. Furthermore, any of the dangers that Torontonians were warned against over the years never materialized. For instance, despite the constant hazard posed by pollution of the water system in the late nineteenth century, there was never a major outbreak of typhoid fever.

Although Toronto's two great fires did not approach the intensity of the conflagrations in many other cities, they were bad enough. Fortunately, both were downtown blazes which did not wipe out residential areas, and the number of deaths and injuries was limited. Also, both fires were followed by the construciton of new buildings which still beautify the city. They differ in that, while the first great fire was probably unavoidable in view of the hazardous conditions of the era, the second could have been easily prevented, or at least controlled, had the civic government been willing to pass the needed building codes or spend the required money on modern fire protection equipment.

Two of the three chapters in the last section of this book deal with the causes and course of the First Great Fire in 1849, and the rebulding of the city afterwards. The third looks at the Second Great Fire of 1904.

Chapter 13

The First Great Fire, 1849 [1]

Almost every city has its record of one or more great fires, and the stories of some of the more famous of these catastrophes have been frequently used as a theme by novelists and script-writers. Most of the great conflagrations, such as the one in Nero's Rome in 64, the London fire of 1666 and the Chicago fire of 1871, began as ordinary central city fires and went out of control because of unusual conditions. Both of Toronto's great fires, which occurred in 1849 and 1904, were of this kind. Other great fires were caused by war or sieges; those in Papal Rome in 1084 and Paris in 1871 are examples. Finally, a few fires were the result of earthquakes, such as the ones at Lisbon in 1755 and at San Francisco in 1906.

Technically, to use an insurance definition, a great fire or conflagration differs from an ordinary fire in that it involves several buildings and causes at least $1,000,000 damage. Large fires involving only one building or object do not qualify as conflagrations. Fortunately, in recent decades modern construction methods and the development of new fire-fighting techniques have virtually put a stop to conflagrations; but up until at least the 1920s approximately one fire in 20,000 reached conflagration proportions. Once that happens, it takes all the skill of even modern fire-fighting techniques to stop its progress. As late as 1918 J.G. Smith described that situation in his *Fire Waste in Canada* :

> No conflagration has every been stopped by organized attempts at extinguishment. The most powerful hose streams are ineffective at more than 150 feet, the exact distance depending on the velocity of the wind. The horizontal reach of the flames driven by a gale has, in many instances, exceeded 1,000 feet, and buildings over one-half mile in advance of the fire have been ignited. Under such conditions, a fire department can

fight the conflagration neither in advance of the flames nor from the rear, because of the trail of hot and burning debris. Operating on each flank of a sweeping fire the efforts of a fire department are again of doubtful value, being spread over too large an area to permit effective work. Without attempting to disparage the efforts of firemen in dealing with conflagration, it should be recognized that their chief value has been in preventing flames from spreading across the wind, and in extinguishing brands that have alighted outside the zone of the fire.[2]

The problem of fighting such a major blaze is complicated by the fact that, since it burns at an average temperature of 1,500 to 2,000 degrees Fahrenheit a conflagration tends to create its own wind currents and atmosphere. To quote an analysis of the American National Fire Protection Association:

Conflagrations create terrific thermal updrafts. The heated air and gases rise and air is drawn in from the side of the burning area so rapidly that a high wind is often reported by nearby observers while the air is relatively calm a few miles away. Frequently large pieces of burning material are carried aloft in several directions and start numerous other fires.[3]

References to high winds, and the outbreak of separate fires, occur in many of the descriptions of the great fires of history, including that of 1849 in Toronto, without, of course, the narrator realizing what was actually happening. Take, for example, this Dutch account of the Great Fire of London in 1666: "It was marvelous that during this great fire a very strong wind should have prevailed. The wind carried the flames in various directions, and drove them along by the river ...."[4] Or this description of the 1871 Chicago fire written by one of the victims:

... no words can give an idea of the horrors of that night. The wind, blowing like a hurricane, howling like myriads of evil spirits, drove the flames before it with a force & fierceness which could never be described or imagined; it was not flame but a solid wall of fire which was hurled against the buildings .... The air was full of cinders; pieces of blazing shingles & boards & great strips of tarred felt fell in every direction, now on the roofs of houses yet unburned & then on the loads of furniture & bedding which people were trying to save .... [5]

One might well think that the cities of North America, with their regular patterns and wider streets, would have a much better fire record than their more congested counterparts in Europe. Actually, because of a far greater number of frame buildings, there have been more great fires on this continent. J.G. Smith estimates that, of the 528 major fires in the world between 1815 and 1915, 290 were in Canada and the United States, and that in Canada alone from 1750 to 1917 there were 61 major fires located as follows: Halifax, 4; Fredericton, 2; Saint John 7; St Hyacinthe, 2; Quebec City, 14; Montreal, 9; Ottawa-Hull, 5; Toronto, 6; other towns, 10; Northern Ontario forests, 2.[6] This list includes some fires which were not of the conflagration type; but it does not take into consideration some of the major fires in Newfoundland, such as the ones that destroyed St. John's in 1846 and 1892. Unfortunately, the incidence of major fires in Canada did not improve to any great extent for some years after Smith wrote. Quebec was subject to fairly frequent conflagrations in its smaller towns — Rimouski and Cabano in 1950 come readily to mind — and there have been bad fires in cities with good fire protection, such as the blaze in downtown Winnipeg which began in a building equipped with sprinklers. Toronto nearly had a third great fire in 1977 when the old Eaton's Annex building ignited several nearby structures.

The six fires that Smith lists for Toronto, beside the great fires of 1849 and 1904, consist of the one that struck University College, University of Toronto, on Feb. 14, 1890 and three others which occurred in early 1895 — in the *Globe* building on January 6, in the Osgoodby Building on January 10 and in Simpson's store on March 3. These last three are interesting in that all began in buildings at least five storeys in height, all were transmitted to the roof by vertical openings, all spread to other buildings, and all were stopped by natural causes and good luck rather than fire-fighting. In every case, the firemen were hampered by the fact that the water pressure was insufficient for the streams from the hoses to reach the upper storeys. Nine years later, when the Second Great Fire of Toronto broke out, a lack of water pressure was again one of the major factors in its getting out of control. The City Council finally authorized the construction of a high-pressure system the following October, stimulated by a seventy-five per cent increase in fire-insurance rates.

The 1849 and 1904 fires had this in common: they were both located in the centre of the city and destroyed an area of some ten to fifteen acres. Here, however, the resemblance ends. The 1904 fire was entirely confined to commercial buildings and did a much larger amount of damage, some $10,400,000. The 1849 fire, although it too destroyed many commercial buildings — and at that time Toronto had none too many — also burned some houses, the principal church, St James's Cathedral, and the offices of two of the leading newspapers, the *Toronto Mirror* and the *Patriot*. As well, it damaged the largest market in the city. and it came very near to burning down the new 1844 city hall, St Andrew's Presbyterian Church and the main fire hall. Thus, it had a much greater effect on the social life of the city, and its aftermath — particularly the reconstruction of St James's Cathedral, involved many of the leading citizens of the era.

Surprising enough, for such an important event, there is only one drawing of the ruins, which was just discovered recently. There are, however, a considerable number of accounts of the fire, both in newspapers and diaries. Probably the best newspaper account is given in the April 11 *Examiner*, where its entire course is described in detail and the names and addresses of most of the people suffering losses noted. There is also a table showing the amounts of loss sustained by the various insurance companies. *The British Colonist*, the *Church* and the *Christian Guardian* gave shorter outlines of the course of fire with insurance- loss estimates.

The *Globe* went to press on the morning of the fire and was therefore able to say little. It did, however, provide the first printed notice:

Postscript

Saturday A. M. - 6 o'clock

With deep regret we announce that a dreadful fire broke out about half-past 1 o'clock this morning ... it is said that some people are hurt. The military are assisting. We shall announce the particulars in an extra by next post. The fire is not yet extinguished.

In its next issue the paper provided another list of the losses suffered by individuals with an estimate of the amount which would be covered by insurance where any was carried.

Other accounts of the fire, based on communications from the Toronto papers, appeared in various out-of-town journals such as the Montreal *Pilot*. The only newspaper description of personal experiences is contained in a letter written by Bishop John Strachan to the Society for the Promotion of Christian Knowledge which was copied in the *Church* on Aug. 9, 1849. In it the bishop appealed for restoration funds for St James's and gave an account of his own experiences during the fire. Unfortunately, it is not too helpful, since in the confusion no one remembered to wake him up until 4 a.m., when the worst was over.

Three other contemporary references to the fire are quite valuable. The first of these is a diary entry by the Reverend Henry Scadding, rector of Holy Trinity Church, in which he describes the size of the burned-out area as well as the destruction of St James's and also provides a detailed report of the weather conditions. The second is architect John Howard's "Office Journal," which says little about the fire itself but provides invaluable notes on the details of the subsequent insurance adjustments in which he played a leading part as one of the city's few surveyors. The last is a petition of the fire brigade to the City Council, written a month later on May 7, which describes the actual fighting of the fire.

Several later reminiscences are generally more detailed. Scadding, in his *Toronto of Old* (1873), gives a much-quoted account of the burning of St James's which is doubtless the best literary effort resulting from the fire. Further minor details together with another eye-witness description of the burning of

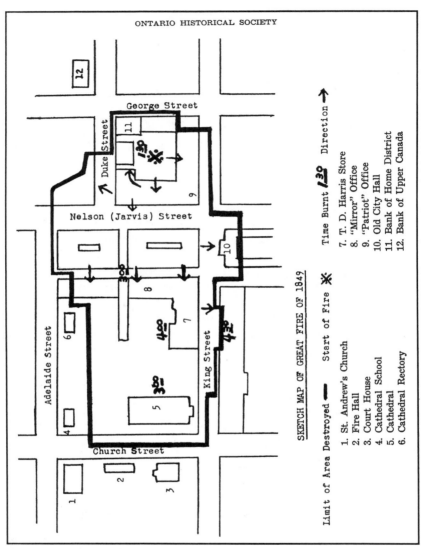

Map of 1849 fire area.

St James's — which must have been really spectacular from the amount of space devoted to it — are provided by C.C. Taylor in *Toronto 'Called Back'* (1888).One of the longest and most detailed descriptions of the fire is that of Samuel Thompson, a partner in the *Patriot*, in his *Reminiscences of a Canadian Pioneer*. Unfortunately, his account is hopelessly inaccurate wherever it can be checked against any other source. The last eye-witness story of the fire is that of William Henry Pearson in his *Recollections and Records of Toronto of Old* (1914), where, in a very short chapter, he describes the burning of the only "fireproof" building in the city, Thomas D. Harris's hardware store.

As well as these personal narratives there are various accounts of the fire by later writers using one or the other of them as sources. John Ross Robertson, in his monumental description of all the fires in Toronto up to his time in the second volume of the *Landmarks of Toronto* (1896), gives an accurate description of the "Cathedral Fire," as he calls it, along with details of the losses largely based on those provided in the *Examiner*. He also gives a rough map of the destroyed area.

One of the most favourable descriptions we have of Toronto in the middle years of the last century comes from the pen of the Reverend H. Christmas, who visited the city early in 1849 shortly before the fire took place, and later wrote:

> Toronto is a noble and promising city, — a young giant of the west, — a proud monument of British energy directed by the fostering care of Providence. And it may be imagined that it was with no little interest that I gazed upon its polished spires and brightly tinned roofs, glittering in the light of the morning sun, as the steamer rounded the point and swept up to the wharf... [7]

Christmas saw a city which was undergoing a rapid expansion, as is exemplified by the population increase from 19,706 in 1845 to 30,775 by 1851. It had many of the amenities of contemporary urbanization: a water system, a sewage system, gas lighted streets, licensed cabs and eight newspapers.

The "noble and promising city" that the good reverend saw was not, however, apparent to all visitors. *The Journal of a Wanderer*, anonymously written a few years earlier, presents quite a different picture:

The appearance of many of the inhabitants of Toronto, would lead me to think that it is rather a dissipated place .... There is wanting that spirit of enterprise which you see in the States. They reckon the importation of immigrants ... as their harvest, and ... pluck them every spring .... I would not advise anyone who has capital, and can live comfortably at home, ever to come here ... a residence of two or three years here sometimes makes a person look ten years older.[8]

Much as loyal citizens might disagree with this analysis, they would have to concede that the "Wanderer's" description of the weather had some merit.

Indeed it has been alleged, and with some correctness, that for two months of the Spring and two months of the Autumn, you are up to your middle in mud, for four months of summer you are broiled by the heat, choked by the dust, and devoured by the mosquitos; and for the remaining four months, if you get your nose above the snow, it is to have it bit off by the frost ....[9]

The main business artery of the city at that time was King Street, already built up solidly practically all the way from Jarvis (Nelson) Street to York Street. It was the section of this street stretching from Church to Jarvis streets where the fire was to wreak such havoc. On the west side of Church Street were the town's first fire hall, built in 1827 and still housing three of the city's six fire brigades, and St Andrew's Presbyterian Church. East of these buildings, across Church Street, was then, as it is today, the property of the Anglican cathedral. The cathedral itself, the fourth of the five St James's to stand on that site, was a new structure built to replace one which had burnt in 1839. It was evidently an object of little beauty, and even Christmas was unimpressed: "...the building as it stands is one with the commonest possible round-headed windows, and but for the ill-proportioned and stumpy attempt at a spire, might answer as well, or, perhaps better, as regards to the exterior, for a corn exchange."[10]

King Street looking east to the spires of St Andrew's and St James, 1846.

On the south side of King, a block to the east of these buildings, was the old St Lawrence Market, the commercial centre of the city. It was a red brick structure which had been erected in 1833 from the plans of James G. Chewitt and which for some years housed both the market and the municipal offices. The latter had been moved in 1845 to a new city hall-cum-fish market which stood immediately to the south. The area surrounding these buildings was largely built up with shops and hotels, although there were a fair number of dwellings interspersed in the section north of King Street.

Josiah Broomfield, an indefatigable representative of the Phoenix of London Assurance Company who toured most of the eastern section of the continent in the mid 1840s to make insurance inspections, has left us a detailed description of the construction of the city, which he visited in 1845. Discussing the centre section he said:

> ... in this and other business parts of the town the Houses are mostly built of Brick — there are some few timber ones, here and there, fronting the Street tho' they are for the most part small dilapidated Buildings. About one fourth of the Brick houses have Tin roofs the remainder of them and the whole of the Wooden Houses are Shingled ... the outbuildings in the rear are invariably of Wood covered with Shingles. The whole of the New Houses that are now building are of Brick and Stone, and are all to have Tin roof.[11]

Although these conditions compared favourably with those in many of the cities of the time, the city's central core generally presented a considerable degree of hazard, in spite of the heavy brick fire walls between the buildings. The inside of the blocks, the most difficult part to reach in fighting any fire, contained the worst construction, frame, and the most inflammable roofing, wooden shingles. Any fire starting in this region could attack the larger brick buildings on the outside of the block at the rear windows.

What was stored in these buildings presented another problem. The majority of the buildings fell into three classes; taverns, hardware stores and dry goods stores. In the first, there were bound to be large amounts of hay and straw for horses, probably largely stored in the frame outbuildings; in the second, stock of oils and other inflammables; and in the third, clothing and linens, which, although not as hazardous as hay, oils and the like, would make fine fuel once a major fire started. The sidewalks were yet another danger; not only were they made of wood but also their elevation above ground level gave fires a good draft. A few years later this type of sidewalk was to be a major factor in spreading the Great Fire of Chicago.

On the other hand, there were several positive features. Besides the fire walls that separated many buildings, there were the large churchyard of St James's; the open gardens outside the immediate downtown area and the proximity of the lake water. Another favourable feature was the Fire Act, which had been passed in 1845 which combined all the various existing ordinances into one amplified set of regulations. This prohibited many obvious fire hazards such as smoking in stables, keeping ashes in wooden vessels and lighting fires near buildings. It also regulated carpenter shops, stoves and stove pipes, as well as chimney sweeping, and provided for a fire warden to make inspections and levy fines where necessary. To make certain that the warden did his duty properly, Section XXIII of the act provided that, should a chimney catch fire as a result of not having been properly swept, the fire warden would be liable for the same fine as the owner.

The act further monitored the volunteer fire department, which consisted of both fire fighters and a salvage division, The Property Protection Company. The firemen were provided with uniforms, exempted from jury duty and given the right to choose their own officers and to nominate the "engineers", who attended to the maintenance of the engines. These were formally appointed by the City Council. Overall control was vested in a chief engineer and the assistant engineers. In addition to these regulars, the act provided that in an emergency any male aged sixteen to sixty could be drafted to help pull engines, demolish buildings, save property or do whatever else was necessary. The city officials were given wide powers in this respect, Section X of the Act stating that: "The Mayor, and alderman of the city, who are to be recognized as bearing a wand with a gilded flame at the top, have authority to command the assistance of others at such fires. Persons refusing liable to be sent to jail."[12] Fire warning was given by ringing both bells of St James's Cathedral, keys for the church being available at both the city hall and the West Market Place (St Patrick's Market on Queen Street). When one considers the amount of time it must have taken for someone to run or ride from the fire to get the keys, unlock the church and ring the bell, to say nothing of the time required for the firemen to assemble and bring the engines to the fire, it is a wonder that any buildings were saved once they were ablaze.

The chief engineer of the Fire Department at the time of the Great Fire was Robert Beard (1807-1882), who held that office from 1842 to 1846 and again from 1848 to 1850. He had had considerable experience as a fireman, having served with the hook and ladder company and then been assistant engineer from 1838 to 1841. He was also involved in municipal politics and was alderman of St Lawrence Ward for some years. The department he commanded in 1849 consisted of six companies, which were named and stationed as follows:

Engine Company No. 1 (York) - Fireman's Hall Church Street.
Engine Company No. 2 (Toronto) - Fireman's Hall Bay Street.
Engine Company No. 3 (British America) - Fireman's Hall Church Street.
Engine Company No. 4 (Victoria) - Fireman's Hall St Patrick's Market.
Hook and Ladder Co. No. 1 (Toronto) - Fireman's Hall Church Street.
Hook and Ladder No. 2 (Hercules) - Fireman's Hall Bay Street.

Except for the "British America", the fire engines were hand-pumped machines of the "goose neck" type, so called because the hose was attached to a pipe which rose about three feet above the deck of the engine and was curved like a goose's neck. Each engine had a water tank with suction hose attached to its rear, which was operated by seven or eight men pumping on a bar or brake on each side. Two of the engines had been with the department since it was founded in 1826, and were probably in an advanced state of decrepitude by the late 1840s. The "British America" had been presented to the city by the insurance company of the same name in 1837 and was a more powerful engine, requiring twelve to fifteen men on each brake. At this period it was quite common for insurance companies to present fire engines to cities in which they did a considerable amount of business, and the engines certainly represented a sound form of "insurance" for the companies themselves.

The firemen were far from satisfied with their treatment by the city at the time of the fire, and shortly afterward — the fire probably having acted as a catalyst in bringing matters to a head — they presented a petition of grievances to Mayor George Gurnett. Basically two complaints were outlined in this document, which was written by William C. Morrison, secretary of the fire brigade, on May 7: lack of financial support from the City Council, and lack of help and moral support from the citizens. As well the firemen pointed out that the only privilege they received — the freedom from jury duty — actually gave them very little, since many of them were too young or did not quality for other reasons. Finally, the funds allocated for uniforms and the like were inadequate and many of them had to spend money on their personal equipment.

The firemen supported their complaint about the lack of funds by pointing out that in 1826 the city, with a population of 1,719, possessed two fire engines, whereas in 1849, with a population of 24,000, it possessed only four, none of them of the latest type. The petition also gave an interesting comparison of the Toronto and Buffalo fire departments; it showed that the Toronto brigade's lack of necessary equipment and inadequate manpower extended into almost all facets of its operations:[13]

Type of Equipment or personnel	Buffalo	Toronto
Engineers	3	3
Wardens	10	0
Members	460	210
Engines	9	4
Hook and Ladder	2	2
Feet of leading hose	4,960	2,500
Feet of suction hose	150	60
Carriages for same	9	4
Lamps	24	4
Buckets	30	2

The complaints against the public highlighted both a lack of interest and a lack of support. For example, the Property Protection Company had had only 25 members the previous October instead of the 200 allowed by law. An attempt made to increase this number by petitioning 300 persons, advertising a meeting in all the papers and holding two meetings resulted only in an increase of five. Further, all appeals for help from gawking spectators at fires met with refusals. As the petition said:

> It has been the painful lot of the Firemen to feel that the Citizens do not participate in or respond to their exertions—while upon duty mingling with the flames or drenched with the freezing water, their blood conjealed with intense cold, with every sinew strained to its utmost tension— the Toronto Fire Brigade have seen—have heard—too often heard-the requests, the supplications of their Engineers or their Captains made for help to thousands of intelligent but idle Citizens—persons who have been more than once saved by the exertion of the Firemen from some former conflagration—they have heard no responsive cheer—they have received no help or succour—but sickening with the unnatural spectacle— ... they have been left to struggle unaided.[14]

The petition ended with another blast at the citizenry over their conduct during the Great Fire. When the petition failed to effect an improvement in conditions, most of the firemen resigned. The city was practically without fire protection until the end of the year, when the City Council offered more generous terms to firemen and new companies could be organized.

In addition to their disagreements with the City Council and citizenry for years the firemen carried on a running battle with the water works. Water to fight fires had originally been provided by bucket brigades and licensed carters. In 1841, however, it was decided to provide a proper water supply to fight fires, and the legislature authorized Albert Furness, James Mason and John Strang of Montreal to form the City of Toronto Gas-Light and Water Company, with capital not to exceed 40,000. By 1843 a reservoir had been built on Huron Street, north of St Patrick

Street, and water was pumped up from the intake at the foot of John Street. From this reservoir the water was led to the twenty fire plugs through a system of improperly installed wooden pipes. Although the sole purpose of the system was to provide water for fires, it proved an almost complete failure in this regard. Even after it had been in operation for over two years, the revised Fire Protection Act of 1845 still included a section (No. XI) making it compulsory for the carters to attend all fires: "Licensed carters to attend all fires with their horse and cart, for the purpose of conveying water thereto, and not to leave without the permission of the officer in command of the department."[15]

Financially, this dual system of water supply was a heavy drain on the city. The Water Company received a flat £250 per annum, and in addition to this the payment to carters for the years 1843-47 was £584/15/0, which does not compare very favourably with the £419/16/3 paid in the years 1839-42 before the company began operations.[16] In 1847 the value of the water works was pretty well summed up by the Civic Committee on Fire and Water, which stated, after an investigation, that: "... so far from contributing to the security of life and property (it) had considerably enhanced the danger to both, by leading citizens to the entertainment of a dependence on a source of supply which had in almost every instance proved defective."[17]

In view of these statements, Broomfield's comments in his insurance report on the subject of the water supply are interesting: "The city is well supplied with Water, from the Mains laid down in all the principal streets, by [the] Waterworks Company — and Fire Plugs are erected at convenient distances."[18] Like all experts paying flying visits, poor Broomfield was at the mercy of the agents of his insurance company on the spot, who were eager to expand business and wanted to present Toronto conditions to their company in a rosy light.

Naturally, the people who were most unhappy with the water supply were the Fire Department. An example of their feelings may be found in the petition of the British America Fire Engine Company on April 5, 1847, written after a house on John Street was destroyed because of a lack of water:

> ... the subject of the frequent deficiency of water
> at fires ... being brought under consideration, it
> was unanimously resolved: That the company

cannot too strongly urge on the city corporation and the various insurance companies the necessity for some immediate and energetic steps being taken to supply the engines with water at fires. The so-called water-works, for which the citizens are taxed so heavily, are, in general, of little service in case of fire, and might with advantage to the safety of the inhabitants be at once shut up .... That if some sufficient means to compel the company to fulfill their obligations to the citizens be not adopted, or some other means be not devised to provide an ample supply of water for the engines at fires, the members of the fire company cannot be expected to remain associated in a service, which, thus rendered inefficient, must be dishonourable.[19]

To present a fair picture, however, both sides must be given, and the Fire Department was often at fault itself. For example, take the following description of the burning of Doel's Brewery at the corner of Bay and Adelaide streets, as reported in the *Patriot* on April 13, 1847.

The hydrant at the corner of King and Bay Streets was the only hydrant open — and from this and the three ponds just mentioned the chief water supply was obtained (there were seven other hydrants available and not used). Round the hydrant just mentioned, there were generally five, sometimes six carts, waiting to be filled, and from the want of a properly managed hose each took about twice as long to fill as was requisite. We do not hesitate to assert that with the pressure of water on the hydrant a hose with a double branch could have filled two carts in about one-half the time occupied in filling one. This is the province of the Fire Engine Department not of the Water Company.

Sometimes it must have seemed to the citizens that both the Fire Department and the Water Works were conspiring to aid the flames. On June 1, 1847 the *Patriot* reported a fire at Yonge and Richmond streets as follows:

> The cistern or assistance as it is called, of (Engine) No. 1, was so defective that of the water poured in fully half escaped at the leaks; and the hose connecting it and the Engine was losing water in as melancholy a proportion ... paralysed at the want of water ... Engines were partially supplied by carters.

The British Canadian on June 5 also discussed this fire: "The hydrants were not supplied there being only three or four feet of water in the reservoir instead of nine or more .... Another fact, much to be regretted, was the defective state of some of the fire engines." The issue of the *British Colonist* on the same day carried two letters which had been written to the City Council. The first pointed out the misuses of the hydrants by the Fire Department, stating in part: "... if the defection appears to originate in the mismanagement of the hydrants and hose, you may adopt an improved system in regard to them ...." The signature was that of "Albert Furniss, For the City of Toronto Gas and Water Co." The other letter was equally disinterested.

> Sir: The want of water last night at the fire being so obvious, and the distressing destruction of property consequent thereon, force me to the duty of once more reporting the total inefficiency of the Water Works, as they are at present arranged, and I sincerely hope the Council will take immediate steps to remedy the evil.

The signature here was James Armstrong, the chief engineer of the Fire Department. The letter makes no reference to the possibility of the trouble being caused by the age and decrepit condition of some of his equipment.

Thus it would appear, not very surprisingly, that relations between the two organizations were anything but satisfactory. On occasion, fortunately, the hydrants worked admirably, and the firemen performed with equal efficiency and success, although sometimes with discouraging results. Take this editorial describing a fire at Rice Lewis & Co., hardware merchants, on Nov. 20, 1847, which appeared in the *British Colonist*:

> It was got under by the Fire Companies, but the goods were very greatly damaged by the water pumped on them. This is said to have been done to a somewhat unnecessary extent. Even firemen should be as careful as they can, consistently with the safety of the surrounding property ....

At times, both parties must have felt that they could not win.

"On the morning of Saturday, April 7, 1849," wrote John Ross Robertson in 1896, "occurred a fire by which more damage was done then by any blaze before or since."[20] It began about 1:30 a.m. in the centre of the block bounded by Adelaide (Duke), George, King, and Jarvis (Nelson) streets, which was then one of the most heavily built-up areas in the city [see map]. The yard where it started was occupied by a collection of frame outbuildings, probably used at least in part as stables. These belonged to Post's Tavern, which stood halfway up the block on Jarvis Street, and Covey's Tavern (formerly Graham's), which occupied a similar position on King Street. The cause was never discovered, and although there had been a suspicion of attempted arson in the area two months before, it was probably either a lantern or careless smoking which set off the blaze. Taverns, at that period, were correctly regarded as fire hazards partly because of the straw problem but also because of the condition of some of their clients. As Broomfield said in relation to St John's, Newfoundland: "The rare occurrence of fire of late years is attributed to the disuse of ardent spirits among the lower classes of inhabitants who are now nearly all teatotallers [sic], the former fires having originated in grog shops.[21]

The fire rapidly engulfed the centre of the block and, as the wind was not yet very strong, began burning in all directions. To the north, it spread up to Adelaide Street, evidently burning some dwellings on its south side, and even scorching some buildings on the north side; for, although no damage is mentioned there in the newspaper accounts, Howard noted in his "Journal" that he was assessing the damage to the Cochrane residence which stood on the north side. To the east, the fire burned down the Bank of the Home District on George Street, although fortunately the records were saved, but did not cross the street to the east side. To the south, the fire burned through Covey's Tavern to King Street at the centre of the block and then spread both east and west along the north side of the street. To the east, it took out four frame houses, and then, after either severely damaging or destroying Sproul's store, it was stopped by heavier construction — and probably the wind — before it reached the corner of George Street. To the west of the starting point, Post's Tavern on Jarvis Street soon went, and from there the fire — with the wind which was now blowing east-north-east to help it — spread southwards to the large brick stores at the corner of King and Jarvis streets. The fire must have reached there fairly quickly — possibly even before it got to the Home District Savings Bank on the opposite side of the block — for there was apparently only a small amount of goods rescued from these structures.

It was at this point that the only loss of life took place. A group of men including Richard Watson, publisher of the recently defunct *Upper Canada Gazette*, were attempting to rescue type from the *Patriot* office when the flames attacked the building. Samuel Thomson, who as a partner in the paper should have known what happened, tells a story at variance with all the others; but, as noted, he is a far from an accurate source. Probably the *Examiner*'s account of the incident presents a reasonably true picture: "Mr. Watson, publisher of the *Upper Canada Gazette*, went into the *Patriot* office to assist in removing some of the materials. He stayed too long and never returned. One of the printers belonging to the office had to be taken out of the window; previously to which Mr. Watson had started down stairs. He must have suffocated by smoke in the passage and so perished." In the confusion he was not missed at the time, and it was not until he failed to return to his family in the morning that a search was made, and his remains discovered.

It was probably about the same time that Charles Donlevy, the owner of the *Mirror*, the other paper to be burnt out, broke his leg in attempting to help with the rescue operations. Although much of this salvage work was probably done by the owners themselves, there must have been — judging from the amount of property saved — a great number of voluntary workers helping to rescue goods. Certainly the Property Protection Company was not large enough to have removed much by itself.

The fire had now completely covered the block in which it originated, except for some buildings at the southeast corner; but it had not as yet spread beyond except where it had scorched the buildings to the north. Now backed by the wind, the flames were threatening to cross Jarvis Street and attack the buildings to the west. This area, now covered largely by the park east of St James's Cathedral, was then solidly built-up except for the cemetery adjacent to the church itself. It was divided into four blocks by two narrow streets — really lanes — Francis (Market) Street (north-south) and Commercial Street (east-west). At this strategic juncture the water supply broke down; the blaze crossed the street without opposition and assumed the proportions of a conflagration. The *Examiner*, after recording that for an hour one of the engines stood uselessly by, goes on to say:

> No one can shut his eyes to the fact that much of the damage resulted from the want of a sufficient supply of water. It is the opinion of many persons who were on the spot that, with a good supply of water, the fire might have been prevented extending further than Nelson [Jarvis] Street.

Thus, with no water to stop it, the fire quickly crossed the street from Post's Tavern, which was of frame construction, to Platt's Tavern, a new brick building at the south corner of Jarvis and Commercial streets. From there, aided by the large amount of frame construction in the area and the rising wind, it soon doubled its area and spread west to Francis Street. Once again, the rescue operations were responsible for the saving of a fair amount of goods, but even more property was destroyed. Ironically, among the sufferers was the Water Company, a tenant in Thomas Thompson's building on the northeast corner of King and Francis streets, whose entire records were destroyed, although some other tenants in the same building managed to save theirs.

By this time (2:00-3:00 a.m.) the fire had covered three blocks with increased intensity because the stores along King Street, from Francis to George streets, most of which were large buildings, must have been nearly all blazing simultaneously. Worse, the wind was now driving embers and shingles over the area to the west. The editor of the *Christian Guardian* found them in the yard of his residence half a mile away, and Bishop John Strachan reported that they were carried two miles. Here we have a typical example of a conflagration creating its own weather. The official records of the government weather office, located in the university grounds a little over a mile to the northwest, show that there was only a mild east-north-east wind of six to nine miles an hour blowing during the entire time the fire was burning.

About 3:00 a.m., one of these pieces of burning shingle caught in the lattice in a window of the cathedral tower and ignited it. Here various accounts disagree and give several different reasons for the fire not being quickly extinguished. Some say that the would-be rescuers were prevented from climbing the tower; others, that the fire engines were busy elsewhere; and still others, that the people were held back by confusion and inertia. However, even if the fire engines had been ready, and the hydrants operating properly, they could not have thrown a stream of water high enough to help. Probably the most accurate account of what happened is that given by the *Examiner*.

> One of the cakes of fire, with which the air was loaded for a great distance, fell into the wooden window of the spire of the cathedral. It was a long time before it burst into flame. Spectators indulged in speculations as to whether the sparks would ignite the wood, some expressing one opinion and some another; while if they had acted instead of idly speculating and talking, the cathedral might have been saved. At length the spark burst into flame and it was not long before some persons were inside wasting pails of water on the flames which a single pail would have prevented when the fire was confined to a mere spark.

This report of mob apathy is confirmed by the opinion of the Fire Brigade, which stated in its petition a month later:

> At the recent terrible conflagration as on every former occasion there were many — too many —

whose exertions consisted in quietly gazing on the extending ravages of the appalling scene before and around them and when requested to assist those who was nearly prostrated to the earth with exhaustion, unfeelingly refused.[22].

From this start, to quote Scadding,

> ... the flames made their way downwards within the tower till the internal timbers of the roofing over the main body of the building were reached. There, in the natural order of things, the fire readily spread; and the whole interior of the church, in the course of an hour, was transformed, before the eyes of a bewildered multitude looking powerlessly on, first into a vast 'burning fiery furnace' and then, as the roof collapsed and fell, into a confused chaos of raging flame.[23]

Fortunately, the fire spread down slowly enough that everything moveable, including the organ, library and even the various hymnals in the pews, were rescued from the building. The fall of the spire must have presented an impressive sight, as Conyngham C. Taylor, a dry goods merchant, described it many years later:

> The writer distinctly recollects the falling of the spire. When the fire had done its work, and the crash seemed inevitable, it was supposed the spire would fall outwards, and the spectators kept a long way off, when, to the surprise of everyone it fell almost perpendicularly, top foremost, the vane on the top striking the flag at the front door.[24]

When the cathedral was first ignited the buildings to the east of it were not yet afire; but practically simultaneously, the fire, as well as spreading to the cathedral, crossed narrow Francis Street, probably on a broad front along its entire length, and also crossed King Street to the south and broke out in the old city hall. The first of these two new areas to be attacked, that west of

Francis Street, was divided into two blocks by Commercial Street. This was a short lane running westwards from Jarvis Street halfway between King and Adelaide Streets, crossing Francis Street on the way. The area to the north of this street was largely occupied by small houses in the part west of Market Street, except for the tavern of Messrs. Bell and Lennox and its outbuildings. All these were quickly levelled but the fire was stopped on the north at Adelaide Street, leaving St James's rectory and some adjacent houses standing.

South of Commercial Street the fire swept up various small structures in the rear of Francis and King streets and then burnt along the line of stores on King Street. Some of the merchants on this street, such as Campbell & Hunter, sadlers, and John Eastwood, clothier, had managed to rescue all or most of their stock by this time (3:30-4:00 a.m.), but one merchant, Thomas D. Harris, refused to allow any goods to be removed on the grounds that his building was "fireproof." The structure was certainly solidly built, with all the windows being protected by iron shutters and the roof covered with tin. For a while it stood intact as the buildings around it burned, but then it, too, burst into flames and was consumed. Some of the newspapers suggested that the fire spread to it through the roof or by a wooden hoisting tackle in the rear, but more likely the structure was ignited by the heat radiated by the surrounding buildings as they burned. One advantage of its superior construction may have been that, by burning slightly later than its neighbours, it did not expose the south side of King Street to as much heat.

The *Examiner* states that by about 3:20 a.m. the wind had switched to blowing from the north. With no evidence from the Weather Bureau to support this change, it is probably a case of the fire, which was burning strongly on the north side of King Street, creating its own eddies. Meanwhile, the fire that had broken out in the old city hall quickly destroyed the northern range of the building facing King Street. This was occupied by various stores and offices, including a depository or storage warehouse of Gooderham & Worts, and the Toronto Athenaeum. The latter, with its more than 1,000 volumes, was the second largest library in the city, the largest being the legislative library. Evidently, most of the books were rescued.

Although unable to save this northern section, the firemen somehow managed to prevent the flames from spreading southward to the wings around the other three sides of the market courtyard, and consequently to the new city hall, which stood immediately to the south of the older buildings. The fire at this time, around 3:30-4:00 a.m., was at its height, with six blocks aflame and sparks and burning pieces of debris being carried over a wide area. It must have been visible for miles, and the editor of the *Church* advised that: "... a friend from St Catharines tells us that not only the lurid sky was seen, but the flames were distinctly visible there."

Toronto was, however, saved by a combination of three developments. The first was a "smart" rain shower, which, although it only lasted for a few minutes, wet down the roofs of the buildings west of the blaze and made it more difficult for flying brands to ignite them. As Scadding wrote in his diary on April 1: "Had this not damped the roofs I think the whole western portion of Toronto from Church Street, would have been in flames simultaneously."[25] The rain fell about 3:30 a.m., and although the shower was localized enough that it was not recorded by the weather office, it was heavy enough for both the *Examiner* and the *Church* to note its appearance and agree with Scadding's opinion.

The second favourable development was that the wind continued from the north and east and thus drove the flames up against the open cemetery around St James's, which broke the in that direction and saved the court house, fire hall and St Andrew's Church to the west of Church Street. The third development was the arrival of the troops from the garrison (about 4:00 a.m.) to assist the firefighters, who must by then have been completely worn out. The firemen themselves attributed the saving of the city to this intervention and stated in their petition: "The Brigade feel had it not been for the timely arrival and assistance of the military in seconding their endeavours on that wild night of woe, Toronto would not now stand as it does and many another monumental ruin would have chronicled that sad event."[26] The troops arrived as both the buildings on the south side of King Street, opposite the cathedral, and the stores to the east of it were beginning to burn. Thanks to their assistance, the south side of King Street in this area was saved, although the roof was burned off one building and at least one other building partly damaged (a few of these stores of the 1830s still stand today as the oldest commercial structures in the city). By 5:00 a.m. the flames were finally under control, and an hour later they were nearly out.

Drawing of St. James's Cathedral shortly after fire.

In 1849 Toronto was extremely fortunate, as it was to be again in 1904. The ruins may have spread over a large part of the heart of the city; but much of the commercial district, as well as nearly all the residential sections, were untouched, a situation only too rarely to be found after a conflagration. For example, when Saint John, New Brunswick, burned in 1877, although it had a much smaller population than Toronto in 1849, the flames destroyed two-fifths of the city covering some 200 acres, including 1,612 houses. Toronto was also lucky in another way. Not only was the area destroyed comparatively small, but the times were prosperous and by the end of the year, except for the ruins of the cathedral and the uncompleted new St Lawrence Market, there were few signs of the recent catastrophe.

Chapter 14

The Rebuilding After the First Great Fire[1]

The First Great Fire of Toronto in 1849 had left some ten to fifteen acres in the heart of the main business district in ruins, the destroyed structures including the St Lawrence Market and St James's Cathedral. The subsequent reconstruction — most of which took place in 1849, although the restored St James's was not completed until 1875 — was probably the most important single alteration to the city's face in the nineteenth century.

The immediate question after any fire, in 1849 as today, is the insurance settlement. Fortunately for Toronto, the fire did not reach a scale where it bankrupted any of the insurance companies involved, as was an all-too-frequent happening in such cases. From 1845 to 1871 about three-quarters of the American insurance companies were put out of business by conflagrations. The Chicago Fire of 1871 alone bankrupted fourteen local companies, and forced the suspension of payments by some thirty-seven other companies with head offices outside the state. Local insurance companies — that is, those operating mainly in one city — were particularly vulnerable to such large fires since they lacked a "spread of risk." Their major liabilities tended to be grouped in their home town, and when it burned, their premium income was insufficient to cover the losses incurred, because too little premium income was available from other areas to help cover the payment of settlements.[2]

Two local companies operated in Toronto at the time of the fire, the Home District Mutual and the British American Assurance Company. Both survived the fire, although with some difficulties — as the first laid assessments on its policyholders of 12 1/2 per cent of their provisional premium on April 7, and a further 2 1/2 per cent on April 20; the latter ordered its shareholders to come forward with an installment on their capital stock payable at 5 per cent before June 18, and 5 per cent before August 6. The reason for these latter charges was the system in vogue at that time of purchasing stock on an installment payment system as the money was required, rather than in one flat sum. The Home District Mutual Fire Insurance Company, to give it its full title, had its office on Jarvis (Nelson) Street and had been in operation since 1837. Its secretary-treasurer, John Rains, had been careful not to accept too great an insurance liability in the central area so that the company's loss in 1849 was only £4,000 or £5,000. The other company, the British American, had been incorporated in 1833 by fifty-two prominent citizens including Archdeacon John Strachan, John Rolph, Henry John Boulton and John Elmsley, and at the time of the fire it had William Allan as its governor and T.W. Birtchall as its managing director. This company was very heavily exposed in the area of the fire and suffered a loss of over £17,000 (at roughly $5.00 to the pound) — more than double the amount paid by any other company.

Besides these companies, which dealt directly with the public, there were other companies with head offices outside the province which were usually represented by local merchants, who operated as their agents in much the modern manner. These representatives were given the authority to accept risks and write policies, but they were usually regulated to an extent by the underwriting instructions of their various principals and by the rates in their companies' manuals. The actual number of these companies operating in the city varied considerably over time. Those losing money in the fire included three British, two Quebec and five American companies. All were evidently able to meet their losses without trouble.

It is not possible to prepare an exact table of losses, since none of the Toronto papers agree completely on the amounts. Their figures are as follows, in pounds:

Insurance Company	Examiner	Globe	Christian Guardian
	April 11		April 12
	April 11		
Aetna of Hartford	3,600	3,600	3,600
Alliance of London	8,150	8,150	8,000
British American	17,000	17,000	20,000
Camden	400	400	400
Columbus	5,307	5,310	5,300

Globe of London	2,050	2,050	2,025
Hartford Fire	3,900	3,900	3,900
Home District Mutual	5,000	4,575	4,500
Montreal Assurance	4,124	2,500	2,500
Phoenix of London	5,850	4,400	5,000
Protection of Hartford	1,300	1,350	1,350
Quebec Fire	2,900	2,950	3,000
Totals	59,581	56,185	59,575

These figures probably should represent the face values of the insurance policies, not the adjusted loss, and those for the *Examiner* do not include the damage to the stores on the south side of King Street — although such losses cannot have been large enough to make much difference to the totals. In most of the cases, the loss was complete and, because insurance was not carried to full value by the majority of the sufferers, the overall direct loss was likely far greater than the amount of the policies. The *Examiner* suggested a grand loss from the fire of at least £100,000, and stated that some estimates went as high as £300,000, which would appear to be excessive. Smith, in his *Fire Waste in Canada*, estimated a total of $50,000. Unlike present-day adjustments, the above would not, of course, include claims for business interruption or for loss of rental income. Calculating figures for a modern equivalent is difficult, but a comparison is possible. The pound then consisted of 20 shillings and the shilling of 12 pence (240 pence to a pound). At the time of the fire, beef could be purchased for between two and a half and four pence per pound and house rent ran from £25 to £50 per annum, so the £60,000 insurance coverage was in itself a vast amount.[3]

An insight into the method of adjusting insurance claims on buildings in this period is given by the "Office Journal" of John Howard, a leading surveyor and architect at the time, who is remembered today for having presented High Park to the city. His many activities described in the journal include several insurance settlements after the fire. Both the company and the insured party appointed surveyors — that is, evaluators — who independently examined and measured the ruins and arrived at an estimate of the loss. If their figures did not agree — and disagreement appears to have been very frequent — an umpire was appointed who examined both their statements and made a decision which was usually accepted by both the assured and the company. The following excerpt from Howard's journal shows how this method operated:

> April 18th. Wed .... at one to meet Mr. [F.W.] Cumberland to measure Mr. Beaty's house to ascertain the amount to be paid by the Hartford Insurance Office, Mr. Cumberland acting for them I for Mr. Beatty [sic]. April 19th. Thurs. — Morning at Mr. Beaty's measurement 2 hours Mr. C. had not made his half so much. Then to Mr. [William] Thomas about the church matter, put all the papers concerning Mr. Beaty's valuation into Mr. Thomas hands to act as umpire back at three.[4]

The principal surveyors in the city at that time were William Thomas, John and Kivas Tully, Frederic W. Cumberland and Howard; and the fee for an adjustment seems to have been £2/ 10/- per case, regardless of whether the individual was a surveyor or an umpire. Adjustments on contents or furniture losses were apparently made by the insured party submitting a list of the destroyed articles to the company or its agent.

Settlement of the claims must have been quite prompt; most of the commercial reconstruction was completed by early autumn, and this must have depended on the availability of insurance money in many cases. The settlement of the city's claim — involving the British America Company — was approved in early June, and the out-of-town companies would hardly have been able to retain their business if they had been much slower in their payments. The efficiency of the insurance system in Toronto is best attested by the following notice, which appeared in the *Globe* on July 5, complimenting an insurance broker:

> A CARD
> To Messrs. Whittmore, Rutherford & Co., Toronto. GENTLEMEN - We beg to acknowledge the receipt of the full amount of our claim on the Aetna, Protection, and Hartford Fire Insurance Companies, for the loss by fire on the 7th

April last, and to thank you and the Directors of the several Offices, for setttlement.

We are Gentlemen,
Your very obedient servants,
Toronto, July 4, 1849. HAYES BROTHERS

With or without insurance payments the burned-out businesses reopened their doors with remarkable speed and energy. For those who were only tenants, especially when a fair amount of stock had been saved, this was a fairly easy matter. Some who owned their own buildings reopened at temporary locations until their premises could be rebuilt, while others — such as Nasmith's Bakery and Platt's Tavern — evidently waited until reconstruction was completed. The first business to resume operations was the printing office of Rowsell & Thompson, who were able to publish an edition of the *Patriot* on April 9 since they had fortunately been able to take over the premises and equipment of the recently defunct *Herald* at 36-1/2 Yonge Street. The firm was able to resume full printing operations in all divisions, although it was a month or two before the paper could be printed in as large a format as previously.

The other paper destroyed by the fire, the *Toronto Mirror*, was not so lucky; for not only were its premises completely wiped out but the proprietor, Charles Donlevy, had severely injured his leg leaping from the roof of a house where he had been trapped while helping in the rescue operations. In spite of his injuries, by April 13 Donlevy was able to prepare a rather pathetic circular which was printed in the *Canadian Free Press* in London, Ontario, on April 24. Chiefly a request for overdue subscriptions, the notice stated in part:

> Fire is a fell destroyer; but a bad paying subscription list is yet worse. We can insure against fire; but no office will undertake to protect us against the losses to which we are subjected by negligent or dishonest subscribers.
>
> We have every confidence in the generosity and honourable spirit of our subscribers. If they fail to help us in this hour of trial then we shall think ourselves truly unfortunate.

Evidently the delinquent subscribers responded nobly, because by May 11 the paper was able to resume operations at the southeast corner of King and Jarvis streets over the store of William Henderson. The pathos of the earlier circular was now succeeded by a happy bumptiousness:

> Alive again, and Kicking
> ... nothing promotes improvement so certainly as a fire ... The suspension of the Mirror was felt by all its readers, as well as by the entire newspaper press of Canada, to be the severest visitation which had befallen the fourth estate for, proba- bly a quarter of a century. From every quarter we received the most flattering testimonials with the most earnest expression of solicitude for an early exhumation.
>
> ... We trust to be able soon to manifest our grati- tude, in our well known old style: — that is, by cudgeling everyone who dares to stand in our sunshine, or in any way to interrupt the even tenor of our reflections. ...
>
> We can not however overlook the circumstances of the burning of the Parliament House [at Montreal] so soon after the destruction of our office. Great events seldom come single. We felt convinced something would go wrong in our absence.[5]

The *Mirror* also promised to cancel the subscriptions of the remaining delinquent subscribers, and "then take other steps."

Meanwhile, the papers were beginning to carry announce- ments of the reopenings of many of the burnt-out stores, some at temporary locations. Between April 9 and April 18 notices appeared for Thomas Thompson's Mammoth House, Geo. H. Cheney & Co., Walter MacFarlane, Hayes Brothers, and Carey & Brown. These were followed by R.C. Gwatkin on May 25 and finally W. Rolph's Black Horse Inn on June 1. These notices were all very simple, except that of Mammoth House. Its enterprising proprietor was something of a nineteenth-century "discount" merchant who never missed an opportunity to bring his name before the public. His notice — which was conspicuously the first from any of the stores — appeared prominently on the front page of all the papers. After emphasizing the new address it proceeded.

> Thomas Thompson, would briefly like to state that he was rapidly recovering from the destructive fire of March, 1848, when he was again a sufferer in the calamitous one, of the 7th April, when the hard earned savings of nineteen years was in a few hours levelled to the ground. His motto, however, is "NIL DESPERANDUM" ! ! ! and from the sympathy manifested by the community in general he is induced once more to try again with the satisfaction that he is able to pay EVERY YORKER! and if the same patronage be extended to him as has during the past 12 months, he hopes to see the Mammoth House, like the fabled Phoenix rise from its ashes, and again rear its majestic form and be as HERETOFORE. "The emporium for Cheap and Fashionable Goods."
>
> In the meantime he will commence SELLING OFF his immense Stock, which with the Spring Arrivals, daily expected, will be as complete as any in the City.
>
> The damaged part of the Stock will be sold off at a GREAT SACRIFICE.
>
> Toronto April 9th. 1849.

By August 13 a large part of the reconstruction was completed, and a group of merchants located on the north side of King Street and the east side of Jarvis Street petitioned the City Council to restore the wooden sidewalk in front of their stores. The signatures — Foy & Austin, John Mead & Co., Carey & Brown, George Brooke, George Harris, and William Henderson Co. — indicate the return of a high percentage of the former businesses, since all except George Harris had been burnt out in the fire. Then on September 17 another group of merchants, including Thomas Thompson, and Sabine & Hughes, sent the Council a petition for the restoration of the sidewalk opposite the market. Their position was even more desperate than the first group since the sidewalk on the south side of the street also was unusable because of the work being done on the new market. The Board of Works approved these petitions on September 24, when it finally recommended that £200 be allocated to replace all fire-destroyed sidewalks in the city. The recommendation was passed by the City Council only on October 29, and with the autumn mud growing deeper day by day, it is to be hoped that new sidewalks were constructed before inaccessibility bankrupted any of the survivors of the fire.

The City Council was also busy with insurance settlements and reconstruction. Its most immediate problem was the replacement of the fire bell, which had been destroyed when the cathedral burned. Fortunately, Thomas D. Harris, some of whose stock must have survived the fire, wrote on April 13 generously offering to supply a new bell at manufacturer's prices (1/9d per pound), and, until a satisfactory bell could be obtained, to lend the city the largest bell he had in stock, which weighed 397 pounds. He suggested that, for the time being, it could be erected on a platform in the churchyard. After ascertaining that there was no insurance on the old bell, the city accepted his offer and voted to spend £25 to install the temporary bell in the court house.

The Great Fire of 1849 naturally brought suggestions for the improvement of fire-protection and for legislation regulating construction in the central areas. The most obvious need was the installation of a proper water supply for fire-fighting. On April 14 the *Patriot* printed an interesting suggestion along this line from John Thomas, a manufacturer of pianos. After explaining that he had lived in the city for eleven years Thomas went on to propound his solution:

> Every large store generally requires a warehouse in the rear; and if one of these, about the centre of each block, were built of sufficient strength 10 to 15 feet higher than the houses, having on top a cistern of sufficient size, with taps and hose attached in such a manner as could easily be conveyed to any part of the block, a small steam

engine made portable with a pump attached, might be used to fill them in any part of the city, at trifling expense. If the water should become foul it could be let off through the hose to the main sewer, and again filled immediately. Space for a stove must be left, to keep the cistern from freezing, in cold weather.

This ingenious system might have provided a valuable secondary water supply for use when the hydrant system broke down, but the city neither took action to add such a secondary system nor installed an adequate hydrant system.

Another hazard was the frame construction of many of the buildings. Evidently a committee under the chairmanship of William Thomas was already discussing the revision of the building acts before the fire, and on April 21, 1849 it was able to submit a report providing a suggested wording of the new act. Since a good portion of the centre of the city was about to be rebuilt, one would have expected prompt action by the City Council. But the ways of municipal bodies can be mysterious and it was not until Jan. 25, 1850, long after rebuilding had been completed for all except the public structures, that a new building act was passed. Fortunately, as was not uncommon, the insurance offices took more effective action. On May 6, 1849 they jointly printed the following notice in all the newspapers:

The Late Fire

NOTICE IS HEREBY GIVEN, that the companies represented by the undersigned, will not grant any Assurance on Wooden Buildings, (or their Contents) erected within the same limits, [or] where Wooden Buildings belonging to them shall be erected in the rear.

This firm stand must have had the effect of forcing rebuilding on more substantial lines, and the new building regulations which came into force in 1850 ruled that in future first-class construction was necessary throughout the whole of the downtown area. During the next few years it was this heavier construction which probably saved Toronto from further conflagrations in spite of the lack of a reliable water supply.

The most interesting suggestion for the improvement of the appearance of the city came from William Thomas who, influenced by the design of the recently constructed Regent Street in London, England, wrote the City Council on April 28 recommending that a general arrangement be made under which the second stories of the new shops would be built three feet back from the fronts of the actual stores. This, he felt, would not only give a wider space and consequently better fire protection, but also it would greatly improve the appearance of the street, especially if a continuous cast-iron balcony was run along the top of the first storeys. Unfortunately, as with so many good ideas, the suggestion was ignored.

The rebuilding, as befitted the city's main shopping area, was of an impressive character, and when new must have presented an imposing appearance, particularly since all the buildings were uniformly constructed with white brick and usually trimmed in stone. There was also an overall uniformity in the design of the gable-ended buildings which may still be seen to a certain extent in the scattered remains of a range of structures across from the cathedral, and also in the then huge five-storey block which still stands on the northeast corner of King and Jarvis Streets.

The two most important structures that arose from the ashes of the fire and still grace the city are the St Lawrence Hall and St James's Cathedral. The story of the construction of the Hall, which was originally part of a plan to update the market, goes back five years before the fire. The original market, built in 1832-33, had also became the city hall on incorporation of the city of Toronto in 1834. In 1844-45 the second city hall was erected just south of Front Street. At the same time a "select Committee on the Proposed New Front of the Old Market Buildings" had been constituted to examine the possibilities of refacing the King Street facade of the old city hall-cum-market. On Jan. 27, 1845 this committee had submitted the following self-explanatory report:

> The Select Committee appointed to advertise for and receive plans, specifications and estimates for the proposed New Front to the Old Market Building beg leave to report that on the day

appointed plans so [sic] were received from the following gentlemen viz

> Wm. Thomas Esq.
> Thos. Young Esq.
> Henry B. Lane Esq.
> and K. Tully Esq.

That subsequently the plans of Mr. Young were withdrawn by that gentleman.

That after the most careful examination and comparison of the merits of the several plans your Committee have unanimously agreed in recommending to Your Worshipful Council that the first premium be awarded to Mr. Thomas and the second to Mr. Lane.

> All of which is respectively submitted.
> James Trotter, Geo. Gurnett, Chairman,
> Robert N. Beard, John Craig.

No further action was taken at that time, probably because the city was unable to afford the project after paying for the new city hall; but when the fire made reconstruction necessary Thomas was automatically called in as architect.

William Thomas (1800-1860) was for many years one of the leading architects in the city. A specialist in ecclesiastical design he built at least eight churches in Toronto. Examples of his work are St Michael's Cathedral, Toronto (1845), and St Paul's Presbyterian in Hamilton (1857). Two other excellent examples of Thomas's style are still standing in Toronto — the former Commercial Bank of Canada (1845) at 15 Wellington Street West, and his last work, the centre section of the Don Jail (1858-65). Like other architects he was also a surveyor and engineer.

At the same time the council was busy with the insurance settlement on the market and the necessary preparations for its reconstruction. With regard to the settlement, Howard reported in his journal:

> Apr. 10, Tu... then with Mr. Gooderham to the Chamberlain's office. Heard that he had sent me a notice to meet Mr. Cumberland on the part of

the Assurance office to value the damage to the
Old City Hall. I am to be on the part of the city,
saw Mr. Cumberland...

Two days later the measuring of the ruins had begun, and a
fortnight later Howard wrote:

Apr. 25 W...back at 11 [.] had lunch and at 1/2
past . went to measure with Mr. Cumberland at
the Old City Hall till 4...

Apr. 26 Th...saw Mr. Cumberland, went to the
British American Assurance office at 12 with him
till 1/2 past 5...

Despite the length of this meeting no agreement was reached,
and on May 21 the Committee of Finance and Assessment,
under the chairmanship of C.A. Ridout, reported to the City
Council that there was a difference of £235/11/9 between
Howard's and Cumberland's estimates. The committee suggested that either the reports be submitted to an umpire, or if the
insuring company was agreeable, they simply split the difference between the two figures. The second suggestion was eventually adopted and a sum of £1252/10/— was duly deposited at
the Bank of Upper Canada in full settlement.[6]
At the same May 21 meeting the Finance and Assessment
Committee recommended offering leases for the proposed new
market. These leases were to be for four store areas, which were
to have a twenty-five-foot frontage on King Street and be seventy-five feet deep. Two were situated on either side of the main
entrance from King Street. Behind them there was to be a fifteen-
foot lane which was not to be built upon. This is essentially the
plan of the present St Lawrence Hall; but at that stage there was
still no intention of demolishing the unburnt southern portion of
the old market building.
On June 22 the same committee submitted another report
suggesting the adoption of a new market structure. Presumably
there had now been a change of opinion and the committee had
decided to demolish the remaining part of the old market and to
build a mall of shops running south from St Lawrence Hall on
King Street to Front Street. These shops were demolished in their

turn in 1904, to make way for a new market which was in turn demolished to make way for the present building in the 1967 restoration. The total construction was estimated at £3,957 plus £543 for a bell, clock and so on, and the committee recommended using debentures to a value of £4,000 to supplement the residue of the insurance money. The rental income from the new building was to be £350 per annum.[7]

The remaining part of the old market building was now demolished, and on August 16 City Clerk Charles Daly advertised for tenders for the construction of the new building. As the lowest tender received was £125 in excess of the estimate, the Council increased the debenture issue to £4,500. Construction proceeded slowly, with some changes along the way. The final result was an "I"-shaped structure with a long north-south corridor and with connecting transverse sections along King and Front streets. The council named the new market and hall the St. Lawrence Buildings after the ward in which they were named. They bacame ready for occupancy in April 1851.

The restored northern section, the St Lawrence Hall, remains one of the most beautiful buildings in the city, and it still contains the hall which seats 1,000 people and served as the social centre of Toronto for twenty years. It witnessed such stirring events as the first Toronto performance of Handel's *Messiah* in 1857, concerts by sopranos Jenny Lind and Adelina Patti, and speeches by Sir John A. Macdonald, George Brown and Horace Greeley. The part of the building demolished in 1904 was much less ornate in design. The corridor or arcade running from north to south, which was 200 feet long by 20 feet wide, was lined by fruit and fancy goods shops at the north end, and by butcher shops at the south.

The last building to be rebuilt was St James's Cathedral. In this case, reconstruction was delayed by a shortage of funds that led to a long and involved controversy over the type of structure that was required. The residue of the insurance money after the payment of all bills — some 5000 — technically belonged to the parish, not the diocese. Although this sum was quite adequate for the construction of a parish church, it was nowhere near the amount required to construct a new cathedral. Accordingly, some members of the congregation led by Alexander Dixon and Vestry Clerk William Wakefield suggested that they should merely build a parish church, seating 800 to 1,000, reusing the

*St. Lawrence Market, view from south-east showing
demolished Front St. section, c. 1898.*

walls of the burnt building if possible. Since such a solution would mean that there would be no building large enough to use for a cathedral for an indefinite number of years, the proposal was naturally opposed by a second section of the congregation led by Clarke Gamble, William Allan, George P. Ridout and Dean Henry John Grassett. The plan of this faction was to lease the southern part of the churchyard, along King Street, in order to secure the funds for a larger building on the north part of the property.

At the vestry meeting of April 19 a committee including representatives of both factions was instituted to inquire into the problem. The vestry meeting of May 19, to which its report was delivered, decided in favour of the more ambitious project. Other resolutions were passed providing for the reburial of those interred in that southern part of the churchyard, and for the submission of an application to the provincial legislature requesting an act that would enable the church to lease the ground. The latter was necessary because the land had been set aside exclusively for the purposes of a church and graveyard by Administrator Peter Russell in 1797. Finally, the meeting authorized the committee to advertise for plans for the new church as soon as it was known how much money was available.[8]

The desired act for leasing the lands was passed by the legislature and on May 30 received royal assent. Meanwhile, however, opposition to the leasing of the land was growing in strength, as is evidenced by the increasing number of letters to the newspapers. On June 1 Howard noted in his diary that he had prepared the advertisement for the plans of the new church, and this appeared in the *Church* of June 21, as follows:

TO ARCHITECTS

THE CHURCHWARDENS AND VESTRY OF ST JAMES'S PARISH IN TORONTO are desirous of receiving PLANS, SPECIFICATIONS, and ESTIMATES for a new church in the GOTHIC STYLE to replace that destroyed by the late fire. The former church was 149 feet long by 80 feet wide, and was capable of accommodating 1800 persons, without including the Aisles, it contained 278 pews, and the intention of the Vestry is, that the NEW CHURCH shall not be on a less scale, and that it shall afford the means of restoring as many pews.

The materials to be white brick, with Cut Stone dressing, cost not to exceed Ten Thousand Pounds.

Exclusive of TOWER and SPIRE which should be of cut stone and sufficient to bear a full Peal of Bells.

Printed instructions can be obtained in application to THOS. D. HARRIS, ESQ. or LEWIS MOFFAT, ESQ Churchwardens, Toronto & at the Office of this Paper. The Plans etc., must be sent to the Churchwardens on or before the 14th August next

The successful Candidate to receive £75, provided that he is not afterwards employed to superintend the Building. The second best to receive £50. The third £25.

The advertisement was also placed in select Montreal and New York Papers. The deadline for the submission of plans was shortly extended to September 1, and a committee composed of the three local architects who had not submitted designs — Howard, Johnstone, and Young — was nominated to judge the entries. The church wardens were obviously planning Toronto's first architectural competition. The eleven entrants included architects from Boston, Hartford, Montreal and New York, as well as Frederic Cumberland, Kivas Tully and William Thomas of Toronto. The committee awarded the first prize to Cumberland. The decision was none too popular, many people evidently preferring Thomas's design, for in the issue of the *Church* on September 20 the editor stated that Cumberland's plans had merely won the contest and would not necessarily be used for the actual construction, although he felt that they should be. Wakefield and his pro-parish group now took action and had Thomas check to see whether the old walls were usable. His report advised that they were sound up to the springing of the arches, and that part of the old tower also could be utilized.[9]

When the vestry met the controversy had reached such a pitch that it was forced to adjourn until Attorney General Robert Baldwin could determine the qualifications for voting. On December 21, when the meeting reassembled, the proceedings were again stormy. The pro-cathedral and pro-Cumberland group managed to pass a motion that the building should be rebuilt as a cathedral, not a parish church. This faction represented the "official" opinion of the church. After another battle over leasing the King Street portion of the property — a battle which the pro-catherdral faction won when the rector, Dean Henry Grassett broke a tie vote, William B. Jarvis and George P. Ridout moved that Cumberland's plans be adopted provided the cost was under £15,000. This was carried after another skirmish, and a building committee representing both sides was then agreed upon. Finally, the official party carried a motion that a 42-year lease at £3 per foot frontage per annum be granted for a strip of land stretching 238 feet along King Street east from Church Street to the stores at the end of the church property.[10]

By this time the citizenry of Toronto was taking an interest in the controversy and on Feb. 23, 1850 a public meeting held at the city hall passed a resolution protesting against leasing the land. This forced the vestry to examine ways and means of raising funds to cover the cost of construction without alienating the land. At the ensuring series of meetings the tide had turned and the opposition was generally in command and the proposed location of the new church moved back to the scorched foundations.[11]

Cumberland and his partner, William G. Storm, were confirmed as architects and asked to submit a new plan for a building on the old site. Storm was to become one of the greatest Canadian architects, building such structures as St Andrew's Church and Victoria College in Toronto. On June 1 Cumberland reported that the structure, less the spire and half the tower, would cost £16,500 exclusive of the value of the old materials. In view of the fact that only £10,000 was available, he alternatively suggested that a "usable" church could be built for £11,463/7/6. Under this plan the tower would be built only to the rooftop and the transepts and pinnacles would be left until later. This less ambitious project was approved, as was a further motion by

Wakefield that the church be built on the centre of the land. Thus, by July 1, 1850, nearly fifteen months after the fire, the way was cleared to begin reconstruction of a cathedral without any leasing of land..

Like so many distant controversies the whole fracas over the rebuilding sounds like a storm in a teapot — considering their talents, it probably does not matter whether the cathedral was built by Thomas or by Cumberland and Storm. However, there was another issue at stake, for a decision that the King Street land be sold off would have deprived Toronto of the green space around the cathedral, since much expanded, which now provides one of the city's finest downtown parks. Altogether the incident provides an excellent example of how remote decisions over often personal issues can have a virtually permanent effect on the fabric of a city. Fortunately, in the case of St James's park it was a decision with which we can be pleased.

Work progressed slowly, but finally on Wednesday, Nov. 20, 1850, Bishop Strachan was able to lay the cornerstone after preaching an appropriate sermon at Holy Trinity and proceeding to the new church in an impressive procession. Construction still moved at a snail's pace, with delays occasioned by inclement weather, the difficulty of obtaining cut stone from Ohio and the "pecuniary embarrassment" of the contractors, Metcalfe & Forbes. At last, however, on June 19, 1853 St James' was ready for services and the congregation moved back from Holy Trinity, which had been its temporary home for more than four years. No further work was undertaken on the cathedral until the autumn of 1865, when 35 feet were added to the tower to contain a new £6,000 peal of bells. The tower and spire were not completed until 1873-74, when the transepts and pinnacles were also constructed. The church clock, purchased by a non-sectarian subscription of Toronto citizens, finally was installed in 1875.

By that date the fire had receded a quarter of a century into the past, most of the population would have forgotten about it, and Strachan and many other leading participants in the reconstructions were dead. However, the rapid rebuilding that followed the fire not only demonstrated Toronto's burgeoning economy but also gave it two of its finest buildings today in the cathedral and market.

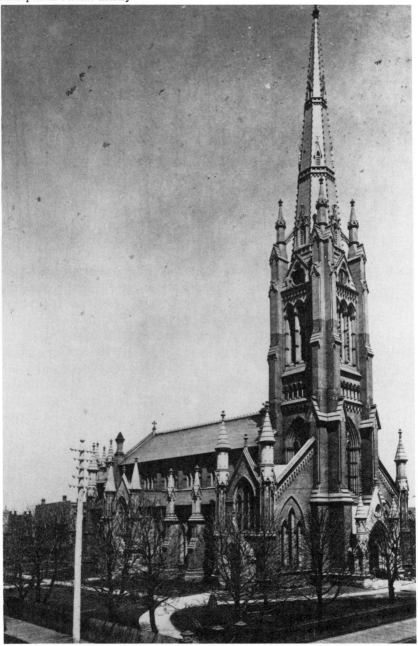

St. James's Cathedral, 1866.

Chapter 15

The Second Great Fire, 1904 [1]

Although conflagrations have been one of the greatest sources of disruption of urban society since man began to live in concentrated settlements, it is only in this century that the danger of such fires has been virtually eliminated. The latter half of the nineteenth century witnessed an enormous number of advances in building construction, but many of them created new fire hazards which were all too often disregarded. As a background to the Second Great Fire of Toronto in 1904 this chapter will first examine some of these advances and show how they interacted with the problem of fire protection. It will then briefly discuss late-nineteenth-century conflagrations in North America, look at the Toronto fire itself, and finally investigate the subsequent rebuilding of the destroyed area of the city.

Late-nineteenth-century fires provide an interesting commentary on human inability to learn from experience. Such conflagrations as that of Toronto in 1904 were completely unnecessary: it was only a total neglect of the obvious, the desire to make a profit and the city fathers' aversion to spending money or to regulating development which allowed them to take place. Earlier conflagrations, such as the first Great Fire in Toronto in 1849, were really not preventable; but the Second Great Fire, and many contemporary blazes elsewhere, could have been avoided. In fact, given the general negligent attitude, it is amazing that more conflagrations did not occur in North America, where a mushroom growth of cities and towns was the normal story of development.

Conflagrations can be described as "sweeping fires that spread beyond control to destroy cities and large areas of built up property." Aside from those caused by natural disasters, or those that arise from war, conflagrations may be divided into four basic categories. The first of these — the type that will be dealt with in this paper — is the conflagration that arises in congested central areas of cities and is spread over and out from the downtown core. Most of the famous great fires of history fall into this category: Rome in 64, London in 1133 and 1666, New York City in 1835 and 1845, Toronto in 1849 or Boston in 1872. The second basic type is the blaze that begins in a residential area and spreads by such factors as frame buildings and wood shingles. Often before it is over, the entire downtown is also engulfed. This is the typical type of great fire in a pioneer boom town, the most famous example being Chicago in 1871. Besides these two types of conflagrations, there is the fire that originates in a neighbourhood forest or brush and spreads into the city — a type still relatively common in California — and the fire that arises from an explosion.[2]

The crucial minutes in fighting any fire come at the beginning, and this is especially true of conflagrations. Until recently, once such a blaze was underway it was virtually impossible to stop it. Flames can be driven for 1,000 yards by the wind, and in the nineteenth century the best fire departments could do was little more than prevent their spreading against the winds. Sometimes even this was almost impossible, for fires create terrific thermal updrafts as the heated air and gasses arise. They thus create their own weather conditions in their immediate vicinity. Such "fire storms" can be erratic, with the wind changing direction and thus creating additional hazards, for the flames spread not only directly but also by means of flying brands and wandering clouds of superheated gasses and combustion. Against the wind, the fire can burn back not only by direct communication, but also by radiated heat.[3]

Why did major fires continue to be relatively commonplace at such a late date? One of the major reasons was the increase in size of the downtown buildings. In mid-century the evolution of both the cast-iron method of constructing buildings and the passenger elevator, which removed the limit on height, meant that structures became larger in core areas, a tendency which was encouraged by the growing value of the land in the centre of the cities.

Even including the older buildings, by the end of the century the average height of buildings in many downtown areas of Toronto was about four storeys and the average ground area about 5,000 square feet. With these larger buildings and consequently greater quantity of contents, intense internal heat could be built up with combustion. Thus a fire was much more likely to spread to adjacent structures by radiation.

This hazard was made worse by inadequate fire-safety measures. Internal fire breaks created by solid walls between adjacent buildings were all too rare. Jast as rare were measures to protect windows from outside heat exposure, even when they faced on narrow lanes at the sides or the rear of buildings. Further, the flat roofs which were developed in the late nineteenth century proved to be combustible; the gravel composition used was not only non-fire resistant, but also was itself inflammable to a considerable extent. Usually such roofs were supported by ordinary wood joists, which could be readily ignited. Almost invariably there were skylights of thin glass set into light metal frames. These provided external fires with an easy method of access to the interior, and a convenient flue if the building ignited internally.[4]

Architecturally, the ornate designs of the buildings facilitated the spread of fires, whatever might be said of their adornment of the city. For instance, the Mansard, or Second Empire style, so popular from the mid-1850s to the 1880s, had high roofs, towers and dormers, all of which could catch flying brands and ignite, unlike upper walls of brick or stone. In all styles the cornices which ran along the front of the buildings, and the window trims, were often of wood and thus easily ignited. At the worst the cornices could be hollow, with metal covering over wood backing. This type of construction could carry the flames internally along the entire front of a block of buildings. Before discovery, such a fire could burn back into the buildings, engaging the roof timbers.

Interior construction presented another host of problems. As well as the lack of solid division walls within buildings, the situation was frequently complicated by the cutting of unprotected doors from one building to another. Worse still were the vertical openings of a variety of types: light wells or shafts to admit light to the interior, staircases, elevator shafts. All were usually open at each floor, constructed of wood and frequently topped by a skylight, so that the chimney effect was complete. Chutes and solid walls pierced by belt holes through which flammable belts could move either horizontally across a floor between compartments, or vertically from floor to floor, or both, were another hazard. Belts can literally carry a flame from one area of a plant or warehouse to another, even if it is only smouldering.[5]

The interior supports of the buildings were normally either wooden or wrought-iron beams combined with cast-iron posts. The wooden posts were not quickly flammable, although when two were nailed together for strength a fire could smoulder between them. The iron beams, of course, as well as the steel beams which were beginning to replace them, were subject to cracking and buckling. The idea of covering these with an insulating material, such as tile, was still in the future. Floors were usually of wood joist construction. Finally, the fittings of many of the buildings were, of course, more hazardous than the actual structure, with plenty of veneers to provide kindling and paper for tinder. Beyond the internal construction there were always the problems of highly flammable contents and danger-ous manufacturing processes.[6]

On the streets such fire conveyors as wooden sidewalks were disappearing, but the development of the telegraph, tele-phone and electricity had ushered in a new problem — the complex festoons of wires that overhung most downtown streets. These prevented firemen from placing their ladders against buildings and in winter they quickly became covered with ice, blocking the play of the hoses on the flames. Trolley wires down the centre of the street frequently complicated this picture. As a fire spread the utility poles could burn like matches and the flames could race along the wires, carrying the conflagration forward on the flammable insulation and creating a pyrotechnic display of brilliant blue and purple flashes. Once the wires were down they caused new problems, threatening fire-fighters with electrocution.

The picture was not entirely negative. Techniques of fire protection made great strides as the century progressed, even if all too often they were not put into practice. Some of the most important developments in the protection of both factories and warehouses had been made by some specialized groups, par-ticularly the New England mutual companies, which carried the insurance on many of the largest factories of that region. Early in the nineteenth century these businesses developed what is called "mill construction." This involved floors and roofs of heavy plank, three to four inches thick, supported on heavy timbers, which were slow to burn. Over this base was a bearing floor for the actual machinery, sometimes with a layer of fire-resistant material between, so that the floor itself could be easily four to five inches thick and provide a good hold in a fire. Roof-construction methods were also improved as the century progressed. The high-peaked roofs of the early mills, with their hazardous attics, were replaced first by the mansards and then with the less hazardous flat roofs.[7]

Internally, the idea of the standpipe and hose came in — that is, a pipe running vertically through the building with hoses on each floor, fed by a roof tank or pumps. Special hydrants and fire pumps were next developed to help augment the municipal water supply. Usually, too, the building was divided into several sections. In 1852-53 one of the greatest breakthroughs came with the dry-pipe sprinklers. These were wrought-iron pipes with holes 16 inches apart, which were staggered on opposite sides of the pipe and so cut that they threw the water upwards towards the ceiling. The sprinklers were controlled by a central valve at ground level, with the disadvantage that water had to be turned on throughout the entire building, or at least a large portion of it. Thus most of the sprinklers played where they were not needed, soaking everything, while the water pressure at the site of the fire was greatly reduced. Still, the dry-pipe sprinklers represented a great advance in fire-fighting.[8]

The first practical automatic sprinkler, with pipes always filled with water and a sprinkler head that was set off by a temperature of about 150 degrees, was invented in 1874. Dry pipes with the same type of head were also perfected for areas that were unheated. In 1881 the modern Grinnell sprinkler head appeared and a new era of fire protection was inaugurated. With the sprinkler came the idea of water curtains to soak down the outside of the building. The protection of exposed windows by the use of iron shutters had, of course, long been known. In 1849 these had nearly saved one of the main stores of downtown Toronto. By the end of the century wired glass appeared, capable of sustaining far greater heat than ordinary panes.[9]

Nor was this all. Volunteer fire departments were being replaced by professional ones by the 1860s. New York, for instance, changed over in 1865. New types of equipment were added. Steam fire engines were introduced in 1854 to replace the hand pumpers, and the first aerial ladder truck — invented by Daniel Hays of San Francisco — appeared in 1870. The water tower, designed to throw a stream of water at a height of forty-five to sixty-five feet from a nozzle controlled at the base, was demonstrated at Baltimore in 1879. Simultaneously, fire boats were developed, both for waterside fires and to pump water into the city mains from the harbour.

The great step forward in spreading the alarm was Samuel F.B. Morse's work on the telegraph in the mid-1840s. In 1852 Boston became the first city to install a complete telegraph fire-alarm system, a feature that spread rapidly and was gradually improved. By the late 1870s telephone exchanges were making their appearance and the telephone gradually supplemented the telegraph.[10]

All these municipal forms of protection were adopted with more or less alacrity in the majority of cities, but the installation of the piece of engineering most necessary to fight fires in congested downtown areas was much slower in gaining acceptance because of its cost to the taxpayer. That was the municipal high-pressure water system, which would both provide the pressure necessary to throw streams of water to the upper floors of the new higher buildings and operate completely separately from the regular city supply system, so that it would not be affected by the breaking of pipes in burning buildings or by other demands placed on the water supply.[11]

In 1874 the first such system was installed in Rochester, New York, where it was relatively easy to pump water from Lake Ontario. Unfortunately, Rochester was copied by few other cities. Buffalo later constructed such a system, but such large centres as Philadelphia and New York put in high-pressure systems only in 1904 and 1908 respectively. As a result, an inadequate water supply remained one of the chief causes of major fires. And even when the water supply proved adequate, there was still another related problem, which caused infinite difficulties and would not be solved in Ontario until recent years. This was the lack of standardization of the sizes of hose couplings. When, as was usual in a conflagration, nearby towns sent equipment to aid in fighting the fire, the hoses frequently could not be connected.[12]

There were other problems. Legislation was not passed, or enforced, by city councils, developers and builders saved money whenever possible and insurance underwriters failed to establish and enforce high rates. As a result, combustible materials and oversized buildings, which would not have been permitted in Europe, were common in North America. In Canada, as late as 1912-15, 1,378 fires involved 6,786 buildings: an extraordinary record! Even when new building laws were enacted they usually did not require that existing structures be remodeled, so that many of the old, sub-standard buildings remained interspersed with the new ones, forming what were called "conflagration breeders." Sometimes, however, as the Toronto fire was to show, small, low buildings dating from an earlier era could be of help in stopping a fire, particularly if they were of solid construction.[13]

Given the changes in building construction and the failure of municipal authorities to take the necessary steps to provide adequate protection, the continued occurrence of conflagrations was to be expected. The surprising thing is that there were so few in the latter part of the nineteenth century — an excellent illustration of the major role good fortune plays in human destiny.

There are no lack of examples of what could go wrong. The Chicago fire in 1871 was not the type of conflagration that spreads from a central business district, though once it reached the downtown area it clearly demonstrated the flammability of the major structures. The great fire of Boston in 1872 was another matter, for it was almost a case study of what could happen in such downtown fires: some 80 acres of the central city was wiped out, encompassing 748 buildings. While the fire-fighting was complicated by the fact that the fire department horses had been weakened by an epidemic, the spread of the conflagration demonstrated all the construction problems inherent in four- and five-storey congested downtown buildings. Even after this disaster, however, fire protection in Boston was not greatly improved, and the city was to suffer similar, but less destructive, conflagrations in 1889 and 1893.[14]

After the Boston fire there was a general lull in spectacular conflagrations in North America. Though this respite may have given a false sense of security, it did not mean that the danger had abated, or that there had been no fires. Smith estimated that in Canada, in the period from 1870 until he wrote in 1918, there had been 21 major conflagrations with a total damage of $73,000,000. This excluded the destruction, or near destruction, of 134 towns and villages. Some of the worst conflagrations, such as the fires at St John's, Newfoundland, in 1892 and Hull-

Ottawa in 1900, were, like Chicago, examples of fires spreading into the main part of the city. In 1901, however, the loss of 30 buildings in downtown Montreal showed that the problem of fires in city cores was still very much present.[15]

Even without these incidents, one city that should not have taken a complacent attitude was Toronto, where, on three separate occasions in early 1895, potential conflagrations had developed and were stopped by luck as much as by anything else. True, Toronto did have some reasons to be satisfied. In the downtown area there were very few frame structures and wood shingles had been abolished under bylaws. Such legislation provided that only certain construction methods would be approved within the limits of the central business district. Further, most downtown buildings were relatively modern structures dating from the 1870s and 1880s. Toronto had also been spending a certain amount on fire-protection equipment. Steam engines had appeared as early as 1861, new equipment, including ladder trucks, was being purchased, and a fire-alarm telegraph system had been set up in 1871, though it was rather out of date by the new century. The paid fire department had been inaugurated in 1874.[16]

Then came the three sudden catastrophes, each of which nearly became the "second great fire" nine years early: the *Globe* was struck on January 6, the Osgoodby Building on January 10 and Simpson's on March 3. The story in each case was much the same, for all three demonstrated the problems of sub-standard construction, lack of water pressure, and the ease with which fire could spread to other structures.

The *Globe* fire started in the boiler room, which was not separated from the rest of the building by fire walls, early on a Sunday morning and within 20 minutes had raced up the two elevator shafts which flanked a wooden stairway in the middle, totally ignited the building and spread to adjacent structures. Fire Chief Richard Ardagh, a man of great experience who had held the office since 1878, was fatally injured when he attempted to reach the rear of the fire from another building, was trapped and had to jump. The water pressure proved insufficient for the streams to reach the fifth storey. The flames also demonstrated that the standard 78-foot-wide streets of downtown Toronto formed no obstacle. The fire was finally extinguished only with great difficulty, the fighters being helped by some good fire walls and low, solidly built, older buildings. The loss was estimated at $715,000.[17]

The Osgoodby fire, four days later, which was blamed on an arsonist, again proved how flames could roar up an elevator shaft, in this case forming a magnificent but terrifying arc across Wellington Street. It also clearly showed how a fire could race out the windows of one building through the unprotected windows of another. The janitor and two women had to leap 70 feet into a net. Once more the city was fortunate: the burning area abutted on the *Globe* ruins, there were some good fire walls, and, possibly most important, a heavy fall of wet snow blanketed the city. This time the loss was $723,000.[18]

Simpson's was in many ways the most interesting of the three fires for it demonstrated that the very latest style of construction was as highly flammable as ever if care was not taken. Simpson's, then as now, occupied a large area on the southwest corner of Queen and Yonge streets, although it had not yet spread out to cover the entire block. It was a new seven-storey store, just opened three months, for its predecessor had burned in 1894. Some of the latest ideas in construction had been incorporated, including a structural steel frame. The boiler room, nevertheless, was not cut off from the rest of the building by fire-resistant walls and ceiling and when fire broke out there early Sunday morning the inside hoses failed to work.

The flames leaped through to the roof within eleven minutes from when the alarm was sounded, the steel girders twisted and in another fifteen minutes the building was a ruin and the fire was burning on all four corners of Queen and Yonge streets. Although the winds were high, blowing brands as far as the Don River, they were also erratic, so that the fire was at times blown back on itself. One of the greatest aids in stopping the spread of the fire was Eaton's store on the north side of Queen Street. Because that store had a well-trained employee fire brigade and a Grinnell automatic sprinkler system which included three hydrants on the roof for hoses, the blaze was stopped to the north. This time the loss was estimated at $744,000, some $400,000 to Simpson's itself.[19]

It would be nice to say that some lessons were learned from these experiences, but regrettably, such was not the case. Nevertheless, a great deal was certainly said about what needed to be done. The Toronto Chapter of the Ontario Association of

Architects prepared a new code of building bylaws and tried to get them passed, only to see them pigeon-holed by the Property Committee of City Council. The architects tried again just after the turn of the century, but were no more successful.[20]

Another untouched problem — wires — was emphasized by Fire Chief John Thompson in his *Annual Report* for 1901, in which he basically repeated what he had said two years earlier:

> There are today a number of places in the heart of the city that it would be almost impossible to raise our aerial ladders, to reach the buildings, even in daylight, much less at night, and should a large fire occur in any of those districts, the existing danger is most serious, and the loss of human life might be appalling.[21]

Fortunately, the fire of 1904 was to come at night, when the downtown buildings were empty, but the Council could hardly have foreseen such luck. It ignored Thompson's warnings that legislation should be obtained to force private companies to remove wires. The whole situation was well summed up by Norman Patterson when he wrote up the great fire for *The Canadian Magazine*: "The conflagration presents the same lessons that go unheeded by the public year after year — the lessons of faulty construction by the individual owner who builds his house upon the sand, of municipal neglect, of postponed precaution."[22]

In 1904 Fire protection was under the guidance of the Fire and Light Committee of City Council, which consisted of the chairman, Alderman Robert Fleming, and six councillors. There were three fire stations in the downtown area: No. 1, at the corner of Bay and Temperance streets; No. 5, on Lombard near Jarvis street; and No. 6, at Queen and John streets. There were also alarm boxes throughout the district.[23]

Water for the city was provided by five pumps at the main station, with a capacity of 40,000,000 gallons in 24 hours, plus a high-level pump at Poplar Plains, with a capacity of six million gallons, and a smaller pumping station on Toronto Island. The central district of the city was supplied by 24-inch feeder mains leading directly to the main pumping station; however, the 36 hydrants in what was to be the fire area were not attached to these mains, but rather to minor 6- and 12-inch mains which led off them. The fire department consisted of 204 men equipped with 5 steam engines, a 65- foot water tower and both 65-and 85-foot hook and ladder trucks, as well as minor equipment. In view of the small number of alarms in the city in the opening years of the century, the fire department may have seemed adequate; for instance, there had only been 867 alarms in the city in 1903, with a total loss of \$273,696.70.[24]

When building construction is considered, however, the picture hardly merited any optimism. The downtown buildings of the city possessed all the weaknesses enumerated above, and very few of the favourable points. Despite their brick construction, internally most were typical open-joist construction. The majority of the buildings in the fire area were over twenty years old; most had no internal fire breaks or any rudimentary protection against flames spreading from other buildings. Only three buildings in the fire area had sprinklers: the Toronto *Telegram* building on Bay Street and the Kilgour Building on Wellington Street West, both of which were to play a major role in stopping the fire, and the Brock Building, at the southwest corner of Bay and Wellington streets, which was right in the centre of the burned-out sector.[25]

The buildings in the core area were an intermixture of offices, warehouses and manufacturing plants, often with several firms in the same building. A large percentage were wholesalers. The most frequent types of businesses were dry goods, printing and binding, and millinery; but there were several men's clothing establishments, and such miscellaneous businesses as a livery stable and a flour mill. All of these were almost guaranteed to produce highly flammable contents. As the architects and the Canadian Manufacturers' Association had pointed out, overall it was a frightening prospect. A typical example of a downtown building of the time was the structure occupied by the printing firm of Warwick Bros & Rutter, at 68-70 Front Street West. Built in 1889, in the fashionable Richardson Romanesque style, it had a 33-foot front and stretched back 208 feet. The four storeys and basement had no internal fire breaks and there was no protection on the windows in the rear. When the fire reached the building through these windows, it gutted the structure in half an hour.[26]

Tuesday, April 19, 1904, was a miserable, wintry day in Toronto. A strong, steady, northwest wind was blowing and by the time the downtown business offices closed at 6 p.m. the temperature had dropped to 24° F. The workers hurried through the snowflurries to the streetcars that would bear them homewards; soon the downtown buildings were solidly locked for the night and the streets in the centre of the city deserted.

The quiet lasted little more than an hour. T.H. Johnson, who for some years had been employed as a nightwatchman by several building owners in the downtown area, was heading south on Bay Street on his rounds after chatting with some of his cronies at the corner of Bay and King streets. Smelling smoke as he reached the corner of Wellington Street, he hurried westwards and saw flames billowing upward from the elevator shaft of the Currie Building on the north side, a few doors west of Bay Street (the present-day Toronto Dominion Centre block). Racing back to King and Bay streets, the better part of a two-block sprint, he turned in the alarm at Box 12. Almost simultaneously the policeman on the beat also saw the flames shooting skyward from the elevator shaft and dashed south to Box 7 at York and Front streets. Johnson out-distanced him by a split second; the alarm registered at Box 12 at 8:04 p.m.[27]

The E. & S. Currie Building at 58-60 Wellington Street West was an all-too-typical example of the "conflagration breeder" that was to be found throughout the downtown. It covered a ground area of 35 by 175 feet, and stood 4 floors high in front and 2 in the rear. Inside it presented all the typical disadvantages of ordinary joist construction, with open staircases and elevators. As well, there were highly flammable contents, for the Curries were neckware manufacturers. The exact origins of the fire will never be known — possibly defective wiring, possibly an overheated furnace flue. Whatever the cause, it apparently broke out in the neighbourhood of the elevator, possibly some twenty minutes before it was discovered, and, roaring up the open shaft, it quickly reached out and engaged all four floors of the structure.[28]

When the alarm sounded, Fire Chief John Thompson was at the Lombard Street Fire Hall, only a few blocks to the east; he arrived with the fire engines to find the entire Currie Building blazing. Despite the fact that much of the downtown equipment answered the first alarm — including three engines, an aerial

View along Wellington Street showing Currie Building.

truck, a hook-and-ladder truck and the water tower —it was immediately obvious that the building could not be saved. Worse, although the fire was still confined to a single location, the general situation was a dangerous one, for the water pressure was low, even at the outset. The pressure was to vary from 60 to 90 pounds per square inch during the fire; comparably, Buffalo, with its high-pressure system, could produce 150 pounds. Also, the 30 m.p.h. wind presented a grave problem, especially since the six-storey Gillespie Fur Company, immediately to the east of Currie's premises across a 12-foot lane, was directly downwind and there were unprotected windows in both buildings. The fire-fighting was still further complicated by a shortage of hydrants in the area, and by the wind deflecting the streams of water and turning them into spray.[29]

The problems presented by nature and construction were soon compounded by errors of judgement on the part of the Fire Department. The fire engines were slow in starting. Then only two of the seven streams were used to prevent the spread of the flames, while the other five were played on the doomed building. Worst of all, Fire Chief Thompson, with some of his men, made the mistake of entering the Gillespie Building to see if it was possible to pour water onto the Currie Building from above. The accounts of exactly what happened next are somewhat contradictory. To follow Thompson's own story, as he narrated it to the *Globe* the next day, he and four of his men broke into the Gillespie Building with three lines of hose. When they reached the fourth floor, they were stopped by dense smoke and, having no laterns, were unable to find the staircase to retreat. They accordingly went to a window, lowered a rope to pull up a hose and slid down it to safety. When it came the chief's turn, he lost his hold, fell and broke his right leg. (Other accounts of the incident state that it happened on the third floor, or that the floor below caught fire).[30]

Norman Patterson, in his account of the fire for *The Canadian Magazine*, analyzed the situation succinctly: "The general who is supposed to direct the Toronto firemen so far forgot himself as to do some scouting which should have been done by a ranker; the result was that he lost his way in one of the buildings, and slid down a waterpipe to safety and a broken leg."[31] After the death of his predecessor nine years earlier, as a result of a somewhat similar accident during the *Globe* fire, Thompson's actions are

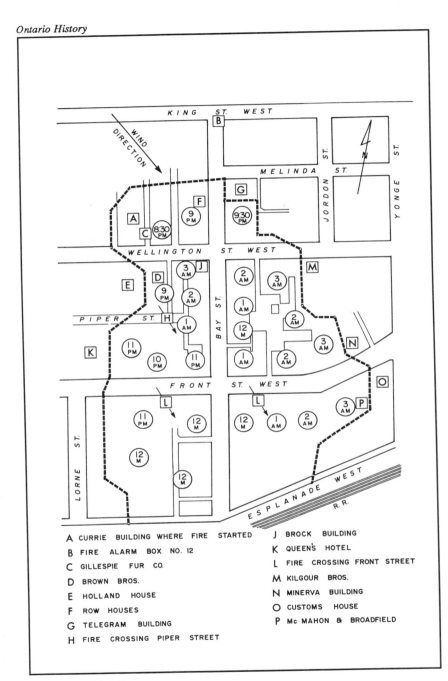

Map of 1904 fire area.

A CURRIE BUILDING WHERE FIRE STARTED   J BROCK BUILDING

B FIRE ALARM BOX NO. 12   K QUEEN'S HOTEL

C GILLESPIE FUR CO.   L FIRE CROSSING FRONT STREET

D BROWN BROS.   M KILGOUR BROS.

E HOLLAND HOUSE   N MINERVA BUILDING

F ROW HOUSES   O CUSTOMS HOUSE

G TELEGRAM BUILDING   P Mc MAHON & BROADFIELD

H FIRE CROSSING PIPER STREET

particularly surprising, especially since he was an experienced fire-fighter, having joined the department in 1876 and become its chief in 1899. He was to continue in office until 1915 and it was most unfortunate that his worst moment came with his greatest fire.

Deputy Chief John C. Noble, a man of equal experience, who had joined the department the same year as Thompson and been the deputy for four years, assumed control. By that time, most accounts agree that the confusion had meant fatal delays in containing the fire. The Gillespie Building was an even larger structure than the Currie factory and soon its 33,000 feet of floor space was entirely alight. From there the flames swept northwards and eastwards to Bay Street. Simultaneously, impelled by the wind, they jumped southward across Wellington Street's 66-foot-width—just as they had done in the Osgoodby fire nine years previously — and burst into Brown Brothers' stationery manufactory through the front windows. Within an hour of the fire's start some dozen buildings were ignited and the blaze had become a conflagration.[32]

The general alarm was turned in at 8:51. Shortly afterwards, Mayor Thomas Urquhart asked Noble if outside help was needed. Receiving the response "we need all the help we can get," he rushed to the Bell Telephone office to contact both the suburban municipalities and all major centres within a reasonable radius: Hamilton, Niagara Falls, Buffalo, Brantford, London and Peterborough. The call for support received the customary willing assistance from all these neighbouring municipalities, and the Grand Trunk Railway cleared its main lines so that the trains with fire-fighters and equipment could race to the city. First to arrive were the forces of the suburban municipalities: Toronto Junction, East Toronto, Kew Beach and the Volunteer Fire Brigade of the Island. They were largely on the scene by 11 p.m. The chief of the Hamilton Fire Department, with a dozen men and some equipment, arrived shortly after midnight, following a forty-five minute trip on a special Grand Trunk train. The Buffalo and London brigades reached Toronto about 2 a.m., within a few minutes of each other, Buffalo in four cars and London in three. They rendered good aid in the late stages of the fire and in the final cleanup operations. Support also arrived in the early morning hours from Brantford, Niagara Falls and Peterborough, and the Waterous Engine Works Company of

Brantford sent an engine. That company had a direct interest in rendering assistance. Having sold Toronto a 600-gallon steam engine in 1896, the owners doubtless saw the opportunity of advertising their latest model.[33]

The usual argument favouring the use of dynamite to clear a fire break was quickly raised and Mayor Urquhart gave his permission. Military engineers were brought in from the Garrison at Stanley Barracks, but the dynamite could not be located. This was probably fortunate. Although sometimes explosives can be used effectively in preventing back-burning against the wind, as was the case when the Tower of London was saved in 1666, they generally do far more damage than good. The fire breaks created by the blasts are never ready in time, or wide enough, as had been shown in Chicago in 1871 and was to be clearly again demonstrated in San Francisco two years later. Chief City Architect Robert McCallum was familiar with this problem and warned that the dynamite might result only in spreading the flames.[34]

The troops remained to help the police control the crowd, for by that time a large part of the citizenry was hastening downtown to watch and this mass of humanity had to be kept back so that they would not impede the firemen, or harm themselves. Safety was a major problem for the streets were becoming increasingly dangerous. A wide swath was littered with pieces of burning wood, plate glass was falling in showers and there were tottering walls, fallen wires and lengths of tin from the roofing and cornices. As well, because of the broken pipes, as much gas was burning as the Consumers Gas Company could make. Basically, the crowds, as Chief of Police H.J. Grasett described them, "were very orderly", however, he added, "of course they were all anxious to see the most of the fire, and we had to be rough with them." Despite the police and the troops, several spectators were injured, some by falling off vantage-points.[35]

Many, however, were not coming to gawk, but rather to attempt to rescue their business records. Some bank clerks told of an expressman's son who took his sleeping father's wagon and horse and made $36.00 removing valuables. Beyond the fire area, the various safety deposit companies were opening their vaults to take in books, documents and costly goods. At the same time, the well-being of the fire-fighters was not neglected. The

Grill Room of the King Edward Hotel was thrown open from the small hours until noon of the next day to provide them with refreshments. For the injured, the police ambulance was stationed at the corner of King and Bay streets and the staff of the emergency hospital were busy. In all, nine were injured besides Chief Thompson; some, as noted, were spectators, not firemen.[36]

The fire now began to spread its talons further. Westward on both sides of Wellington Street, the combination of the opposing force of the wind and fortunate fire breaks stopped it. On the north side of Wellington Street (now the southern end of the Toronto-Dominion Centre), there was a forty-foot gap, with blank walls on each side, just to the west of the point of origin. The flames could not jump this break against the wind. On Wellington Street's south side (site of the present-day Royal Bank Plaza), one of the last of the Family Compact mansions, "Holland House," built by Attorney General Henry John Boulton in 1831, was still standing, though long dispossessed of its view south to the lake. Its open gardens served to stop the flames' inroads.

Eastwards, towards Bay Street, the fire, to an extent, had to burn back against the wind. When it broke through on the west side of Bay Street, about 9 p.m., it was stopped because the firefighters were able to prevent its northward spread at some small, mid-nineteenth century row houses (roughly the site of the old Stock Exchange). These had been converted to commercial use, but their solid fire walls remained. Across Bay Street, on the east (Commerce Court) side, the fronts of the buildings north of Wellington Street were ignited. On the east side, the wind direction did not favour the flames, which were stopped at the offices of the *Telegram*, just south of Melinda Street, although the Office Specialty Company, immediately south of the newspaper building, was burned out. The *Telegram* building was one of three buildings with sprinklers, but the sprinklers were not required, although the front windows were broken by the heat, for the system also included a roof hydrant and inside standpipe and hand hoses, which the employees used effectively to douse down the window frames and the side of the building. John Ross Robertson, the proprietor, was to provide substantial bonuses for their efforts. Noble was able to place firemen at the rear of these buildings and their efforts, aided by the wind, were sufficient to prevent the spread of the flames eastward along the north side of Wellington Street.[37]

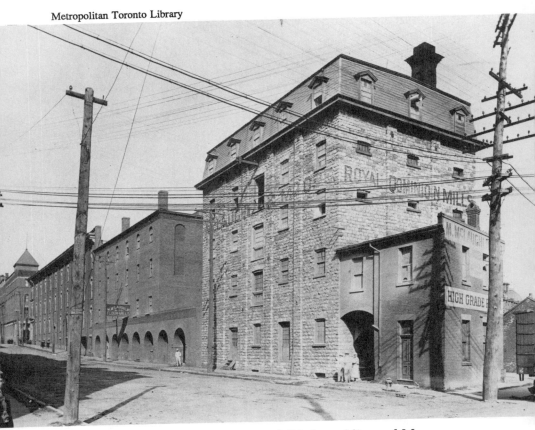

Foot of Bay Street before fire with McLaughlin and Moore Flour Mills.

The same, immediately after 1904 fire.

It was to the south side of Wellington Street that the real danger lay, for, with the flames propelled by the wind and the insufficient water pressure, the firemen could literally do nothing. From Brown Brothers, the first building ignited on the south side of Wellington Street, the flames spread east to Rolph, Smith & Company, lithographers and printers, and then soared out the back windows of both structures, with the wind behind them, to blow across Piper Street, a narrow lane parallel to Wellington Street, and burst through the unprotected rear windows of the buildings on the north side of Front Street West. By 10 p.m. these structures were burning furiously. At Warwick Bros. & Rutter, some 2,500 pages of type for provincial government publications were destroyed, including proofs for journals, reports and statutes.[38]

To the east of the Rolph, Smith property on Wellington Street stood the Brock Building, at the southwest corner of Wellington and Bay streets (the northwest corner of the Royal Bank Plaza). This was a wholesale dry goods warehouse, which possessed a sprinkler system supplied by both the city mains and a gravity tank on the roof. It also had outside sprinklers on the west side, facing the fire, and these provided a water curtain. Almost immediately the structure became a "wet sponge" enveloped in clouds of steam and the fire was held in bay for six hours until the buildings to the west and south had been destroyed. Then, at about 3 a.m., the private water supply ran out and the lowered pressure from the city mains allowed the flames to enter. Even then the fire was a slow one and the building was to provide one of the main sources of salvage. If an example of the efficiency of sprinklers had been needed, a better one could not have been found.[39]

Meanwhile, on the north side of Front Street, the most romanticized episode of the fire unfolded when the flames were prevented from spreading westward to the old Queen's Hotel, long Toronto's finest inn, which occupied the present site of the Royal York Hotel. The hotel was upwind from the fire and protected by a sixty-foot garden that stood between it and Warwick Bros. & Rutter's blazing building. Also, the firemen under District Chief Frank Smith, including some of the Hamilton brigade, were ready, stationing themselves on the roof and extinguishing fires that started there. Much of the credit, however, went to the distinguished guests resident in the building, in those days the usual stopping place for out-of-town members of the Legislative Assembly, which was then in session. As soon as the Warwick premises ignited the ladies at the Queen's were quickly removed to other hotels, a procession of Verral Transfer Company express wagons arriving to take their baggage and the hotel silver. Some of the gentlemen fled with them. Others stayed, such as James Pliny (later Sir James) Whitney, the leader of the Ontario Conservative opposition who the next year was to become premier. Whitney was content to move from his water-soaked room overlooking the garden to another wing, even though the fire still raged.[40]

The real fight inside the building was led by Manager Henry Winnett, assisted by Robert L. Joynt (the Conservative MPP for Grenville) and Major John R. Barber (the Liberal MPP for Halton), who, together with some firemen, organized an amateur brigade which filled the bath tubs, soaked blankets and then hung them down from the tops of the upper window sashes to prevent the wood from catching fire. By working rapidly and in a coordinated fashion they kept the windows cool enough to stop the entrance of the flames. In the end, only slight damage was done and the old landmark was to serve as Toronto's great hostellery for another two decades.[41]

To the south of Front Street (now Union Station), in the direct path of the fire, there was no saving anything. Driven directly by the wind, the flames quickly leaped that 78-foot-wide street and by 11 p.m. almost the entire block was aflame from Bay Street west to Lorne Street and south to the railway tracks and the open land beside Lake Ontario. The firemen did save some low sheds and stables to the extreme southwest because they could throw water over them and the wind was in their favour. The railway signalmen's sheds on the Esplanade were burnt, as was The Grand Trunk Railway shed, although the cars were removed safely before the flames reached the building.[42]

There were some rather comic incidents. At the Eckhard Casket Company on the Esplanade the employees rescued five or six completed hearses and, attaching them together, tried to have one horse pull them away. The horse persisted in hawing when told to gee, until finally the spectators enjoying the show took pity and dragged the hearses to safety. At the Hendrie Transport Company the men rushed out the horses and the first harness that they could find, but then the process of trying to harness the horses in the deep mud of the Esplanade quickly degenerated into chaos. Ultimately, they were rescued by their western location as the fire moved away.[43]

While the area south of Front Street was being ignited, the fire was crossing Bay Street on a wide, two-block front, which stretched from almost Wellington Street southward to the railway tracks. First, propelled by the heat and its own wind currents, it burned back northwards from Front Street, spreading up the west side of Bay Street until it reached the Brock Building about 2 a.m. In crossing Bay Street it was aided by the high Mansard roofs of the Barber, Ellis building and the Robert Darling Company on the east side, which once ignited could not be put out from either the ground or the roof. Within five minutes the flames were within these buildings.[44]

East of Bay Street, on the north side of Wellington Street, the adverse winds meant that little damage was done. On the south side of Wellington Street, however, the fire quickly burned half way to Yonge Street, jumping yards and lanes in the process, until it reached the Kilgour Brothers bag and paper box factory, the third building equipped with sprinklers in the central area. This was a long, narrow edifice, four and five storeys high, which was divided by fire doors into two sections. The fire protection was excellent. To feed the sprinklers there were two gravity flow tanks on the roof to supplement the city water system in case there was a drop in pressure. Outside the structure there was a water curtain with city connections and an auxiliary pump. Although the buildings right under the Kilgour's windows burnt out completely, the sprinklers were able to contain the fire, except on the top floor at the north facing Wellington Street. In one case, where an automatic fire door stuck, leaving a gap six feet wide, six sprinkler heads opened on the endangered side and prevented the spread of the fire. The Kilgour Brothers might well have been among those thanked officially by the city, for their sprinklers not only saved their own premises, but also prevented the flames from breaking through to Yonge Street.[45]

In the south half of the same Wellington-Front block (the future Bell Telephone Centre), the advance of the fire parallelled its course on the north. By 2 a.m. it had nearly reached Yonge Street, destroying a dozen large factories and warehouses and reaching the structures immediately south of the Kilgour building. In that area the heat was intense and any fire-fighting had virtually proven impossible. The flames roared hundreds of feet into the air over these buildings and the heat buckled the asphalt streets into great hummocks, which broke up under the tread of feet. The water pressure was halved, for there were some fifty streams of hose going and there was, of course, a constant leakage from the innumerable broken pipes in the buildings.[46]

With the Kilgour Building creating the first break on the north side of the block, the fire-fighters hoped to stop the flames from breaking through along the south side to Yonge Street at Front Street. Across Yonge Street there were more unprotected facades and behind them more blocks of similar, and occasionally older warehouses and factories, some of them frame, stretching on past the St Lawrence Market. The wind was now somewhat in the firemen's favour and there was a possible place for a stand at the Minerva Building next to the Bank of Montreal at the corner of Yonge Street. Originally built in the 1860s by Senator William McMaster, the founder of the university that bears his name, the Minerva Building was a massive four-storey mansard structure that served as an underwear factory. To its northwest the fire had been deflected by the Kilgour sprinklers; its west side was a blank wall which rose two storeys above the adjacent warehouses, and its open windows and ornate facades faced south and east away from the fire. Here the firemen finally scored a victory.[47]

The first round was fought by the building's staff, led by the engineer, W. Wingfield, who had been about to leave his home to see "An English Daisy" at the Princess Theatre when he noticed the flames and rushed downtown. Equipped with their own standpipe and 250 feet of hose, the employees poured water down on the Wool Exchange building to the west, which had quickly become a "perfect cauldron." As the flames roared up, Frank Smith and some eight or ten men, some from the Hamilton and Toronto Junction Departments, took over and made what Smith described as their "grand stand finish," pulling the hose to the top by ropes. Although the top of the building was burned out, and they once had to retreat, they succeeded in stopping the fire with a loss of $50,000 to the stock and $15,000 to the machinery, which was fortunately covered by insurance. The Minerva Building, somewhat unsympathetically repaired, was to survive until the 1960s when it was replaced by a parking lot (now, in 1988, under development) [48]

To its immediate east, at the corner of Yonge and Front streets stood — and still stands — the magnificent Bank of Montreal, built in 1885. Although the roof caught on fire it was saved with the help of the Buffalo fire-fighters. Meanwhile, as the fire headed towards the Minerva Building and the bank, the merchants of Yonge Street had hurriedly begun removing their goods. Simultaneously, the firemen from Buffalo and Hamilton played water on the buildings on both sides of the street to cool the structures and prevent burning brands from igniting them. When the fire was safely stopped north of Front Street, Acting Chief Noble told the press that "if it had got a hold in Yonge Street, God knows where it would have stopped." Certainly, the fire could have easily run to Church Street and possibly as far as the St Lawrence Market.[49]

But the danger was equally grave south of Front Street where the flames burned east from Bay Street without opposition, while brands flew over the railway tracks and set fire to the wharfs along Lake Ontario. At the harbour front there was further confusion, particularly when "a man with a load of paper soap labels drove out to the wharf, and when the flames reached these fire flew everywhere in chunks." Fortunately, there was little to ignite. There were some small fires in goods on the dock and an oil store burnt, but, basically, the steamer offices and warehouses on the wharves had iron roofs and were thus spared.[50]

The flames billowing towards the wharves endangered a number of vessels moored to the piers. These mostly belonged to The Montreal and Chicago Merchants Shipping Company, or The Richelieu and Ontario Navigation Company (now the Canadian Shipping Lines), and included the *Ocean*, *Kingston*, *Persia*, *Mazeppa* and *Cuba*. The tug of the Clark Brothers Ferry Company rescued some vessels, while others were able to move under their own power. The *Mazeppa* and *Cuba* at the Yonge Street wharf were particularly endangered. The former was towed to John Street west of the fire, but before the *Cuba* got up its own steam to flee into the bay it was surrounded by a storm of flying embers from the blazing flour mill at the foot of Bay Street.[51]

Along the south side of Front Street itself (now the 1930 Federal Building) eighteen warehouses, three to five storeys in height, burned in a row. These buildings had replaced the "Iron

Block," one of Toronto's first cast-iron structures, which had gone up in a spectacular fire in February 1872, with a damage of $400,000. The masonry warehouses proved no more resistant to fire, possibly because unprotected openings had been cut through their eighteen-inch-thick brick party walls over the years. Some sources state that dynamite was used here in an attempt to stop the fire, but without success. This may have been just as well, for one of the buildings was H.S. Howland Sons & Co. warehouse, used to store powder and cartridges. As the *News* reported when the fire reached this building, "there must have been thousands that went off. What with the noise and the reports, and the roaring of the fire, you could not hear yourself shout." The last of these warehouses, McMahon & Broadfield's crockery business, had a solid wall on its east side and then there was a forty-foot gap before the ornate mansard Customs House was reached at the southwest corner of Front and Yonge streets. Stretching south of it and to the southeast of the warehouses, again separated by a thirty-forty foot lane and protected by blank walls and iron shutters, was the Customs Receiving and Examining Warehouse, which was jammed to the ceiling with flammable materials, some of which were hastily moved out.[52]

It was here that District Chief Charles Smedley decided to make his stand on the south side of Front Street, about an hour after the Minerva Building had been saved. His own tired men were reinforced with fire-fighters from Hamilton, Buffalo and London, who also continued to soak down the buildings along Yonge Street and hold the fire there. Considering the highly flammable state of the sheds and the old wooden railway station beyond them to the east of Yonge Street, it was, as he said, "the only thing we could do." Because of the direction of the wind, despite its ornate exterior, the slate-roofed Customs House itself was in less danger than the warehouse. Fortunately, Smedley was able to play streams of water over the warehouses's exposed sides by placing firemen in the lane and by stationing men with hoses inside and on the roof. The battle lasted for two hours with the flames seeming almost to engulf the warehouse at times. Then, when the engagement seemed lost, the McMahon-Broadfield Building suddenly collapsed, the firemen fleeing to safety from the alley, one of them, Nicholas Sweetman, being seriously injured. The flames then died down. At 4 a.m. the fire was under control, though it was to burst out at times for another two weeks.[53]

Statistically, although totals differ, the conflagration had destroyed between 98 and 104 separate buildings, housing some 220 firms. It encompassed 19.7 acres, if the 4.4 acres of street allowances are included. Over 230 firemen had poured nearly 3,000,000 gallons of water on the blaze. Aside from Chief Thompson, four others had been fairly seriously injured, with another 20 slightly overcome but able to continue on duty. Happily, there were no deaths, and no dwellings were destroyed. The loss was estimated at $2,070,000 on buildings and $8,280,000 on contents, for a total of $10,350,000. Insurance was to cover $8,383,500: $1,345,500 on the buildings, and $7,038,000 on the contents.[54] Some 5,000 to 6,000 people were thrown out of work, a large proportion of them women and girls. Many of them arrived for work at 8 a.m. the next morning only to find their premises destroyed. At least 14 of the firms that were destroyed had over 100 employees. These included: E. & S. Currie, where it all started, 300; the Minerva Manufacturing Co., 280; Warwick bros. & Rutter, 250; Kilgour Bros., 200; and W.R. Brock, 100.[55]

The insurance companies, which were probably at least partly at fault for not giving proper credits for superior construction in their rating system, now finally moved swiftly, both to settle the loss and augment their income. The fire insurance premiums for all Canada in 1903 had been about $11,000,000, which was very close to the actual loss in the 1904 fire. As a temporary measure, until the rate structures could be examined, two days after the fire the Toronto Board of Fire Underwriters added $1.00 loading, or additional charge, per $100.00 insurance on all building and contents rates in the congested areas of the city centre and .50c in the less hazardous districts. Reductions were allowed for sprinklers, fire-resistant construction or the use of co-insurance. This last is a clause that requires the owner to carry insurance up to a stated percentage, usually 80 per cent, of value. On the average the rates went up 75 per cent.[56]

The organization of the settlement was quickly and efficiently arranged; nearly all the 48 companies involved joined to form an overall Loss Committee within the week. Subsidiary committees for each separate loss were also established, composed of representatives of the companies involved; standard forms were printed; joint use of adjusters arranged and an overall salvage system agreed upon. The largest sufferers were the Royal with $755,000 insurance in force, the Alliance with $370,000 and the Scottish Union and the North British and Mercantile with $350,000 each. The Underwriters' Salvage Company of New York was retained to examine the ruins and it quickly established offices with the necessary equipment for drying and storage. The amount of salvagable material proved to be limited, for only 10 of the 41 ruins examined yielded anything that warranted the expense of handling. The most valuable recoveries were the dry goods stocks, particularly from such basements as that of the Brock building, where much material had been too soaked to burn.[57]

While the settlement was still taking place the owners of most buildings were beginning to plan reconstruction. The mood, far from being despondent, was one of optimism. Bryon Edmund (later Sir Edmund) Walker, general manager of the Canadian Bank of Commerce, set the tone when he said that the fire "was merely a halting moment in the prosperity of Toronto" and he expected to see the buildings destroyed "rise triumphantly from their ashes, stronger and more vigorous than ever." He also noted that nothing seemed to have been learned from the *Globe*, Osgoodby and Simpson's fires and that the city needed an adequate water supply and good building arrangements. The president of the bank, Senator George Albertus Cox, who was also president of The Canada Life Assurance Company and the Western and the British America Fire Assurance companies, agreed, recommending a high-pressure system, an idea endorsed by the editor of the *News*. [58]

The only really sour — and rather modern — note came from one G.R.R. Cockburn, who stated that he would not rebuild his Bay Street premises as "there was too much socialism abroad; the property tax was too high and he could invest his money to better advantage than rebuilding." Most Toronto businessmen demonstrated exactly the opposite outlook. The W.R. Brock Company was typical; by the 21st it was advertising that it had a large Montreal warehouse with exactly the same stock as Toronto and could fill orders immediately. Also, it had set up temporary offices at 8-10 Wellington Street East and was negotiating for the Mutual Street Rink. Soon businesses were reopening in temporary locations scattered throughout the city.[59]

Services were quickly restored wherever possible. For some, such as gas and water, the mains had to be turned off in some areas until the broken pipes could sealed. The electricity had been cut off in half of the western part of the city, but new poles were being put up while the fire was still burning and by noon of the 20th the power was on north of Wellington Street. By the 21st the power was pretty well back in service. The telegraph companies were simultaneously rooting out burnt stumps and putting in newly shaved poles while the ruins were still smoking; but it was a few days before their services were fully restored. The urgent task of demolishing the dangerous walls began on the 21st under the supervision of City Architect McCallum. Dynamite was used and those streets with streetcar lines, such as Front Street, were cleared first.[60]

At the same time, urgent calls were going out for experts to open the safes and vaults as soon as they were sufficiently cool. These "safe crackers," as the workmen cleaning up the ruins came to call them, were frequently assisted by such calls as "let us know when you get to the stuff old man; we'll keep an eye on the cops." In most cases the safes had held back the heat and the waiting clerks soon busied themselves in passing out the books and papers, "knocking and blowing the dust from them, at the same time sadly damaging their patent leathers in the mess underfoot, and keeping one eye open for additional contributions to the scrap heap from the crumbling walls projecting overhead" — an unhappy note on the necessity of faultless dress for the underpaid clerk of the era. In a few cases the results were decidedly unfortunate. Buntin, Reid & Co. found only a United States silver dollar welded to a Canadian quarter; books, tin boxes and all other contents were completely destroyed.[61]

The City Council, too, was finally activated. Making provision for burnt-out companies to resume business as soon as possible was an obvious need. On April 20 the Board of Control recommended the suspension of the fire limit bylaw, which controlled construction, "to enable sufferers of the fire to erect temporary one storey premises in any part of the City to enable them to resume business with as little delay and inconvenience as possible." The board then approved the application of Johnston and Sword, tie manufacturers, to make temporary use of a vacant school at Bathurst and College streets until they could obtain other premises. The controllers also asked the city legal department to ascertain whether or not the city could compel the removal of poles and the placing of all wires underground.[62]

But more than temporary changes to the building code were necessary. The obvious haste of most companies to rebuild meant that any new building regulations would have to be enacted quickly. On April 25 a special committee was set up to amend the building bylaw. It consisted of the mayor, two controllers and four aldermen, including Fleming, and was instructed to consult with the Board of Trade and the fire underwriters. The committee immediately went into action, possibly too quickly, for Toronto's architects were not consulted, although they offered their services. On July 6 the new bylaw passed all three readings at one session. In some ways it did not satisfy the architectural critics. For instance, there was no height-limit and no demand that mill construction as a minimum be used in rebuilding. Certain other provisions were rather too drastic and had to be modified. Some obvious controls were missed, such as that on vertical openings, with the result that the fire underwriters were quickly demanding action on more requirements. Finally, despite the Board of Control's interest, there was no provision for placing wires underground and these were to remain as hazards to fire-fighters into the 1920s.[63]

Legislation for fire protection was a little more successful; the inadequacies of the water supply had been obvious. The city was finally ready to consider an auxiliary high-pressure system, without private connections, for congested districts, as the National Fire Protection Association highly recommended. The Canadian Manufacturers' Association seconded this demand in a letter to the Council on June 13. In the summer the Council sent a deputation to visit four American cities which had high-pressure systems: Detroit, Cleveland, Buffalo and Philadelphia, as well as Boston and New York where such systems were not yet in use. Its report in September recommended such an installation, as well as an improved alarm system to shorten delays, and more equipment. In November the City Council passed an enabling bylaw, authorizing the city to borrow $700,000 for these improvements in fire protection, subject to a referendum for the electors to approve. As an added incentive, at the end of December the Toronto Board of Fire Underwriters promised a 20 per cent reduction in dwelling rates — to say nothing of commercial risks — when the system was in operation. On Jan. 2, 1905, a citizen's plebiscite approved the borrowing of the then huge sum of $700,000 by 8,379 to 3,234, a clear majority of 5,145.

The high-pressure system was nearly completed in May 1908, when a broken valve held up completion till the year end. It went into operation in 1909.[64]

By that time, although there were still some open spaces for years, the rebuilding of most of the burned-out area north of Front Street West had been largely completed. Many of the businesses had resumed full operations in remarkably quick time. Warwick Bros. & Rutter, for instance, had obtained the use of another factory building before midnight on the 20th. Before long they had added five more locations and were operating their office and printing plant, partly in shifts, from six scattered temporary quarters throughout the downtown. In February 1905 the company began a new building at King Street West and Spadina Avenue, "entirely of brick, steel and concrete construction, reinforced with expanded metal and thoroughly fireproof."[65]

This combination of both speed and concern for solid construction was typical of most of those companies that had suffered loss, though the majority of them preferred to remain at their downtown location. Before the area destroyed by the fire was again largely rebuilt, in the burst of construction since the 1950s and 1960s, many buildings could still be seen bearing the dates 1904 and 1905. Generally, these were much less ornate architecturally than their predecessors, but they had the advantage of being largely constructed of reinforced concrete and steel.[66]

The last edifices to rise, on the public land to the south of Front Street, were the new Union Station (1915-30) and the 1930 Customs House (the Federal building), which still add a rare monumental touch, one almost reminiscent of imperial St Petersburg, to the face of downtown Toronto. Thus, while the First Great Fire in 1849 had left St James's Cathedral and the St Lawrence Market as its legacies to the city, the second added another fine touch with Union Station and the Customs House. When Union station was officially opened by the Prince of Wales in August 1927, the Second Great Fire was already a memory of the rather distant past, an unhappy incident from what was coming to be regarded as the golden age that had preceded World War I.

But the incident had left its largely hidden legacy. On the morning after the fire, T.H. Johnson, the watchman who had turned in the first alarm, told a reporter that "all the buildings I have been watching so long are gone." In 1904 the city had at least learned a lesson; the new construction methods, coupled with the better public protection and some good luck in the unburned older areas, meant that his lament would not be repeated again.[67] On May 9, 1977, when the third great fire of Toronto nearly broke out in the old Eaton's Warehouses and Annex, the combination of sprinklers, an adequate water supply and efficient fire-fighting prevented a recurrence of the horrible events of 1904.

Notes

Chapter 1

1. This chapter originally appeared in *The Canadian Geographer*, vol. 8, no. 3, 1966, 172-84, under the title "Toronto in 1834." J.W. Simmons made many helpful suggestions in the preparation of the original article.
2. *Courier of Upper Canada*, Nov. 28, 1833.
3. George Walton, comp., *York Commercial Directory* (York, 1833), 56.
4. "Soldier's Diary," Metropolitan Toronto Library, 15.
5. David Boyle, ed., *The Township of Scarboro: 1796-1896* (Toronto, 1896), 112-3. There were various later changes in the Danforth route; see Robert A. Given, *The Story of Etobicoke* (n.p., n.d.), 13; and Patrick Shirreff, *Tour through North America* (Edinburgh, 1835), 104.
6. Anna Jameson, *Winter Studies and Summer Rambles in Canada* (Toronto, 1923), 17.
7. *Ibid.*, 21.
8. W.H. Pearson, *Recollections and Records of Toronto of Old* (Toronto, 1914), 113.
9. *Ibid.*, 112-13; City of Toronto Archives (CTA), Toronto City Council Papers (TCCP), Nov. 24, 1842; John Ross Robertson, *Landmarks of Toronto* 6, vols. (Toronto, 1894-1914), vol. 2, 762.
10. Pearson, 23. TCCP, May 8, 27, 1834.
11. "Soldier's Diary," 14.
12. Robertson, vol. 1, 362.
13. Pearson, 143.
14. Robertson, vol. 1, 218-9.
15. *Ibid.*, vol. 2, 672.
16. *Ibid.*, vol. 5, 63.
17. J. Armstrong, ed., *City of Toronto and County of York Directory* (Toronto, 1850), 1xxi, 1xxv.
18. Archives of Ontario (AO), Minutes of the Quarter Sessions of the Peace of the Home District, January 6, 1834.
19. Pearson, 23, 110; "Soldier's Diary," 15.
20. *Courier*, June 23, 30, 1832.
21. Pearson, 13.
22. *Courier*, April 17, 1833.
23. Audrey Murton Saunders, "Studies in Yonge Street Settlement Based on the O'Brien Diary" (M.A. thesis, Dept. of Hist., Univ. of Toronto, 1943), 175.

Chapter 2

1. The original version of this article appeared under the title "Metropolitanism and Toronto Re-examined, 1825-1850" in the Canadian Historical Association (CHA), *Historical Papers*, 1966, 29-40.
2. See Harold A. Innis, *The Fur Trade in Canada* (New Haven, 1930); Arthur M. Lower, *Colony to Nation* (Toronto, 1946); Donald G. Creighton, *The Commercial Empire of the St. Lawrence* (Toronto, 1937); and J.M.S. Careless, "Frontierism, Metropolitanism and Canadian History," *Canadian Historical Review* (*CHR*), vol. 35, no. 1, 1954, 1-21.

3.   The most recent discussion of this subject, which includes a valuable bibliographical survey, is by Jim Sentence, "Reconsidering Toronto's Emergence as a Metropolis: Some evidence from the Census," *Urban History Review*, vol. 13, no. 2, 1984, 9-18. Using the Gras model, which he feels has been given a "simplistic" reading by some authorities (including this writer), whom he feels are "confusing form for substance," he proceeds to attempt to gather data on labour from the constantly changing categories of the census and organizes it into sectorial groupings. The sectors do not include everyone and the data itself is hardly up to the modern standards of accuracy. Not surprisingly, his conclusion is just as inconclusive as he deems the findings of all the earlier writers, and he decides that more work is needed (17).

It seems strange that while Sentence thus attacks the former writers for using the "analytical method," which he claims lets everyone place Toronto's metropolitan emergence where they want it, he still uses the ancient (1922) and anecdotal Gras thesis himself as the basis of his statistical analysis — with its quite unsatisfactory statistics. Towards the end of his account he does note the possibility that "the whole model should be evaluated" (17). With all the accurate data we can ever collect from this era at hand, the anecdotal approach can be just as precise as the statistical analysis. Previous historians might perhaps be accused of "confusing form for substance" if there actually were adequate statistics to be had. When there are not, the substance cannot reasonably be quantified and what facts we can collect, both anecdotal and statistical, have to direct us to an answer. As I say in the text, by the mid-1830s Toronto was clearly the major city of a burgeoning province, had bypassed its rivals and was on the way to assuming metropolitan status: the geographic basis was there; the people were rapidly gathering; the transportation and industrial phases were under way; and the breakout point had been passed. It was settled by then that Toronto was going to be a metropolis. Exactly when it achieved that dignity really rests on whatever set of criteria for metropolitan status each individual analyst wants to use.

The Gras thesis, moreover, ancient as it may be, provides an adequate and easily comprehensible guide, given the data of the period. Sentence is trying to build another thesis out of a very inadequate pile of census building blocks. Everything is not subject to adequate quantification, however much money is spent, as Michael Katz proved unintentionally in the case of Hamilton.

4.   N.S.B. Gras, *An Introduction to Economic History* (New York, 1922).
5.   *Ibid.*, 302.
6.   The Macaulay Papers in the AO provide many interesting examples of this trade.
7.   *Courier of Upper Canada*, Sept. 29, 1832.
8.   See *Constitution*, Nov. 7, 1836 for Mackenzie's list of agents.
9.   4 William IV, c. 23.
10.   AO, Minutes of the Quarter Sessions of the Peace of the Home District, March 26, 1836.
11.   TCCP, May 6, 1835.
12.   D.C. Masters, *The Rise of Toronto, 1850-1890* (Toronto, 1947), 15.
13.   *Courier of Upper Canada*, April 27, 1833.
14.   Robertson, *Landmarks*, vol. 2, 677.
15.   Henry Scadding, *Toronto of Old* (Toronto, 1873), 548.
16.   *The Upper Canada Land, Mercantile and General Advertiser* was published from June 1834 to August 1835.
17.   *Patriot*, Feb. 1, 1833.
18.   *Ibid.*, Aug. 9, 1836.

Chapter 3

1. An expanded version of this chapter appeared in *Ontario History* (*OH*), vol. 58, no. 1, March 1966, 21-42. The writer would like to thank Dr. R.C. Overton, professor emeritus of American history at the University of Western Ontario, for his help in preparing the original paper. Where specific reference is made to a document in this paper, and no footnote given, the document or report is in the Allan Papers in the Baldwin Room at the Metropolitan Toronto Library (MTL).
2. Thomas Ralph, *A Brief Account* ... (Dundas, U.C., 1836), 176.
3. *Courier*, July 19, 1832.
4. *Patriot*, Aug. 1, 1834.
5. *Ibid.*
6. Allan Papers, Aug. 28, 1834; *Ibid.*, July 18, 1836; *Ibid.*, Sept. 23, 1834; *Upper Canada Gazette*, Oct. 9, 1834; Allan Papers, Dec. 23, 1834.
7. Allan Papers, Dec. 23, 1834.
8. *Ibid.*, undated but after Nov. 1.
9. *Patriot*, March 3, 1835; Allan Papers, Feb. 21, 1835.
10. *Patriot*, Aug. 28, 1835.
11. *Courier*, Oct. 22, 1835.
12. 6 William IV, c. 5, article II.
13. Allan Papers, July 18, 1835.
14. *Correspondent and Advocate*, July 20, 1836.
15. *Patriot*, Aug. 2, 1836.
16. Ralph, 176; Allan Papers, Sept. 1, 1836.
17. *Correspondent and Advocate*, Aug. 31, 1836.
18. Allan Papers, Oct. 19, 1836. The original article has far more details on the second survey, including extensive quotations.
19. *Patriot*, Feb. 17, 1837. Full details are given in the original article.
20. Allan Papers, undated draft.
21. TCCP, March 5, 1837.
22. Victor E. Lauriston, *Lambton's Hundred Years, 1849-1949* (Sarnia, 1949), 33-4.
23. *Patriot*, April 4, 1837.
24. *Ibid.*, April 7 and 12, 1837; Allan Papers, Shareholders' Books; *Ibid.*, April 19, 1837.
25. *Ibid.*, April 23, 1837.
26. TCCP, April 27, 1837.
27. Allan Papers, May 23, 1837.
28. Allan Papers, April 18, 1837.
29. *Ibid.*, July 3, 1837.
30. *Patriot*, July 14 and Sept. 21, 1837, and *Constitution*, July 26, 1837; Allan Papers, July 31, 1837.
31. Allan Papers, Aug. 21, 1837; *Patriot*, Sept. 21, 1838.

Chapter 4

1. The original version of this article appeared in (*OH*), vol. 55, no. 2, 1963, 61-72. The author would like to thank Morris Zaslow and Cecil H. Clough for reading the original manuscript and making many helpful suggestions. Charles P. Stacey also suggested certain changes.
2. Charles Lindsey, *The Life and Times of Mackenzie and the Rebellion of 1837-38* 2 vols. (Toronto, 1862), vol. 1, 219; *Ibid.*, vol. 1, 233; Aileen Dunham, *Political Unrest in Upper Canada, 1815-1836* (London, 1927), 129; Lindsey, vol. 1, 241-2.

3.   From a letter given to the writer by Frank W. Campbell of Royal Oak, Michigan.

4.   For a more detailed account of the formation of the British Constitutional Society, see the chapter on the Carfrae family.

5.   James Lesslie diary, in the collections of the Dundas Museum, Dundas, Ontario, entry for March 22, 1832; Lindsey, vol. 1, 250.

6.   There is no complete copy of the *Courier* for this date extant, but the account of the riot is in the Carfrae Scrapbook in the Metropolitan Toronto Library. See also Lindsey, vol. 1, 245 ff.

7.   At this time Ryerson was still generally backing Mackenzie, and Gurnett was just as anti-Methodist as he was anti-Reform, which accounts for his coupling the two together.

8.   For further accounts of FitzGibbon's activities see J.K. Johnson, "Colonel James FitzGibbon and the Suppression of Irish riots in Upper Canada", *(OH)*, vol. 57, no. 3, 1966, 139-55.

9.   Lindsey, vol. 1, 245 ff.; J.C. Dent, *The Story of the Upper Canadian Rebellion*, 2 vols, (Toronto, 1885), vol. 1, 244-5.

10.   Lindsey, vol. 1, 244-5.

Chapter 5

1.   The original version of this essay appeared in the *CHR*, vol. 48, no. 4, 1967, 309-31, under the title "William Lyon Mackenzie, First Mayor of Toronto: A Study of a Critic in Power." It is somewhat changed in this version, and I am currently preparing a new overview of Mackenzie's place in Canadian history. This overview, following up on both my papers for the Ontario Historical Society's Rebellion Conference on Oct. 3, 1987, replies to the criticisms of Paul Romney and Michael Cross — the two historians who have attacked the view of Mackenzie put forward by Ronald J. Stagg, Colin F. Read and myself in recent years, and earlier by such authors as Aileen Dunham and Gerald Craig.

2.   *Advocate*, March 20, 1834.

3.   *Ibid.*

4.   *Patriot*, March 21, 1834; *Advocate*, March 20, 1834.

5.   AO, John Macaulay Papers, April 16, 1834.

6.   Jesse E. Middleton, *The Municipality of Toronto*, 3 vols. (Toronto, 1923), vol. 1, 95. See also the votes recorded in *CTA, Journal of the City Council*.

7.   MTL, Carfrae Scrapbook, and Henry Scadding and John Charles Dent, *Toronto Past and Present: Historical and Descriptive* (Toronto, 1884), 154.

8.   Scadding and Dent, *Toronto Past and Present*, 154.

9.   Carfrae Scrapbook.

10.   *Ibid.*

11.   Journal of the City Council, Oct. 20, 1834.

12.   *Ibid.*, April 8, 11 and 14, 1834.

13.   *Ibid.*, May 19, 1834.

14.   AO, Minutes of the Court of the Quarter Sessions of the Home District, April 29, 1834.

15.   TCCP, May 20, 1834; *Ibid.*, Nov. 21, 1834.

16.   MTL, S.P. Jarvis Papers, Jarvis to A. McLean, May 29, 1834; *Canadian Freeman*, July 20, 1834; Journal of the City Council, May 19, 1834.

17.   *Ibid.*, June 7, 1834; TCCP, June 18-21, 1834; *Ibid.*, June 20, 1834.

18.   *Advocate*, June 26, 1834; Scadding and Dent, *Toronto Past and Present*, 162.

19.   AO, Macaulay Papers, Robert Stanton to Macaulay, Aug. 6 and 9; *Patriot*, Aug. 12; and Carfrae Scrapbook; Macaulay Papers, Aug. 21, 1834.

20. *Patriot*, Sept. 9, 1834; *Christian Guardian*, Sept. 10, 1834; *Advocate*, Sept. 9, 1834; Carfrae Scrapbook; and *Patriot*, Sept. 19, 1834. The promissory note is in MTL. See also Charles Lindsey, *The Life and Times of William Lyon Mackenzie*, vol. 1, 318-19.

21. Journal of the City Council, Aug. 18, 1834, and TCCP, Aug. 26, 1834; *Patriot*, Nov. 14 and 21, 1834; CTA, City Council Cash Book, Item #48, Aug. 26, 1834 and Item #63, Sept. 24, 1834; Journal, Jan. 25, 1835; TCCP, Aug. 3, 1835.

22. Carfrae Scrapbook, clipping from the *Courier*, Nov. 25, 1834; TCCP, Nov. 12, 1834; *Patriot*, Nov. 28, 1834. The following account of the incident is based upon the entries in the Journal of the City Council, the *Patriot* (Nov. 28, 1834), the *Courier* (Nov. 27, 1834), and the Carfrae Scrapbook.

23. Aileen Dunham, *Political Unrest in Upper Canada*, 137.

24. Journal of the City Council, Jan. 31, 1835; Cash Book, Feb. 5, 1838.

25. Scadding and Dent, *Toronto Past and Present*, 163; *Correspondent and Advocate*, Feb. 6, 1835.

26. Dunham, *Political Unrest in Upper Canada*, 106.

Chapter 6

1. The writer would like to thank some of his colleagues at the University of Western Ontario — Fred A. Dreyer, A.H.J. Hyatt and Peter F. Neary of the Department of History and J. Peter Denny of the Department of Psychology — and also J. Donald Wilson of the University of British Columbia, for their advice in the preparation of this paper. Sally F. Zerker's complete history of the Toronto Typographical Union, 1832-1925, provides a full account of that organization's activities.

2. Lillian Gates, "The Decided Policy of William Lyon Mackenzie," *CHR*, September 1959, vol. 40, 185-208.

3. Alice F. Tyler, *Freedom's Ferment* (New York, 1944), 214.

4. H.A. Logan, *Trade Unions in Canada: Their Development and Functioning* (Toronto, 1948), 23.

5. *Ibid.*

6. *Star Weekly*, Oct. 27, 1923; the account which follows here is taken from this source.

7. *Ibid.*

8. For a description of the pre-Confederation papers of Toronto, see Edith G. Firth, *Early Toronto Newspapers, 1793-1867* (Toronto, 1961).

9. *Patriot*, Oct. 25, 1836.

10. *Correspondent and Advocate*, Oct. 26, 1836.

11. *Patriot*, Nov. 1, 1836.

12. *Constitution*, Nov. 2, 1836.

13. *Patriot*, Nov. 18, 22, and Dec. 2, 1836.

14. *Star Weekly*, Oct. 27, 1923.

15. R.A. MacKay, "The Political Ideas of William Lyon Mackenzie", *Canadian Journal of Economics and Political Science*, vol. 3, no. 1, February 1937.

Chapter 7

1. This chapter originally appeared in the *Journal of Canadian Studies*, vol 6, no. 3, 1971, 21-36. A mimeographed description and history of the monuments at Queen's Park is available at the information desk. In describing the Mackenzie memorial as the most recent, I have not included the equestrian statue of Edward

VII in the north section of Queen's Park. This is qa in fact a transplant from New Delhi, not a work chosen by the Ontario government.

2. See F.H. Armstrong, "William Lyon Mackenzie, First Mayor Toronto: A Study of a Critic in Power," *CHR*, vol. 48, no. 4, 1967, 309-31, revised as chapter 5 of this book. Paul Romney strongly attacked this interpretation in "William Lyon Mackenzie as Mayor of Toronto" in *CHR*, 56, no. 4, 416-36. As already noted, I am currently preparing a general review of interpretation of Mackenzie following the burst of interest and activity commemorating the sesquicentennial of the Rebellion.

3. Aileen Dunham, *Political Unrest in Upper Canada* (London, 1927), 105.

4. *Ibid.*

5. Charles Lindsey, *The Life and Times of Wm. Lyon Mackenzie*. The scope of this chapter does not permit an examination of such questions as whether or not the rebellion in Lower Canada would have been sufficient to attract British attention, or the extent to which Great Britain had demonstrated an interest in colonial reform prior to the Rebellion.

6. William Kilbourn, *The Firebrand* (Toronto, 1956), vii.

7. F.H. Armstrong, "Reformer as Capitalist: William Lyon Mackenzie and the Printers' Strike of 1836," *OH*, vol. 59, no. 3, 1967, 187-96, revised as Chapter 6 of this book. The introduction and conclusion of this article mention certain of the ideas which are amplified here.

8. Gerald M. Craig, *Upper Canada: The Formative Years, 1784-1841* (Toronto, 1963). For his evaluation of Mackenzie, see p. 210.

9. If there was a recognized Reform leader the honour would go to Marshall Spring Bidwell, who was elected speaker by the moderates in the Reform Assemblies of 1828-30 and 1834-36.

10. See Craig, 210.

11. Dunham, 105-6.

12. Another good example is the tale of the beatings he received which he often brought on himself. See F.H. Armstrong, "The York Riots of March 23, 1832," *OH*, vol. 55, no. 2, 1963, 61-72, revised as Chapter 4 of this book, and J.K. Johnston, "Colonel James FitzGibbon and the Suppresssion of Irish Riots in Upper Canada," *OH*, vol. 43, no. 3, 1986, 139-55.

13. Paul Romney has recently written an article in *OH*, vol. 79, no. 2, 1987, 113-44, which would dispute the adequacy of the compensation for the printing press incident on theoretical not financial considerations.

14. Dunham, 108-9, 112-13.

15. Moreover, a libel suit was not necessarily disastrous, and could provide good publicity. When the secretary of the Welland Canal Company successfully sued Mackenzie for libel in 1837 he was given an award of two shillings as "compensation for loss of his character." Mackenzie, who took up a collection to cover his own expenses and the fine, had soon gathered £31.7.6 (*Constitution*, Nov. 8, 1837). Had donations not been cut off by the outbreak of the Rebellion he might have done even better.

16. *Constitution*, Aug. 10, 1836.

17. Viscount Goderich was colonial secretary in 1827 and again in 1830-33, and thus dealt with Mackenzie during his visit to England.

18. *Patriot*, Aug. 10, 1836

19. Dunham, 106.

20. R.A. MacKay, "The Political Ideas of William Lyon Mackenzie," *Canadian Journal of Economics and Political Science*, vol. 3, no. 1, 1937, 1.

21. "Mackenzie was to some extent the victim of a filing system. A voracious reader and a 'clipper' by habit, he acquired abundant stores of ammunition for whatever issue arose." *Ibid.*, 2.

22. Dunham, 106.

23. Lillian F. Gates, "The Decided Policy of William Lyon Mackenzie," *CHR*, vol. 40, no. 3, 1959, 208.

24. Dunham, 137. They had no idea of long-term financing.

25. See footnote no. 7.

26. MacKay, 3.

27. *Constitution*, July 26, 1837.

28. *Ibid.*

29. *Advocate*, July 10 (12), 1834.

30. Gates, 208.

31. His appointment of Bidwell as city solicitor, at a high stipend, when such an official was not really needed, was a particularly flagrant case of patronage. See *CHR*, December 1967, 324-5.

32. *Ibid.*, 317-27 and 322. Francis Collins, who although a reformer had little sympathy for Mackenzie, commented on his "despotic disposition." *Canadian Freeman*, July 17, 1834.

33. P.E. Trudeau, *Federalism and the French Canadians* (Toronto, 1968), 105.

34. For newspaper activities after 1837, see Lillian F. Gates, "Mackenzie's *Gazette: An Aspect of W.L. Mackenzie's American years*," *CHR*, vol. 46, no. 4, 1965, 323-45, and her "W.L. Mackenzie's Volunteer and the First Parliament of United Canada," *OH*, vol. 59, no. 3, 1967, 163-83. An interesting contrast is provided by John S. Moir, "Mr. Mackenzie's Secret Reporter," *OH*, vol. 55, no. 4, 1963, 205-13. The customs scandals were covered in Mackenzie's *The lives and opinions of Benj' Franklin Butler, United States District Attorney for the Southern District of New York, and Jesse Hoyt, Councillor of Law, Formerly Collector of Customs for the Port of New York* (Boston, 1845), and Van Buren in the *Life and Time of Martin Van Buren* (Boston, 1846).

35. A.G. Bradley in *British America* in "The Nations of Today" series ed. by (John Buchan, series ed.) (London, 1923), 100.

36. Ramsay Cook, *Canada and the French-Canadian Question* (Toronto, 1966), 120.

37. John Robert Colombo, *The Mackenzie Poems* (Toronto, 1966), 14.

38. Cook, 120.

39. Colombo, 14.

40. *Toronto Daily Star*, Nov. 30, 1968.

41. Carl F. Klinck, ed., *Literary History of Canada* (Toronto, 1965), 208-50, 496-519. Windsor discusses the Whig interpretation specifically on 225 ff. Also worthy of note is J.E. Rae, "Rebellion in Upper Canada, 1837," *Transactions of the Historical and Scientific Society of Manitoba, Series 3*, no. 22, 1965-66, 87-94, for an examination of the bibliography related to the Rebellion.

42. This estimate is based on the various editions of *Canadian Book-Prices Current*.

43. Or sympathetic to the Family Compact. In addition, a portrait of Mackenzie was chosen as the frontispiece to vol. 2.

44. Vol. 2, 44-53.

45. Page 53. Lindsey is referred to as "a work indispensable to the student of Canadian History." On p. 51, Dent does note that Mackenzie could be wrong, but there his pro-Whigism would seem to be more powerful than his pro-Rolph outlook. In addition, Dent's *Story* was immediately attacked by another Mackenzie son-in-law, John King, with *The Other Side of the Story* (Toronto, 1886).

46. Kingsford was still being remaindered by a Montreal book dealer for only $25 as late as 1964.

47. Bethune's work, *Memoir of the Right Reverend John Strachan* (Toronto, 1870), was still in print through the Toronto Central Library in the early 1960s. Allison Ewart and Julia D. Jarvis, "The Personnel of the Family Compact," *CHR*, vol. 3, no. 3, 1926, 209-21.

48. See Klink, 227 ff. for Kenneth Windsor's excellent analysis of Mornag's attitudes and the background of the selection of the Lindsey work for reissue. The number of copies of Lindsey sold is noted on p. 228.

49. *Ibid.*, 227.
50. See Viola E. Parvin, *Authorization of Textbooks for the Schools of Ontario, 1846-1950* (Toronto, 1965). Canadian History has largely been taught in the old Junior and Senior Fourth, or Grades 7 and 8. Modern Canadian history, that is post-1890, has been taught in Grade 10 of high school.
51. Ontario Department of Education, *Public Schools Manuals: History* (Toronto, 1912), 7.
52. George M. Wrong, *Canada, A Short History* (Toronto, 1921), 222.
53. *Ibid.*, 227.
54. *Ibid.*, 247.
55. George M. Brown *et al.*, *The Story of Canada* (Toronto, 1950), 250-2, 253-6, 263.
56. *Ibid.*, 67, 69, 72-3.
57. Space does not allow comment on fictional works with a historical background, whether designed for reading in schools or not. Naturally many of these present a markedly pre-Reform picture which can completely lack historical perspective. For southwestern Ontario, Gladys Frances Lewis *Joshua Doan* (Toronto, 1956) is a remarkable example.
58. James L. Hughes, Gage and *Co's Examination Primer: Canadian History*, 3rd ed. (Toronto, 1881), 40.
59. *Ibid.*, 38.
60. A good example of this can be seen by comparing the article on Mackenzie in W.S. Wallace's *The Encyclopedia of Canada*, vol. 4 (Toronto, 1936), 200-1, with the article in the edition of *The Grolier Encyclopedia of Canada*, vol. 6 (Toronto, 1970), 277-9. In the latter the wording has been changed slightly here and there; a note has been added that his daughter Isabel was the mother of S.L.M. King; Kilbourn has been put in the bibliography; and several older works have been deleted. That is about the total of the changes. The date at which Mackenzie was mayor of Toronto remains incorrect.
61. An example of the type of study we need is J.E. Rea, "William Lyon Mackenzie — Jacksonian?" in *Mid-America*, vol. 50, no. 3, 1968, 223-35. At the same time it would be interesting to have similar examinations of the other reform leaders. The main statements from the Marxist view are Stanley B. Ryerson's books 1837, *The Birth of Canadian Democracy* (Toronto, [1937]) and *Unequal Union* (Toronto, 1968).

Chapter 8

1. The original version of this article, which contains considerably more detail on family relationships, wills and minor posts, appeared under the title "The Carfrae Family: A Study in Early Toronto Toryism" in *OH*, vol. 54, no. 3, 1962, 161-81. In preparing the original article the writer was assisted by Miss M. Cartwright and Larrry Ryan of the Toronto Public Libraries; Miss J.M.L. Jackson, librarian of AO; F.H. Burkholder, secretary-treasurer of the Toronto General Burying Grounds; and A.R.N. Woadden, archivist of the City of Toronto. Further information on the family is provided by the writer's "The Carfrae Family of Toronto and London, Ontario," *The York Pioneer*, vol. 80, Spring 1985, 45-54.
2. For recent studies, as well as *Dictionary of Canadian Biography* articles in vol. 9 (1976) on Robinson (668-79) by Robert E. Saunders and on Strachan (751-66) by Gerald M. Craig, there is Patrick Brode, *Sir John Beverley Robinson: Bone and Sinew of the Compact* (Toronto, 1984), and two good but short biographies of the bishop: John L.H. Henderson, *John Strachan* (Toronto, 1969) and David Flint, *John Strachan: Pastor and Politician* (Toronto, 1971).

3. The Carfrae-Campbell Papers, which were donated to the Ontario Historical Society, were transferred to the Metropolitan Toronto Library at the writer's suggestion. They provide a great deal of valuable information on both the family and local politics of the 1830s. The scrapbook of Thomas Carfrae Jr. contains many unique clippings from Toronto newspapers, particularly from the Toronto *Courier* whose editor was Thomas Carfrae's friend George Gurnett. There are also political handbills, copies of wills and miscellaneous papers. These papers passed from Carfrae's widow, Margaret Jane Brooks, to grandson William Carfrae Campbell, who added further documents belonging to himself and his family. There are about forty-five items altogether. Several paintings were also included inthe collection.

4. John Ross Robertson, *The History of Freemasonry in Canada* 2 vols (Toronto, c. 1900), vol. 1, 524-25.

5. *Journal of the House of Assembly of Upper Canada, 1805-1811*, in AO *Report* no. 8, part 2, 1911, 48, 110 and 480. Minutes of the court of the General Quarter Sessions of the Home District, 1800-1911, in AO *Report* no. 21, 1932, 69.

6. *Ibid.*, 84, shows Eliphalet Hale appointed constable in April 1806. Appointments to the Home District offices were regularly made in April. Hugh Carfrae succeeded Thomas R. Johnson in 1807 (*Ibid.*, 105), and his last expenses were paid in April 1811 (*Ibid.*, 105), and his last expenses were paid in April 1811 (*Ibid.*, 181). William Knott was keeper of the Home District Gaol in May of the same year (*Ibid.*, 186), see also 147-8, 166, 168, 171. The fence cost an additional £16.9.6-1/2.

7. *Ibid.*, 161-2. See also *St. James' Baptismal Records* April 5, 1807, in John Ross Robertson, *Landmarks of Toronto*, vol. 3, 376, Robertson, *Freemasonry*, vol. 1, 885; *Quebec Almanac*, 1813, 150, *Appendix to the Journal of the Legislative Assembly, 838-40*, 13.

8. Minutes of the Court of the Quarter Sessions, volume for July 1822 to December 1827, 41. He still held office in December 1828 (*Ibid.*, volume for November 1828 to May 1833, 15). See also Scadding, *Toronto of Old*, 41.

9. A list in the Carfrae papers, dated 1823, shows Thomas Sr and Janet were married on Oct. 22, 1789, and had six children: Janet, born Feb. 10, 1791; Jean, July 14, 1792-June 14, 1793; Jean, Aug. 1, 1793-Jan. 23, 1795; Johanna, born March 14, 1795; Thomas, born Nov. 29, 1796; and Mary, born Jan. 29, 1801. Janets death is recorded in the Carfrae papers. For the windup of the business, see *Courier*, June 20, 1832.

10. *Ibid.*

11. Robertson, *Freemasonry*, vol. 2, 377; *St. James Parish Register*, in Robertson, *Landmarks*, vol. 3, 425.

12. Register of the York General Burying Ground, 1826-1855.

13. M.A. Hodgson, comp; *Toronto Fire Department* (2nd ed., Toronto, 1960), 215. Robertson, *Landmarks*, vol. 2, 563-4.

14. *Observer*, Oct. 1, 1827, in Carfrae Scrapbook.

15. Carfrae Scrapbook, his copy of notice.

16. *Ibid.*

17. *Ibid.* Minutes of the General Court of the Quarter Sessions of the Home District, volume for November 1828 to May 1833, 111.

18. Robertson, Landmarks, vol. 4, 225; *Register of Marriages of Knox Church in York Pioneer*, 1962, 50.

19. J.E. Middleton *et al.*, *The Municipality of Toronto*, 3 vols. (Toronto, 1923), vol. 2, 703; Robertson, *Landmarks*, vol. 4, 121; Rev. Stuart A. Parker, *The Book of St. Andrews* (Toronto, 1930), 3-4; Walton, *York Commercial Directory*, 120.

20. *Colonial Advocate*, July 10 (12), 1834 notes Mackenzie's resignation.

21. This account of the activities of the British Constitutional Society is largely based on clippings and other items in the Carfrae Scrapbook.

22. A copy is in the Carfrae Scrapbook.

23. *Ibid.*

24. *Ibid.*

25. *Ibid.*, clipping from *Courier*, April 17, 1833.

26. Parker, *The Book of St. Andrews*, 8. TCCP, Feb. 25, 1836.

27. Carfrae Scrapbook.

28. Journal of the City Council, April 8 and 14, and June 9, 1834.

29. *Patriot*, Jan. 20, 1834; Carfrae Scrapbook, clipping from *Recorder*, Jan. 17, 1835.

30. The Carfrae Papers contain the letter of the appointment, which was also noted in the *Patriot*, Sept. 22, 1835.

31. Carfrae Papers; *Royal Standard*, Jan. 10, 1837; Journal of the City Council, Feb. 6, 1837, and Feb. 19 and 27, 1838; *Patriot*, May 11, 1838.

32. Burial Register of St. James's Cathedral, 1835-1850.

33. "Observations of Thomas Carfrae on Collections of the Revenue of Customs, December 18, 1839", in *Appendix to the Journal of the Legislative Assembly, 1839-40*, vol. 2, 121.

34. *Ibid.*, 122; *Constitution*, Aug. 10, 1836.

35. *Ibid.*, Oct. 25, 1837.

36. Robertson, *Landmarks*, vol. 1, 334-5.

37. *Patriot*, Sept. 29, 1837, from the *Constitution*.

38. *Upper Canada Gazette Extraordinary*, Sept. 17, 1837.

39. *Patriot*, Dec. 15, 1837.

40. Minutes of the Court of the Quarter Sessions, volume for October 1837 to September 1846, 1; *Patriot*, July 5, 1836, May 9, 1837 and May 11, 1838.

41. Carfrae Papers, various clippings, October 1839.

42. Carfrae Papers, Parker, *The Book of St. Andrews*, 32.

Chapter 9

1. This article originally appeared as "The Toronto Directories and the Negro Community in the later 1840s," *OH*, vol. 61 no. 2, 1969, 111-19. In preparing it I was greatly assisted by two of my colleagues at Western, Professors Fred Landon and Peter F. Neary, who made helpful comments. Professor Ian Pemberton of the University of Windsor was kind enough to let me read his M.A. thesis on the Anti-Slavery Society.

2. Daniel G. Hill, "Negroes in Toronto, 1793-1865," *OH*, vol. 55, no. 2, 1963, 73-91. This most useful article briefly surveys the facts in the *1846 Directory* but the scope of the article briefly surveys the facts in the *1846 Directory* but the scope of the article does not permit any detailed analysis.

3. Other sources of the period are not as useful for ethnic studies. As noted, the breakdowns for the Upper Canada Census of 1848 and the Canada Census of 1851 have not survived. The municipal records are not helpful since the assessment rolls do not show racial derivation and the Board of Education records only begin in the 1850s. With regard to Black religious records, the first Baptist Church at Toronto does not have membership lists and there is no detailed material available in either the Canadian Baptist Historical Collection at McMaster University or the Archives of the United Church of Canada in Victoria College in Toronto. All these organizations have been most helpful in providing information.

   See Fred Landon, "Social Conditions among the Negroes in Upper Canada before 1865," *Ontario Historical Society Papers and Records*, vol. 22, 1925, 147-8, and Ian Pemberton, "The Anti-Slavery Society of Canada," unpublished M.A. Thesis, Toronto, 1967, 33, for some further details on this subject.

4. The *Globe*, of course, was the leading Reform newspaper. Pemberton provides a very interesting discussion of the Society in which he suggests that the Tories seem to have been less interested than the Reformers in the welfare of Blacks.

5. Mrs. R.W. Stuart MacKay, ed., *MacKay's Montreal Directory, New Edition, corrected in May and June, 1857-58* (Montreal, 1857), n.p.

6. That of the 1850 *City of Toronto and County of York Directory* (lxxiv) gives a total population, of 25,166 while the *Province of Canada census of 1851-2* (vol. 1 66 French ed.) states that there were 30,775. The difference seems rather large, though the provincial census may include some categories — lunatics at the provincial asylum and students at Upper Canada College — which were not counted in the directory. The *Toronto City and Home District Directory* of 1846 (22) states that as of Sept. 15,1845, the total population of the city was 19,706.

7. The 1850 population statistics are on page xxiv of the *Directory*. The 1848 census figures are in *Canada, Census of 1871*, vol. 4, p. 169. The 1851 Census figures do not show the "coloured" population of Toronto. See vol. 4, p. 183.

8. [G.P. Ure], *The Handbook of Toronto* (Toronto, 1958), 167.

9. See Hill, pp. 77-8 for description of the development of the churches. *Ibid.*, 78.

10. Sylvester, Alfred, *Sketches of Toronto* (Toronto 1858), 67.

11. *Ibid.*, 54. This is a smaller church, about thirty by forty feet in dimensions.

12. *Ibid.*, 55. The Second Methodist Church building was about the same size as the other Methodist church.

Chapter 10

1. This article originally appeared in *Inland Seas*, vol. 31, no. 1, 1975, 35-40, 42 and 49-50.

2. Obituaries of Richardson appeared in the *Globe* and the *Daily Telegraph*, both of Toronto, on Aug. 3, 1870. For Richardson's London career Mr. Donovan Dawe, the Principal Keeper at the Guidhall Library, had the possible directories and parish records checked. Mr. S.E. Higbee, Parish Clerk of All Hallows Berkynge-chirche by the Tower, London, England, checked the relevant birth records. For property records see London, Ontario, City of, Registry Office, Instrs. 3373, 4554 and 28, New Series.

3. AO, Sir John Beverley Robinson Papers, Richardson to Robinson, Toronto, Jan. 13, 1833.

4. *Globe*, Aug. 3, 1870, *Patriot*, Sept. 2, 1834 and TCCP, Dec. 14, 1836 and May 1, 1837.

5. Public Archives of Canada (PAC), State Papers of Upper Canada, E 3189, #212, Sept. 8, 1838.

6. *Patriot*, April 28, 1835; John Ross Robertson, *Landmarks of Toronto* (Toronto, 1896), vol. 2, 861; *Patriot*, May 6, 1836 and May 6, 1837.

7. AO, Street Papers, Receipt from James Lockhart, May 3, 1839; Robertson, vol. 2, 872, 878; and Scadding, *Toronto of Old*, 575

8. Erik Heyl, *Early American Steamers* (Buffalo, 1956), vol. 2, 37; vol. 6 (Buffalo, 1969), 53.

9. Robertson, vol. 2, 874; Heyl, vol. 6, 70.

10. Niagara *Chronicle*, April 10, 1844. See also Elgin-Grey Papers, vol. 3, 1272-73 and Street Papers, Dec. 28, 1844.

11. Peter A. Baskerville, "Donald Bethune," *Dictionary of Canadian Biography*, vol. 9 (Toronto, 1982), 49-50.

12. AO, Robinson Papers, Richardson to Robinson, Montreal, May 29, 1848.

13. *Ibid.*, Dec. 9, 1849; MTL, Maurice Roberts Vaughan Papers, vol. 3, 9; Walter Havinghurst, *The Long Ships Passing* (New York, 1942), 223.

14. MTL, Roberts Papers, vol. 3, 65.

Chapter 11

1. This essay was presented as a paper at the Conference on the Scottish Role in the Development of Canada, Pugwash, N.S., June 29, 1979, and in a more expanded from at the Bermuda-Canada Conference, Hamilton, Bermuda, Feb. 24, 1984. I have written short biographies on Hay for the *Dictionary of Canadian Biography*, vol. 9, 391-93 and the *Macmillan Encyclopedia of Architects*, 4 vols. (New York, 1982), vol. 2, 347.

   My research on Hay has been greatly assisted by a large number of individuals in Canada and abroad. These include several members of the Hay-Henderson-Reid family: Mrs Sheila Sloane and Mrs Estelle S. Phillips of Edinburgh, and Mrs Margaret Henderson and Ted Lea of Toronto. Several architectural historians have provided information: John Bland, Montreal; A.J.H. Richardson of Ottawa; Stephen Otto, Douglas Richardson and Robert Hill of Toronto. The last has always been unstinting in providing information from his extensive architectural files. Information has also been received from: Peter Savage and Anthony P. Sherman of Edinburgh; L.J. McDonald and Mrs Joyce D. Hall of Bermuda; and Gary D. Shutlak and Shirley B. Elliott of Halifax.

2. Such collections provide colourful insights into the scope of their wanderings.

3. Scotland General Register Office, birth certificate of William Hay, May 17, 1818; *Scotsman*, June 1, 1888.

4. *Canadian Architect and Builder (CAB)* July 1888, vol. 2; *Hart Family Diary, 1842-1966* (Toronto, privately published), 2.

5. *CAB*, vol., 2; Basil F.L. Clarke, *Anglican Cathedrals Outside The British Isles* (London, 1958), 55-6, 126-7.

6. MTL, Hay Plans (in Howard and Langley Plans); T.A. Reed "Toronto's Early architects," *Journal, Royal Architectual Institute of Canada*, February 1950, 47, 49-50; [G.P. Ure], *A Handbook of Toronto* (Toronto, 1858), 234-6, 258-9; William Dendy, *Lost Toronto* (Toronto, 1978) 120-1.

7. Reed, 47; Ure 268-9; Dendy, 30-3.

8. For examples of Hay's writing, see *The Anglo-American Magazine*, vol. 2 (Toronto, 1853), 70-3 and 253-5; Marion MacRae and Anthony Adamson, *Hallowed Walls: Church Architecture of Upper Canada* (Toronto, 1975), 168, 171; Eric Arthur, *Toronto: No Mean City!* (Toronto, 1964), 116; Ure, 269; Reed, 47; John Squaire, *The Townships of Darlington and Clarke* (Toronto, 1927), 310-1.

9. Reed, 47; Arthur, 85; MTL, Mechanics Institute Papers; William Stewart Wallace, *The Royal Canadian Institute, 1849-1949* (Toronto, 1949), 196; various Toronto directories. Douglas Richardson has prepared a paper on Hay's role in Ure's book.

10. David Murray Lyon, *History of the Lodge of Edinburgh (Mary Chapel), No. 1* (Edinburgh, 1873), 349, 353.

11. Reed, 47; Arthur, 249.

12. Various Halifax directories; *CAB*, 2.

13. Thomas S. Reid, *Trinity Church, Bermuda, A Sketch of its History* (Bermuda, 1886), 8-9, 11; Lyon, 349-53.

14. *CAB*, vol. 2; Reed, 47; Royal Commisssion of the Ancient Monuments of Scotland, *The City of Edinburgh* (Edinburgh, 1951), 25-34.

15. T.S. Reid, 15-7; *Bermuda Almanac, 1884*, 72; *1886*, 70; *1889*, 118.

16. *CAB*, vol. 2; Scotland, General Register Office, Will and Inventory of William Hay, 1888.

Chapter 12

1. The writer presented this paper as the president's Luncheon address at the Ontario Historical Society meeting at Orillia on June 16, 1979 and incorporated part of the information in a public lecture at Laurentian University, Sudbury, on Nov. 1, 1979. A short biography was written for the *Dictionary of Canadian Biography*, vol. 10 (Toronto, 1972), 509-10. Miss Leslie J. Greenhill of Chickester, West Sussex, England, Henry Pilon of Toronto, and the Archives of East and West Sussex were of great help in preparing this article.
2. For Small and Millar, see Fred McClements *The Strange Case of Ambrose Small* (Toronto, 1974) and Mark M. Orkin, *The Great Stork Derby* (Toronto, 1981).
3. *Globe*, Nov. 25, 1875.
4. *Quebec Gazette*, No. 20, 1800; University of Western Ontario, Orlo Miller Papers.
5. AO, Russell Papers, William Osgoode to Peter Russell, Jan. 21, 1801.
6. AO, RG 22, Probate Court Records, Series 6-1, Will of Thomas Scott, probated July 25, 1838.
7. Scadding, *Toronto of Old* (Toronto, 1873), 269; John Ross Robertson, *Landmarks of Toronto*, vol. 1, 48; PAC, RGI, E 1, vol. 47, 283, 291; RGI, L3, vol. 332; MG/37; RGI, E14, vol. 10, 158-9; RG7, G16C, vol. 9, 48.
8. PAC RG5, C678, 172b-c; C690, 166-6a, A1, 26686-87 and RG8, C1203, 28, 67, 73.
9. Land petitions include: PAC, RGI, L3 vol. 332, M6/37; 335a, M10/51; 336, M10/150; 337, M 11/57.
10. Ontario Sessional Papers, vol. 4, no. 38, 1978, Mercer Estate Case, Feb. 20, 1878, Mowat summary.
11. Scadding, 84. Henry Melville, *The Rise and Progress of Trinity College* (Toronto, 1852), 85. University of Trinity College, Minutes of the Council, vol. 1, 27, Feb. 20, 1851.
12. The complete story of their relationship is discussed in both Sessional Paper no. 38, 1878, and in Chancery Case #55 of 1875.
13. William Henry Pearson, *Recollections and Reflections of Toronto of Old* (Toronto, 1914), 47.
14. Sessional Paper no. 38, 1878, includes the evidence. Wrights statement is on p. 13.
15. *Ibid.*, 3, 65. The Sessional Papers provide much of the detail of the estate wrangles. Ontario Sessional Paper no. 34, 1880, 1, 4.
16. Sessional Paper no. 38, 1878, 4, 15, 26, 47.
17. *Ibid.*, 12, and in *Escheats for Want as Heirs; The Provinces are Entitled to them, The Argument for the Provincial view in the Mercer Escheat Case* (Toronto, 1881) 26-27.
18. University of Western Ontario, Orlo Miller Papers, "Memorandum" by John Robertson of Edinburgh; Sessional Paper, 1878, no. 38, 3.
19. In 1969 the writer checked with both the East Sussex Record Office at Lewes, and the West Sussex Record Office at Chichester — the county was divided in 1888 — and also, at the suggestion of the latter, had Miss Leslie J. Greenhill of Chichester do a more in-depth investigation. Although various Mercers turned up none fitted in with Andrew. The Genealogical Society of the Church of Jesus Christ of the Latter Day Saints were also good enough to check their records, which show that there was an Andrew Mercer born at Currie, Midlothian (now in Lothian), on Aug. 17, 1778. The same reference appears in the John Robertson "Memorandum" (4) in the Orlo Miller Papers at Western, but as noted in the text, there is nothing to connect the two Mercers. There were a number of other Andrew Mercers born in Scotland at the period.
20. See footnote 19.

21. Sessional Paper no. 38, 1878, tells the story. Cherrier, Kirwin and McGowan's *Toronto Directory for 1873* (Toronto, 1873), 249, shows a James Smyth, flour, feed and grain dealer, at 46 King Street West, which would be quite close to Mercer's cottage, and to Charles Unwin's (260), an insurance agent and lawyer.

22. The account of the trial and distribution of the estate is basically from Ontario Sessional Papers no. 38, 1878, and no. 34, 1880, as well as from John Ross Robertson, *Landmarks*, vol. 1, 433; *The Globe*, Nov. 15, 1875 and Jan. 14, 1876; and *The Mercer Escheat Case*.

23. AO, Mowat Papers, Mowat to Sir Alexander Campbell, Ottawa, May 31, 1883.

Chapter 13

1. A more detailed version of this article originally appeared in *OH*, vol. 53, no. 3, 1961, 201-21.

2. J. Grove Smith, *Fire Waste in Canada* [Commission of Conservation, Canada] (Ottawa, 1918), 103-4.

3. National Fire Protection Association, *Conflagrations in America since 1900* (Boston, 1951), 12-3.

4. W.G. Bell, *The Great Fire Of London, 1666* (London, 1951), 319.

5. Chicago Historical Society, *The Great Chicago Fire* (Chicago, 1946),48.

6. Smith, 277-89.

7. Rev. H. Christmas, *Canada in 1849*, 2 vols. (London, 1850), vol. 1, 67.

8. [F. Burton], *Journal of a Wanderer: Being a Resident in India and Six Weeks in North America* (London, 1844), 162-63.

9. *Ibid.*, 163.

10. Christmas, 84.

11. J.J. Bloomfield, *Visits to Canada and Newfoundland in 1845-1846* (Photostat of ms. is in The Library of the Insurance Institute of Canada, Toronto), 36.

12. Henry Rowsell, *City of Toronto & County of York Directory*, 1850-51 (Toronto, 1850), 29.

13. CTA, TCCP, 1834-96.

14. *Ibid.*

15. Rowsell, 29.

16. J.E. Middleton, *The Municipality of Toronto, a History*, 3 vols. (Toronto, 1923), vol. 1, 129.

17. *Ibid.*

18. Broomfield, 36.

19. Robertson, *Landmarks*, vol. 2, 573.

20. *Ibid.*, 620.

21. *First in the Field* (Toronto, 1954), 25.

22. TCCP, 1834-96.

23. Scadding, *Toronto of Old*, 173.

24. C.C. Taylor, *Toronto 'Called Back'* (Toronto, 1887), 52.

25. MTL, Henry Scadding Diary, 1844-1848.

26. TCCP, 1834-96.

Chapter 14

1. The story of the rebuilding of Toronto, which originally appeared in *OH*, vol. 52, no. 4, 1961, 233-49, has been considerably revised and shortened for this book. The original article contains far more informations, particularly on the rebuilding of St. James's. Morris Zaslow's suggestions were most helpful in the preparation

of the original article and Robert G. Hill has provided valuable advice for the revision.

2. Insurance Institute of Montreal, *General Insurance* (Montreal, n.d.), 6; J.W. Shehan and G.P. Upton, *The Great Conflagration, Chicago: Its Past, Present and Future* (Chicago, 1871), 30-3.
3. J.G. Smith, *Fire Waste in Canada*, 278.
4. [Darling, W.S.], *Sketches of Canadian Life* (London, 1849), 296-8. The Howard Mss. are in the Reference Division of the MTL.
5. The reference is to the wanton destruction by fire of the Parliament House of the United Province of Canada on April 22, 1849, during the Montreal riots following the enactment of the Rebellion Losses Bill.
6. TCCP.
7. Minutes of the City Council, June 22, 1849.
8. Minute Book of St. James's Cathedral, Vestry Minutes 1842-1907, 20-1.
9. The editorial in the *Church* on Sept. 13 provides a detailed architectural discussion, part of which is included in my original article in *OH*. See also the *Globe* for Oct. 13, 1849.
10. Minute Book, 25ff.
11. *Ibid.*, 33.

Chapter 15

1. The original article on the Second Great Fire appeared in *OH*, vol. 70, no. 1, 1978, 3-38. The Toronto Fire Department has been helpful in providing cetain details.
2. National Fire Protection Association *Conflagrations in America Since 1900*, (Boston, 1951) [hereafter NFPA *Conflagrations*], 9.
3. NFPA *Conflagrations*, 11; J. Smith, *Fire Waste in Canada*, 100.
4. G.W. Shorter, *Toronto Fire of 1904* [National Research Council Fire Study, No. 13] (Ottawa, 1964), 6; NFPA *Conflagrations*, 39.
5. Smith, 105, 125; Shorter, 7.
6. *Ibid.*
7. *Arkwright Mutual Fire Insurance Company: 1860 — Fifty Years — 1910*, (Boston, 1912), 66-8.
8. *Ibid.*, 6-8, 16.
9. *Ibid.*, 42; Armstrong, "First Great Fire," 219; Smith, 124.
10. John V. Morris, *Fires and Firefighters* (Boston, 1955), 169, 260, 263; John B. Laidlaw "The Conflagration Hazard," *Proceedings of the Insurance Institute of Toronto, 1904-05*, 233; Morris, 381.
11. Laidlaw, 232-3.
12. Morris, 271.
13. Smith, 26; Laidlaw, 231.
14. *Ibid.*, 196-77, 203-5.
15. Smith, 99, 282; Laidlaw, 221-2.
16. Robertson, *Landmarks of Toronto*, vol. 2, 592, 596.
17. Robertson, vol. 2, 660-3; Smith, 281. The earlier Robertson figures have been taken for these three losses.
18. Robertson, vol. 2, 663-6; Smith, 281; Laidlaw, 200.
19. Robertson, vol. 2, 666-71; Smith, 282; Laidlaw, 200.
20. Edmund Burke, "Building Construction in Connection with Fire Risk," *Proceedings of the Insurance Institute of Toronto, 1905-05*, 140, 142; City of Toronto, *Minutes of the Proceeding of the Council of the Corporation, 1904* (Toronto, 1905) [hereafter Minutes], Feb. 22.
21. *News*, July 7, 1902.

22. Norman Patterson, "Toronto's Great Fire," *The Canadian Magazine*, vol. 23, no. 2, 1904, 135.

23. City of Toronto, *Municipal Hand-Book, 1904* (Toronto, 1904) [hereafter *Handbook*].

24. *Ibid*; National Fire Protection Association, "The Toronto Conflagration," *Journal, 1904* [hereafter NFPA *Journal*], 38; Handbook, 42-3.

25. Shorter, 6, 12.

26. Shorter, table 1: Charles E. Goad, *Atlas of the City of Toronto and Vicinity* (Toronto, 2nd ed. March 1890; fourth revision, September 1903), plates 3, 6; Warwick Bros. & Rutter Limited, *The Story of the Business 1848-1943* (Toronto, 1923), 43.

27. *The News*, Toronto, April 20, 1904; Norman Patterson, "Toronto's Great Fires," *The Canadian Magazine*, vol. 22, no. 2, 1904, 132.

28. National Fire Protection Association, *Journal, 1904*, 37; John B. Laidlaw, "The Conflagration Hazard," *Proceedings of the Insurance Institute of Toronto*, 224.

29. G.W. Shorter, *Toronto Fire of 1904* (Ottawa: N.R.C. Fire Study no. 13, 1964), 11; Patterson, 132, 135; NFPA, *Journal*, 37-8.

30. *Ibid.*, 37; *Globe*, Toronto, April 20, 1904; Shorter, 1.

31. Patterson, 132.

32. City of Toronto, *By-Laws, 1890-1904*, 572; Smith, 284.

33. Shorter, 11. Globe and News, April 20, 1904; Shorter, 2 and table 4; Patterson, 134; City of Toronto, *Minutes*, 111-5. These sources are not in complete agreement. See also *History of Toronto Fire Department* (Toronto, 1923), 33.

34. Shorter, 13; Walter G. Bell, *The Great Fire of London in 1666* (London, 1951), 160; Gordon Thomas and Max M. Witts, *The San Francisco Earthquake* (New York, 1971). This work has many good examples of what happens when over-enthusiastic people are let loose with dynamite. See, for instance, 179 and 231.

35. Fergus Kyle, "Incidents at a Great Fire," *The Canadian Magazine*, vol. 23, no. 2, 1904, 137; *News*, April 20, 1904.

36. Kyle, 138; *Globe*, April 20, 1904; *Star*, April 20, 1904; *News*, April 20, 1904.

37. *Canada's Great Fire, A Souvenir Booklet* (Toronto, 1904), pamphlet, no pagination; Shorter, 4; *Globe*, April 20, 1904.

38. *Star*, April 20, 1904.

39. Shorter, 2; NFPA, *Journal*, 38.

40. *News* and *Globe*, April 20, 1904.

41. *Globe*, April 21, 1904.

42. Lorne Street ran south from Front West halfway between Bay and York. It was closed when the present Union Station was built. NFPA, *Journal*, 38; *World*, April 20, 1904.

43. *Star*, April 20, 1904.

44. *Globe*, April 20, 1904.

45. NFPA, *Journal*, 38; Shorter, 4; Laidlaw, 226; NFPA, *Bulletin*, no. 76, May 19, 1904.

46. NFPA, *Journal*, 38; Shorter, 10.

47. *Globe*, April 21, 1904.

48. *News*, April 20, 1904; *Globe*, April 21, 1904; *World*, April 21, 1904.

49. *Globe*, 20 and 21, 1904; *Canada's Greatest Fire*; *News*, April 20, 1904.

50. *Ibid.*

51. *World*, April 20, 1904.

52. *Globe*, April 20, 1904; *News*, April 20, 1904; NFPA, *Journal*, 38; *Star*, April 20, 1904.

53. *Canada's Greatest Fire*; *News*, April 20, 1904; Kyle, 139-40.

54. Shorter, 7-8, 17; City of Toronto, *Municipal Handbook, 1905* (Toronto, 1905), 71.

55. *Globe*, April 21, 1904; *Star*, April 20, 1904.

56. Patterson, 128; NFPA, *Conflagrations*, 7.

57.　These details were obtained from copies of letters, forms and reports in the possession of the Gore District Mutual Insurance Company, Cambridge-Galt, courtesy of Mr. William N. Marritt; Shorter, 9.

58.　*Star*, April 20, 1904; *News*, April 21, 1904.

59.　*Globe*, April 21, 1904.

60.　*Ibid*; *News*, April 20, 1904; *Star*, April 21, 1904; Kyle, 138.

61.　Kyle, 138-39; Patterson, 129.

62.　City of Toronto, *Board of Control Minutes*, April 20, 1904.

63.　These activities are taken from the Minutes; Edmund Burke, "Building Construction in connection with the Fire Risk," *Proceedings of the Insurance Institute of Toronto, 1904-05*, 142-3, 155; Smith, 122, 137.

64.　NFPA, *Journal*, 39; *Minutes*, Appendix A, 315-6, 337, 926-39; appendix C, 136. certain of the systems may not have been fully operative.

65.　*History Toronto Fire Department* (Toronto, 1923), 42; Shorter, 11.

66.　Warwick, 51-2, 55; Burke, 143.

67.　*News*, April 20, 1904.

Selected Bibliography

1.. BIBLIOGRAPHICAL SOURCES

Aitken, Barbara B., *Local Histoires of Ontario Municipalities: A Bibliography: 1951-1977* (Toronto, 1978).

Armstrong, Frederick H., Alan F.J. Artibise and Melvin Baker. *Bibliography of Canadian Urban History,* part 4: *Ontario,* in *Vance Bibliographies* (Monticello, Ill., 1980).

Artibise, Alan F.J., and Gilbert A. Stelter. *Canada's Urban Past; A Bibliography to 1980 and a Guide to Canadian Urban Studies* (Vancouver, 1981).

Bishop, Olga B. *Bibliography of Ontario History, 1867-1976,* 2 vols. (Toronto, 1980).

Morley, William F. E. *Canadian Local Histories to 1950: Ontario and the Canadian North* (Toronto, 1978).

Neary, Hilary Bates and Robert Sherman. *Ontario Historical Society: Index to the Publications, 1899-1972* (Toronto, 1974).

Toronto Public Library. *Early Canadian Companies* (Toronto, 1967). *Urban and Regional References,* 1945-1969 (Ottawa, 1970).

2. GENERAL WORKS

Adam, Graeme Mercer. *Toronto: Old and New* (Toronto, 1891, reprinted. 1972).

Armstrong, Frederick H. *Toronto: The Place of Meeting* (Los Angeles, 1983).

Careless, J.M.S. *Toronto to 1918: An Illustrated History* (Toronto, 1984).

Dictionary of Canadian Biography, vols. 4, 5, 6, 8, 9, 10 and 11. Vol. 7, 1836-1850, is in preparation.

Firth, Edith G. *The Town of York, 1793-1834,* 2 vols. (Toronto, 1962-1966).

Glazebrook, George P. de T. *The Story of Toronto* (Toronto, 1971).

Goheen, Peter G. *Victorian Toronto, 1850-1890* (Chicago, 1970).

Guillet, Edwin C. *Toronto: from Trading Post to Great City* (Toronto, 1934).

Hathaway, Ernest J. *The Story of the Old Fort at Toronto* (Toronto, 1934).

Illustrated Historical Atlas of the Country of York (Toronto, 1878, reprinted, 1965).

Kilbourn William, ed. *The Toronto Book* (Toronto, 1976).

Kyte, Ernest C., ed. *Old Toronto: A Selection of Excerpts from "Landmarks of Toronto" by John Ross Robertson* (Toronto, 1970).

Masters, Donald C. *The Rise of Toronto, 1850-1890* (Toronto, 1974).

Middleton, Jesse E. *The Municipality of Toronto, A History,* 3 vols. (Toronto, 1923).

_____. *Toronto's 100 Years: The Official Centennial Book 1834-1934* (Toronto, 1934).

Mulvany, Charles Pelham. *Toronto: Past and Present* (Toronto, 1884, reprinted 1970).

Pearson, William H. *Recollections of Toronto of Old* (Toronto, 1914).

Robertson, John Ross. *Landmarks of Toronto* 6 vols. (Toronto, 1894-1914, reprints, vol. 1, 1976, vol. 3, 1974).

Scadding, Henry and John Charles Dent. *Toronto: Past and Present* (Toronto, 1884, reprinted, 1970).

Spelt, Jacob. *Toronto* (Toronto, 1973).

_____. *Urban Development in South-Central Ontario* (Assen, the Netherlands, 1955, reprinted, 1972).

Taylor, Conyngham Crawford. *Toronto Called Back* (Toronto, 6 editions, 1886-1897).

Timperlake, J. *Illustrated Toronto, Past and Present* (Toronto, 1877, reprinted).

Walker, Frank N. *Sketches of Old Toronto* (Toronto, 1965).

West, Bruce. *Toronto* (Toronto, 1967).

3. SPECIAL STUDIES

Arthur, Eric. *Toronto: No Mean City!* (Toronto, 1964).

Dendy, William. *Lost Toronto* (Toronto, 1978).

De Volpi, Charles P. *Toronto: a Pictorial Record,* 1813-1882 (Montreal, 1965).

Filey, Michael. *A Toronto Album; Glimpses of the City That Was* (Toronto, 1970).

Jones, James Edmund. *Pioneer Crimes and Punishments in Toronto and the Home District* (Toronto, 1924).

Martyn, Lucy Booth. *Aristocratic Toronto: 19th Century Grandeur* (Toronto, 1980).

_____. *The Face of Early Toronto: An Architectural Record: 1979-1936* (Sutton West, 1982).

_____. *Toronto: 100 Years of Grandeur: The Inside Story of Toronto's Great Homes* (Toronto, 1978).

McHugh, Patricia. *Toronto Architecture: A City Guide* (Toronto, 1985).

Russell, Victor L. *Mayors of Toronto, vol. 1, 1834-1899* (Toronto, 1982). The second volume will appear shortly.

St. Lawrence Hall (Toronto, 1969).

Thom, Ron, *et al. Exploring Toronto* (Toronto, 1972).

Thompson, Austin Seton. *Jarvis Street: a Story of Triumph and Tragedy* (Toronto, 1980).

_____. *Spadina: A Story of Old Toronto* (Toronto, 1975).

Toronto Board of Education, Centennial Story, 1850-1950 (Toronto, 1950).

Wallace, William Stewart. *A History of the University of Toronto, 1827-1927* (Toronto, 1927).

Zerker, Sally F. *The Rise and Fall of the Toronto Typographical Union, 1832-1972: A Case Study of Foreign Domination* (Toronto, 1982).

4. LOCAL OR BOROUGH HISTORIES

Bonis, R.R., ed. *A History of Scarborough* (Scarborough, 1965).
Boyle, David. *The Township of Scarborough, 1796-1896* (Toronto, 1896).
Boylen, J.C. *York Township, 1850-1954* (Toronto, 1954).
Given, Robert A. *The Story of Etobicoke, 1850-1950* (Islington, 1973).
Hart, Patricia W., ed. *Pioneering in North York: A History of the Borough* (Toronto, 1968).
Johnson, James. *Aurora: Its Early Beginnings* (Aurora, 1972).
Mathews, Hazel. *Oakville and the Sixteen: the History of an Ontario Port* (Toronto, 1953).
Mitchell, John. *The Settlement of York County* (Toronto, 1952).

List of Illustrations

All illustrations are from the Metropolitan Toronto Library except where otherwise noted.

INDEX